THE GOOD HIKE

D1648992

Published by Mission Point Press
2554 Chandler Lake Road, Traverse City, MI, 49696
MissionPointPress.com

No part of this book may be reproduced, stored in a retrieval
system, or transmitted in any form or by any means electronic,
mechanical, photocopying, recording or otherwise, without the
prior consent of the publisher.

ISBN: 9781943995226
Library of Congress Control Number: 2016918305

Cover design and illustration by Brett Stenson
Maps by Brett Stenson

Printed in the United States of America

THE GOOD HIKE

A STORY OF THE APPALACHIAN TRAIL, VIETNAM, PTSD, AND LOVE

TIM KEENAN

MISSION POINT PRESS

March 28, 2009 | Heading to the Appalachian Trail Approach, Georgia

September 16, 2009 | The end of the Trail

To my children: Larinda, Jonathon, Colin, Morganne, and Jacob.

In memory of my nephew Evan,

and in memory of my good friend Jim Kulczyk, who died of complications from the effects of Agent Orange.

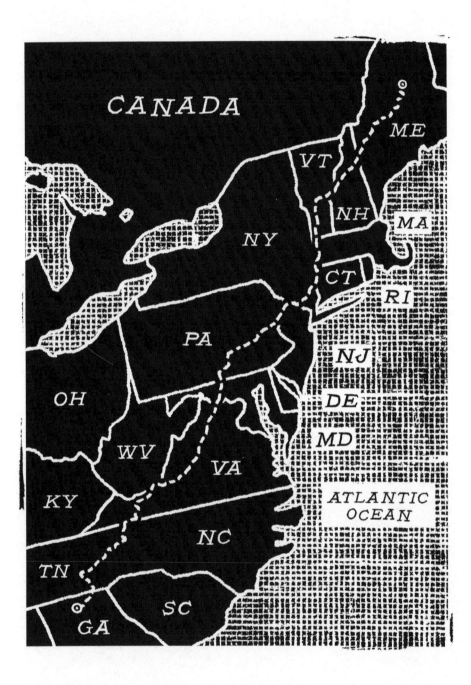

Contents

AUTHOR'S NOTE:

For reasons only a "grunt" would understand, the events I relate in these pages are not in chronological order. A combat veteran's "flashbacks" can occur and reoccur, triggered randomly as we try to make our way through life, as we try to manage our inner wound. A wound no less real just because it cannot be seen. According to our company commander, Captain David Foye, I and the men I fought with made more contact with the enemy than any other company in Vietnam from November 1967 to February 1968.

1 | MICHIGAN

I'd been working for months and months selling greeting cards door to door. I was eleven years old and trying to earn enough for a Daisy BB gun. With a scope! By April I'd reached my goal. The gun came in the mail and I was alive with excitement. I was young, but I was still self-aware enough to treasure what I had earned and the work it took to hold this gun in my hands. It was bliss.

One afternoon I was upstairs in my bedroom with the Daisy. Should I have had my gun up there? My parents never would have let me if they knew. I looked out my window, scanning the backyard in a new way. What could I shoot at? Through the screen I could smell the cherry blossoms on both of our trees. I could hear the songs the sparrows and blue jays made, sitting in the branches. I smiled and, as if a sniper, took aim at a lowly sparrow. I placed the front of the barrel carefully against the screen, put the crosshairs over the bird, held my breath and carefully, carefully squeezed the trigger.

I watched the BB's flight from the barrel of my gun until it entered the sparrow's body. And then I watched the bird tumble out of the tree. I was stunned. I'd meant to shoot it, but I hadn't meant to hurt it.

I ran from my room. *I didn't know! I didn't know!* I thought, as my legs carried me down the hall, down the stairs, through the living room and kitchen, and finally out the back door. I found the bird on the ground and got down on my knees. Its eyes were still open, and they blinked for just a moment, and then they closed. Forever.

I carried the bird behind the garage and buried it. I never shot the Daisy again.

APPALACHIAN TRAIL JOURNAL, MARCH 27, 2009

My dream of attempting a thru-hike of the Appalachian Trail (AT) is nearing reality. For 18 months I have randomly picked up various pieces of equipment. Two years of telling anyone who cared that I was going to attempt to hike the trail. Two years of reading all sorts of books and materials. Two years of talking to others who have completed this journey. I'm feeling anxious and a little scared of what lies ahead. What about my post-traumatic stress disorder (PTSD) from Vietnam, and the uneasiness I feel in the woods? What about the miles that lie ahead? And physically, can I even do this? My knees are a worry, especially the right one, which still hurts from combat assaults. I've had two back surgeries. How many people hike the trail at 62? Will missing my family and friends take its toll on my psyche? What about wild animals? What about wild *people*?

Friends and acquaintances say the word *"Deliverance"* and ask if I'm bringing a gun. The bears and the backward types will just have to content themselves with pepper spray. I have no gun. I don't want a gun. I left guns behind when I left the Army.

I've driven just past Chattanooga, TN, and have entered Georgia. My son, Colin, and his friend, Josh, are along for the drive, and good enough to take turns at the wheel. We're already a long way from our home in Traverse City, Michigan. They'll drop me at Springer Mountain, GA, the southern beginning of the AT. Head-banging music--courtesy of Colin, who's at the wheel--fills the cab. I guess this is the price I'm willing to pay for a ride to the trailhead!--. I dozed in the backseat after taking my driving turn and woke up to find him texting. The dad in me became wide awake "I am begging you not to text and drive," I said.

I think of myself when I was his age. Of my judgment, or lack of. I think of some of my decisions. Things I would do differently if I were given the chance.

To entertain Colin and Josh, and in hopes of getting them to turn down the head-banging noise coming from the dashboard, I told them a Vietnam story.

> I'd just arrived, I think the city was Bien Hoa, and we were trucked to an area of tents that would be our home while we waited for further orders. The area was wide open, unlike the jungle I'd experience all too soon. The first day as we were unpacking, another green soldier excitedly entered our tent. He had news. "There's a work detail here worse than KP (kitchen police)," he said. "Burning human waste." I was confused. What did he mean, "burning

human waste"? The other soldiers looked puzzled as well, and he must have noticed. "Burning shit, man! Burning shit!" he hollered. "There are no fucking flushing toilets here."

I went outside to look and sure enough, there was a wooden building not far from our quarters, maybe fifteen yards long, and five yards wide. I walked over and looked inside. There were about fifteen holes on each side cut into plywood, each big enough to seat an ass.

The next day, after breakfast, we had a formation with all the new, rookie soldiers. An officer explained that we would not be staying here permanently, but as long as we were here we would keep this place "squared away." We would stay busy. We would have details, such as KP, supply duty, and policing the area for trash.

Then he started choosing guys for the various details. This group will be doing this, he said as he pointed to a few guys, and this group will do that. When there were only four of us left, including me, I was thinking, "Perfect, I got out of detail. Time to go back to my tent and write some letters home." I started walking away to do just that.

"Wait a minute troop," the officer said. "Where do you think you're going?"

I said I was going back to my area. The officer shook his head with a slight smirk on his face. "Nope, come with me." The four of us followed. I noticed right away we were heading straight for the shit building. "You gotta be kidding me," Josh said, his face in a look of disgust.

"I wish," I told him.

We ended up behind the building and were introduced to the swinging doors that were under and behind each hole in the "shitter." I was instructed to swing the door up and squat down, letting the door rest on my back. Then I had to reach in and drag out a metal barrel a quarter full of shit and piss. And let me tell you, it was heavy. Oh, God. I tried not to gag as I held my breath. Once I got the barrel clear of the door, I let the door drop. Then I had to drag the barrel to a site away from the building. The four of us had to repeat this process until all the barrels were out of the building. Then we stacked them in a pyramid, poured gasoline in each barrel, and lit them on fire.

That shit lit up like charcoal. Once the flames subsided, we had to stir the shit with a stick. Yes, stir the shit in each barrel. And we kept stirring until everything turned to ash. When that was accomplished, we had to put the barrels back into their proper places.

That soldier was right. There was something worse than KP.

I had that detail for three days. Then I got my orders. I was headed to a base camp in Vietnam's central highlands to join the rest of the Army's 4th Infantry Division. I arrived in the evening and remember feeling scared, but also relieved. At least my shit-burning career had come to a close, right? Wrong.

Even though the latrine was a lot smaller, bright and early the next day one person was chosen for "shit burning." You guessed it: me. There were fewer barrels, but they still needed to be pulled out and dragged to a fenced-in area and burnt. And I still had to try not to gag or puke. I stacked the barrels in a moderated pyramid, but this time I was determined to get the job done as soon as possible so I really could write some letters home. I loaded up each barrel with an extra dose of gasoline, lit a match, and threw it at the barrels.

BA-BOOOOOOOM!

I blew the galvanized fence down, blew the barrels all around, and blew shit everywhere. I scared the shit out of everybody in the company area as well. They thought we were taking mortar fire. I ducked behind the latrine in hopes of becoming invisible. Instead, I got my ass chewed out. I was also relieved of my burning duty. Yes! I thought at the time. Mission accomplished. As it turned out, I would have volunteered to burn shit my entire tour, rather than end up in the infantry. But I was still that eleven-year-old kid, shooting a sparrow out of a tree. I didn't know.

All hikers of the AT either choose a trail nickname, or are given one by another hiker.

I decide my trail name will be "Naneek." My last name spelled backwards. I live in Michigan and the name makes me feel like "Naneek of the North." Trail names provide the hiker with a new and different identity. A chance to leave their life in the regular world behind. No more worries about work, about relationship issues, no more errands to run, no more bills to pay, no more politicians, no more breaking news. People don't hike the trail to talk about their jobs, their degrees, or their relationships. The most dedicated are on the trail to thru-hike, to meet their true selves, and to meet others doing the same. We are on the trail to think about our lives and where we are headed. Perhaps even to make future plans. Perhaps hiking the trail fulfills a dream. Perhaps hiking the trail allows hikers to "get lost" in nature.

For me, the hike is a combination of all these reasons. As Colin drives south into Georgia, I feel excited. I'm nearing the reality of meeting a variety of folks with the same mission as mine: eat, drink, walk the trail, and sleep. And of course, keep the sleeping bag dry.

The boys and I will seek out a town near Amicalola Falls State Park, which has the distinction of being home to the AT trailhead. I will take them out to dinner and then we'll find a motel for the night. On the way I notice a billboard on the highway that says, "Jesushealedmywife.com," and I think, a miracle must have happened for someone. It's a miracle I am alive today. It's a miracle I survived 11 months, 26 days, and 13 hours in a combat zone. It's a miracle I'm about to walk the AT to see if I can stop thinking so much about the horrors of war when I walk in the woods.

We locate Amicalola. I feel like a combination of a child the night before Christmas waiting for Santa Claus and a high school sophomore about to give his first memory selection in speech class. No doubt I will have problems sleeping tonight. Colin and Josh helped me sort out my electronic stuff (iPod, phone charger, etc.) before we turned in. The weather report says rain and cold tomorrow.

I lie in bed and the war hangs over me. I feel real concern about hiking the AT. I have committed to attempt this journey, but second thoughts dance in my head. "Humping" hills was the phrase we used in Vietnam, humping being another word for hiking. I have not hiked or camped overnight since my final day in the bush, way back in July of 1968.

When I was a kid, I loved the woods. Since Vietnam, I'm no longer comfortable there. Northern Michigan is full of trails and I've tried to hike them and relax, but I cannot. I take a step into the woods and feel the crosshairs. I break into a sweat. My heart pounds. I could never shake the feeling that enemy lurked. Walking on a trail, happy-go-lucky, like most people do when hiking would have been welcoming an ambush in Vietnam. When I try to hike, my palms sweat. The intensity level is not quite as high as when I was actually engaged in war, but the edge was always there. I can't help but wonder if the journey I've dreamed of will be stifled by thoughts of past horror. I try to sleep. Tomorrow is a big day.

But I tossed and turned in bed that night, some 41 years later, revisited by flashbacks of Hill 1338. In July 1967, I'd been assigned to A Company, 3rd Battalion, 12th Infantry, 4th Infantry Division. I was in for a year, if only I was fortunate enough to survive it. I ended up in light weapons infantry, "MOS 11B10" in military jargon. My MOS (Military Occupational Specialty) was supposed to be 11C10, heavy weapons (mortars), but when I arrived in base camp they were short-handed in infantry.

Hill 1338. The number is a military signifier denoting the height in meters to the summit. Why I was consumed with Hill 1338 the night before my first day on the trail, I do not know. Such is the nature of PTSD.

It was November 17, 1967, and we had been "taking" hills, engaging in combat, since earlier that month in the Dak To area, near the Cambodian and Laotian border. We knew enough to be fearful with every step we took. I remember thinking even then how wrong this war was. What are we accomplishing by taking hills, by killing and being killed? How exactly would maiming people, inflicting severe and permanent wounds on them and their country, bring peace? Uncle Sam and the media told us we needed to stop communism before it spread to the coast of California. I thought that was bullshit. All the men in my platoon felt the same. I think most of the men in my company felt the same. I wanted to feel the patriotism my dad felt in World War II. Instead, I felt only the need to survive.

On November 16, 1967, A and C companies, led by a reconnaissance unit, humped to within about 2,500 meters of Hill 1338. According to "intelligence," there was supposed to be a mass contingent of NVA (the North Vietnamese Army) soldiers atop the hill. We set up for a sleepless night, knowing the next day would bring battle.

Early, maybe 5 a.m., we got our orders to move out. My good friend from Grand Rapids, Lloyd Slack, was in C Company. We moved in the dark, getting to the base of the hill near dawn. Colonel Jamie Hendrix, whose radio call sign was Grizzly, ordered us up the hill. He was in a helicopter (a "sky pilot") throughout the day, peering at the area below with high-powered binoculars. C Company was to be adjacent to us as we moved. The hill had been peppered with air strikes and artillery the day before and again just before we moved out. This was good news and bad. The good? Air support may have crippled the enemy. The bad? They knew we were coming. "Intelligence" said the NVA was dug in, meaning they had trench lines the entire circumference of the hill, along with spider holes big enough for one man and his weapon.

I have a hard time, even now, trying to describe the fear I felt as we headed up. There was silence among all the troops. Our platoon was second in line as we moved. We tried to maintain visual contact with C Company as we moved, but the dense jungle made it difficult. It was eerily quiet as we advanced. We were close to three-quarters of the way up the hill and had encountered no resistance. I hoped the NVA were gone. I fantasized they were gone. I prayed they were gone. If the NVA didn't think they would give you an ass whipping, they disappeared into the jungle, and I was just daring to believe this is what had happened on Hill 1338. Then, five hundred meters from the summit, insanity struck.

Machine gun and AK-47 fire filled the air. We returned fire but they were dug in on top, occupying trench lines and spider holes. We were crawling and firing, praying and moving, trying to hide behind anything, but we were mostly exposed. We were taking casualties. A guy toward the front took a direct hit from some type of heavy weapon and was blown apart, his body flopping like a rag doll. Others were wounded and in need of medics. Even in the midst of fighting, there were tears of sadness, tears of fear, tears of bedlam, and tears of horror. The medics were in chaos, not knowing whom to treat first.

We were losing. We stopped well short of the summit and called in more air strikes. Suddenly the small arms and rocket fire stopped, as if the battle was over. This was the way of the NVA. Let the GIs think about what is happening in silence. Let them become uncomfortable in their sweat and dirt. It was so quiet all I could hear was my own heavy breathing. I could do nothing but brace for the bullet that was sure to find me. I grasped the St. Christopher's medal friends back in Michigan--Jack, Frank, and Gary--had given me the day I left for this hellhole. I prayed. I prayed to be invisible.

Our CO, Captain Foye, got Grizzly on the radio and frantically reported, "We're suffering too many casualties. We need to pull back." The response from Grizzly? "You don't come down off that hill until you've taken the son of a bitch." Grizzly was a mile above us, safe in his helicopter. Captain Foye obeyed the order. We would continue on.

The noise from the F4s pierced the air. They were so close it seemed like they were going to collide with the hill. They dropped tons of bombs. I could hear shrapnel whistle through the air. The big hunks sounded like a whoosh, then a thud. Smaller pieces of shrapnel were just as deadly. You could not hear them, but each little piece could tear a body up just the same.

One of our squad leaders was huddled in the fetal position against a huge tree. I heard shrapnel and then its follow-up thud. Sergeant Fischer screamed in agony. A medic, a fellow platoon member named Palmer, and I, crawled over to him. Oh my God! The shrapnel had torn into him, severing one of his legs from the knee down. I wanted to scream. I wanted to cry. But there was no time. There was never time for any emotion. The medic immediately secured tourniquets on both his legs and Palmer and I concocted a stretcher out of bamboo. An eternity later we made it to the bottom of 1338. We set Fischer down as gently as we could. He was surrounded by other wounded, and I looked around, hoping not to see Lloyd, my friend from Grand Rapids.

The first person I did see was Lieutenant Terrell. He'd been hit and hit badly. Terrell was a big man. A former Division 1 football player. He was lying on his back, bleeding. His insides were pouring out of him. A medic was working on him, frantically trying to jam his innards back inside his abdomen. Terrell, an African-American, was clutching a photo of his family and begging the medic, "Please don't let me die!" A slightly wounded grunt from C Company happened by, took one look and said, "Man, you are fucked up." The rest of us within earshot cringed and tried to reassure the lieutenant that he was going to make it, even though we knew differently. At least he didn't seem to be in pain. The medic had pumped him full of morphine.

There were many others wounded. The most severe were being attended to, including Fischer. The less wounded tended to themselves. Two men, one from A Company, one from C, were hanging out by a tree, sobbing uncontrollably. They had permission to come down off the hill, as they were mentally incapacitated. At the time, I didn't know what to think of them.

Palmer headed back up the hill and I was following when an officer, I cannot remember who, ordered me to stay with the wounded, help cut an LZ (landing zone) for a medivac (helicopter), and secure the area so the chopper could land and evacuate the wounded. I was extremely reluctant, both because I wanted to stay with my friends who were heading back up 1338, and because I was afraid of getting hit from the rear. Everyone down here was wounded, and could no longer fight, except me and a few others who were helping with the tasks at hand.

We frantically cut down trees using our machetes to open up an area for the chopper. Machine-gun fire, AK-47s, M-16s, and the explosions of grenades filled the air from atop 1338. When the firing stopped for moments at a time, I could hear nothing but the wounded moaning and screaming. The dead were silent. I had just turned 21. And I was considered an older guy.

With each chop of my machete I worried about my friends up on that hill. My senses were on high alert and my eyes darted about, looking for the enemy. I thought at any minute they would come attack us and try to finish off the wounded.

It took an hour, maybe more, but we finally had made enough space for a chopper to land. Lieutenant Terrell had died. So did others. We loaded the most severely wounded onto the first chopper. The non-life-threatened wounded soldiers were put on the following choppers with the dead.

Eventually, word came from the top that we had taken the hill. There were more casualties atop, but we could bring a chopper in up there because air strikes had stripped the terrain of trees.

After getting all the wounded onto medivacs, what was left of us went up the hill. When I reached the top, I saw no foliage. The hill was leveled. The smell of small fires smoldering and dead bodies haunts me to this day. I walked over spider holes and complex trench lines that stretched the circumference of the hill. These trench lines were equipped with tunnels, hospitals, and a room similar to a kitchen. The rest of the hill was nothing but bomb craters, GIs and dead NVA. I walked around in a daze. I looked at the bodies of the NVA. I looked at the wounded GIs. I looked at the medics treating the wounded. One medic (we called them all Doc), a conscientious objector, was treating a wounded NVA. A few guys objected and wanted to kill the wounded enemy, but they had too much respect for Doc to do it. My mom would have been proud of him. Oh, how I thought of home as I wandered. A year ago I was partying with friends in Grand Rapids, Michigan, and now I was in a place so bad I could not have imagined it in my worst nightmare.

After getting the last of our wounded out, we dragged the dead NVA soldiers over to a bomb crater and threw their bodies in the hole. Then we ate some C-rations. As we ate, we told stories of home. We talked of our families. We talked about sports. We talked about girls. Never once did we talk about what had just transpired. Never once did we mention our friends who'd just been killed or wounded.

We stayed on Hill 1338 for a couple of days, sending out patrols and securing that jungle hilltop. Then we took another hill, 1294. It was the day before Thanksgiving, 1967. No casualties, plenty of fear. Then on Thanksgiving Day, our squad was sent out on patrol. I received two calls on the radio. One was to tell me that hot Thanksgiving chow and our mail (packages from home, we hoped) was being choppered to our perimeter. The second, roughly 30 minutes later, was to inform us the NVA were back on Hill 1338.

Our company had been called on to retake it. "Get back here as soon as you can, eat some fucking turkey, get your mail and packages, and get ready to move."

We did retake 1338 that day…. But why were we here? What were we doing? What had my friends died for? Damn the war.

2 | GEORGIA

TRAIL JOURNAL, MARCH 28, 2009

Up early, 7 a.m., making sure everything is in order in my pack. I am feeling hyper.

Colin, Josh, and I arrive at Amicalola Falls State Park about 9:30 a.m. I signed in at the Ranger Station using my real name in one column and my trail name in another, NANEEK. Colin took a couple of photos of me at the base of the trail, which turned out to be an approach trail, not the AT. I couldn't believe I had to walk 8.8 miles to get to the beginning of the AT. Uphill!

The weather is as predicted: rainy, foggy, windy, and chilly. I have no idea what the temperature is, but I am bundled. My pack feels like it weighs a ton. I give Colin a huge hug and say my goodbye, with a great deal of apprehension. Part of me is saying, "What are you doing, Tim? Biting off a bit more than we can chew, are we?" But another part is saying, "You have been promising for at least a year that you were going to do this, so no turning back now!"

Like many first-timers, I have a mentor for this trip. Her name is Marilyn and she was a former thru-hiker. Her basic instructions: "Do not quit until you have hiked for at least thirty days. And keep your sleeping bag dry."

SPRINGER MOUNTAIN | 8.8 MILES AHEAD

It was 10 a.m. at Amicalola Falls State Park, elevation 1,820 ft., as I started up the approach trail to Springer Mountain, the official beginning of the Appalachian Trail.

Colin had a little smile on his face as I left, shaking his head as if to say, "Dad, you are crazy." As I walked up the "steps" of the mountain towards Springer, close to nine miles away, I thought I heard someone's voice. I had to stop and listen, because I was breathing so heavily I couldn't hear. I thought I heard someone yelling something. Maybe it was the universe, trying to give me a final message?

Nope, just Colin yelling "DAD!" in the distance.

I called back, and then he yelled, "YOU FORGOT SOMETHING."

I hollered back through the fog, "IS IT IMPORTANT?"

He said, "YES, IT'S IMPORTANT."

"CAN YOU MEET ME HALFWAY?" I didn't want to have to go backwards on day one.

He met me halfway up. I had forgotten my trekking poles, which are similar to cross-country ski poles, and much needed.

Colin shook his head once again and gave me a hug. "Call me when you want a ride home."

I was sure he thought this hike wasn't going to last long. Maybe it won't, I thought. Last night as I laid in bed, I felt like I didn't have it together at all. As my drill sergeant used to say, "Keenan, you do not have your shit wired tight."

I am such a novice. I am concerned, but still think I have what I need. If I do have problems, I will get off the trail, plain and simple.

Rain, sleet, fog, high winds, and snow greeted me as I walked. A dreadful day to hike, especially on day one. I saw nary a soul this day on the approach trail. With my adrenaline pumping, I had little trouble reaching the summit, although it did take a while.

I made it to the starting point of the AT, Springer Mountain (3,730 feet elevation) close to 4 p.m. Six hours after my start time. One and a half miles per hour. Felt like a dream. When I got to the top, I found several people milling about. I wondered how they got up here. I'd left early and nobody passed me. I didn't see anybody in front of me, and I hiked quickly because of the cold. I was confused. I asked a guy at the top, who pointed his finger and said, "There's a parking lot right down there." Turns out, I could have had Colin drive me to within a mile of the summit. Rookie!

It is extremely foggy up here. I looked at my watch to mark the time. I hadn't planned on bringing one, but a friend from home, TJ, gave me one as a gift before I left.

I was thirsty from climbing the steep hill and got water from a stream using my new filter. I patted myself on the back because I had never used it before. I pitched my tent. Another pat. Got my thermarest (sleeping pad) and sleeping bag squared away. Pat. Put all my dry clothes in a stuff sack to use for a pillow. Pat. Made a meal (pasta) and cooked it on my new stove. Pat. Hung my food (including toothpaste and anything sweet) from a tree so the bears and critters couldn't get it. Major pat. I actually felt proud of myself, I mean extremely proud, for completing these tasks. Simple basics for any experienced hiker, but an accomplishment for a rookie like me.

If I'm fortunate enough to stay healthy for the six months it will take to walk the trail, these tasks are sure to become second nature.

> When I was getting my water from the stream my eyes and mind were back in Vietnam. I caught myself looking about quickly into the forest. I couldn't help it. I took a deep breath. The hike with full pack is a first since 1968. No weapons this time, I reminded myself. No grenades. No extra ammo. No radio. No claymores. No sandbags. No hole to dig.

It is cold up here. I tried to speak to my special friend Kinsley on the phone, but the cell service went in and out. I became emotional talking to her, even though our conversation was brief. I look forward to the day she joins me on the trail, which she's planning to do in late April or early May.

I spoke to a fellow hiker for an hour or so. His trail name is Super Tramp, after the character in Jon Krakauer's book, *Into the Wild.* Super Tramp is a big guy, maybe 6'2", two hundred fifty pounds, with an easy smile. He was laid off from his job, but had saved a few thousand dollars and decided to hike the trail. I met a couple other people as well. One guy forgot his gloves. He's a big dude, too, with a round face, and has to weigh in excess of three hundred pounds. He was all smiles when he said he needed to lose a few pounds, and that this hike should do it. He had a plan all mapped out as to when he would get to Damascus, Virginia, close to 500 miles away.

A slight rain began falling, so I turned in early. I hope to go close to eight miles tomorrow. After just one day's hike, my hip is sore and my feet are cramping. My knees, the main physical worry on this journey, felt strained as I hiked, but seem okay now. I am feeling very comfy in my warm sleeping bag.

As I write the time is 1:20 a.m. I am having trouble sleeping. The rain pours down and the wind howls. *Please tent, don't fold on me. Please let me stay dry.*

Neil Young on the iPod put me to sleep. Mother Nature woke me up. I am still dry.

MARCH 29, 8 A.M.

Oh, it is cold, so very cold. I have no desire to exit the warmth of my sleeping bag. *I need to tear down in the rain the very first day?* Yesterday was the first time I hiked and camped overnight in my entire life, not counting Vietnam, and now I have to tear down in the rain.

After staying dry all night, I didn't want to get the inside of the tent or my sleeping bag wet. I realize before I exit this six-month home of mine that packing up all my gear in the rain and cold is not something I'm going to be fond of. First I put on my shirt and shorts, then my rain gear, in the confines of my little one-person tent. Then I put on my wet socks and boots. Ugh. This was because Marilyn (trail name, Peach), the former thru-hiker, now my mentor, gave me lots of advice in the months prior to this hike. One of the things was to put on my wet clothes when the weather is foul. Psychologically, having the warm and dry stuff for when I am in my tent for the evening can be comforting. Save my dry clothes for a dry day.

I exited the tent and retrieved my bear bag full of food and made my way back into the tent. I stuffed my sleeping bag into a waterproof stuff sack and wrapped it in a garbage bag. Then I stuffed it deep into my backpack. The thermarest was packed on top of the sleeping bag. Then my food. I took a deep breath and made my move out of the tent. What a sight I must have been as I scurried, frantically rolling up my tent quickly to keep the floor dry and then getting everything closed up and snug. I covered my pack with a rain cover. Done.

Items I carry on my back: backpack, tent, poles and stakes, sleeping bag, thermarest, water filter, water bladder, water, five days worth of food, stove, fuel, lighter, cooking pan, spoon/fork, toothpaste and toothbrush, first aid stuff, long underwear, fleece, rain gear, two pairs of socks, journal, book, lighter, baggies, garbage bags, headlamp, camp shoes, thru-hiker handbook and map, baggies for litter, toilet paper, duct tape, iPod and charger, cell phone and charger, camera, rope, and multi-tool. I should have packed some hot chocolate to warm my innards.

As it turned out, I sent anything I didn't use the first week, back home except the first aid stuff. The multi-tool (a.k.a. shit-hole digger), the iPod and charger all went home. Anything to lighten the load.

Items I carried on my back in Vietnam: rucksack, poncho, poncho liner, air mattress (for maybe three days before it got torn up, then it was sleep on the ground for the rest of the tour), iodine tablets for water purification, seven canteens of water if possible, heat tabs or C-4 for cooking, nine meals of canned C-rations when resupplied, toothpaste and toothbrush, letter-writing stuff, maps, instamatic camera, fifteen sand bags to be used multiple times, entrenching tool (shovel), machete, knife, one hundred rounds of machine gun ammo, four hundred rounds of M-16 ammo with bandoleers, one pistol belt, four hand grenades, two trip flares, one claymore mine with cord and detonator, one M-16. Later in my tour, I carried one AN/PRC 25 radio that weighed twenty-five pounds and one extra battery that weighed five pounds. Carrying this much weight coupled with the stress? No wonder I lost fifty pounds in my first two months in Vietnam. In Vietnam, I could not lighten the load. Everything I carried I needed to survive.

MARCH 29 | HAWKS MOUNTAIN SHELTER, 7.8 MILES AHEAD

I arrived at Hawks Mountain Shelter (actually a three-sided lean-to) at about 5 p.m. Elevation is 3,260 feet. My first shelter on the trail! I find I need simply to follow the white blazes painted on the trees. The white blazes are about six inches long and two inches wide. They're painted on the trees every hundred meters or so on both sides of the tree, for north and southbound hikers. I notice a register in the shelter. Another veteran hiker informed me these are available at every shelter. Hikers sign in as they wish and leave notes for other hikers behind them on the trail, or share something significant witnessed that day. I imagined that, as time passed and I hiked further and so did other hikers, I'd see the same names again and know just how many miles certain hikers were ahead of me.

When I saw the first sign on a tree signifying the AT, the real AT, I was mesmerized. I stopped, took a picture, and stared, hardly able to fathom I was actually hiking the Appalachian Trail.

Super Tramp hiked out earlier than me this a.m. and is here, but he and another hiker are pushing on. Danger, danger. One shouldn't go too far, too early. He feels good, he says. "Why stop?"

My hands are so cold I am having difficulty writing. The temp is 30 degrees. This was according to the folks with the high-tech equipment, who informed the lean-to group the weather is supposed to warm tomorrow. I pitched my tent behind the shelter and then made myself some hot pasta. I trembled as I ate. There are lots of good folks here. Seems to be a young crowd. Many are carrying huge packs.

I find it interesting seeing all the different types of cooking devices. Some heat with natural fire. Some heat with alcohol. I use propane. Someone had built a fire before my arrival and Wrath, a hiker I just met, is cooking his food on the "borrowed" fire.

Some of the people I met on the trail today include:

Doctor Bob, a bespectacled middle-aged doctor who looked quite fit. He warned me against doing too many miles too quickly, because I would pay for it later. He said he tried thru-hiking last year, but broke down from walking too many long distances, too soon, too much. Adrenalin. I will heed his advice.

I'm Fine, is the trail name of a young dude with lengthy dreadlocks and a warm, childlike smile. He had thru-hiked last year by himself, at only 17. Wow! He is hiking in the cold, clad in shorts and a tank top.

Jersey is 6'3," from New Jersey, with an abundance of tattoos. He is very animated and loud, with that Jersey accent, and very friendly. He says he has enough pot to get him back up to New Jersey, at which time his wife will meet him with a fresh supply.

Wrath, who resembles a Southern California surfer, is of average height and weight, with blonde dreads. He is hiking in Converse All Stars and a trench coat. A philosopher is he, in fact, a rather bizarre dude. I can't see him going too far. He seemed miserable, but had told Jersey he was going to hike thirty miles tomorrow, barefoot. Unless I am missing something, it appears he does not even have a pack.

> Areas of the trail today reminded me of Vietnam, the foliage being similar. I found myself at times looking around for movement, or any clues of the enemy, but kept gently telling myself to relax. People who were never in a war sometimes ask how long war stays with people. The answer is, forever. I think those who start wars, or send children to wars, or prolong wars should have some experience in fighting them.

The hike was beautiful, but the day was dreary, with little sun and some rain. No cell service to call my family or Kinsley.

There are lots of tents here. I count fifteen, and the shelter is full. The day seemed surreal, as I smiled many times, just grateful to be here. I wondered if all these trail activities and feelings would become routine for me. The hiking and the day-to-day became routine in Vietnam. Not the fighting, but the setting up.

> The first day on the AT was a bit different from my first day in "the boonies" of Vietnam. Back then I was intimidated by the men and boys who had already been in country for months when I arrived via helicopter. Most did not seem to welcome me, but laughed and

asked, "How many days you have left, new guy?" They always knew their exact number. "I have 59 days and a wake up." Or, "26 days and a wake up." "Short," they called it.

I was scared and nobody gave a shit. I felt so alone. I missed my family. I missed my friends. I did not smile my first day in the bush in Vietnam; I longed for home. And I knew no job in the military could be worse than this.

On the AT, people are friendly, inquisitive, and supportive. Everyone has the same 2,178.3 miles to walk with a full pack. All are in the same boat. *I guess all were in the same boat in war as well, but here nobody is suffering, at least not like grunts suffered. People are wary of what lies ahead, but not scared of losing their lives. Nobody is "short."*

MARCH 30 | DAN GAP, 14.6 MILES TODAY, 22.4 MILES TOTAL

I tossed and turned a little last night, but generally had a good night's sleep. I can see a pattern forming with me turning in early, waking up early, and moving on.

Today was glorious. The songbirds are magnificent. The walk is soothing, but I didn't heed Dr. Bob's advice and hiked too far, almost 15 miles. I am now at a place on the map that looks like Dan Gap (elevation, 3,300 feet). I'd planned on stopping sooner, thinking there was a hostel at Woody's Gap, 2.5 miles ago, but I must have missed it. Humped to this point at 5 p.m. I should get into the Neels Gap outfitter and hostel relatively early tomorrow, as I have "only" 8.3 miles to go. The .3 will be a big part of this journey. Kind of like a marathon runner. People ask the runner, "You ran 26 miles?" The runner replies, "No, I ran 26.2 miles." The .2 is huge.

I look forward to a rest and a shower at the hostel. I had heard if one gets there early they may have cheeseburgers on the grill. I can practically smell them.

I saw a "ridge runner" (conservation officer) speaking with Wrath on the trail. I was going to join in the conversation, but the ridge runner acted indifferent towards me. I overheard her say to Wrath that at this stage of the journey, hikers on the trail are a "bunch of wannabes." I vow to steer clear of negativity.

I hiked 14. 6 miles to get where I am, planning on camping with some other human being, but dusk arrived and here I sit in the middle of the woods, alone. It is so very quiet. So quiet I can hear a leaf drop. I find myself a wee bit scared. I told myself to relax countless times today. My mind swirled with thoughts of the "enemy." Now, before turning in, I had thoughts of putting out trip-flares, clearing a field of fire, and placing claymore mines strategically in front of trees.

I'm on the trail and I so want to feel serenity, but I do not feel safe. I feel tired, but I know I will sleep with one eye open. This is a first since the war. I must continue to tell myself over and over not to worry about being shot at, not to worry about someone sneaking up on me. I continue to tell myself, "There is no enemy, Tim." But I do have my poles, a knife, and pepper spray at the ready position next to my sleeping bag just in case.

I was very hungry upon arrival. After I pitched the tent and got everything prepared for bed, talking to myself all the while, I ate a meal of pasta, followed by a Snickers candy bar for dessert.

It neared dark. I have always been afraid of the dark.

I hiked today with several folks, but they stepped up their pace after seven miles or so. I see these gung-ho people starting to suffer already. They seem to want to charge down the trail. This is rough travel. Going up one mountain and down, up another and down, with the trail being an array of pointy, jagged rocks. I pray my body holds up. Like the rookie I am, I asked I'm Fine, who I hiked with for a bit, how long the terrain stayed like this. He smiled gently, as if to say, "You are already asking this type of question only fifteen miles into your hike?" I'm Fine is such a nice dude. He has so much knowledge for an eighteen-year-old. He gave me good advice. "Keep a positive attitude and a smile on your face. You will have lots of bad days. Push through them, savor the good ones, and you will be rewarded." Then he said I had "about four or five hundred miles to go before Virginia, where the terrain is not quite as tough."

Four or five hundred miles!

I took several breaks today, but still hiked close to ten hours. Stopped and got water at a beautiful stream. Others were there, including Wrath. A couple, Schooner and Megan, were also filling their water filters. Wrath waded in to retrieve a penny he saw on the creek's floor.

I haven't really connected with anyone yet. That's okay. I think being alone with myself will be good for me.

Every once in a while I see a sign that reads, "Appalachian Trail," and I smile and pinch myself. The signs keep me motivated as I'm finding I get extremely winded on the uphills, while the downhills are tough on my knees. As I hiked today I was having second thoughts about this journey, thinking it may be impossible for me to go over 2,000 miles, but tonight I feel better, physically, at least. I wonder if this is the way it will be for me mentally. I will tell myself to remember the advice given by I'm Fine. Attitude. Smile. Relax.

The rains are supposed to continue for the next four days. *Please be warmer. Please.* I wish myself a peaceful night. I want to sleep.

MARCH 31, 8:20 A.M.

I feel like Super Tramp in the book/movie. Alone. Peaceful. No bear bothered me last night. No enemy. No dudes from *Deliverance* showed up. Hiking with Kinsley would be nice, but alone and sometimes with strangers will have to do. I actually had a decent night's sleep. I stayed warm.

I sense rain in the air. I will be bundling up because the temp is forty degrees or so. *Am I doing the right thing by being out here?* So far, I feel good.

I did do a lot of swearing and yapping to myself this morning, trying to pack up. I need a system. Takes me a good hour to tear down and pack. Then I have problems remembering where things are when I do pack them. I get all packed up and ready to go only to forget to brush my teeth. And then I don't recall where I packed the toothbrush and toothpaste and have to tear the whole pack apart looking for them, cussing all the while. If it were raining right now, that would not be good, but the sun shines.

I made myself breakfast, hoisted the loaded pack on my back, grabbed my trekking poles, and headed down the trail.

NEELS GAP | 8.3 MILES, 30.7 TOTAL MILES

I made it to Neels Gap hostel and outfitter. I walked in here with my head high and feeling strong. I am actually beginning to think of myself as a thru-hiker, albeit, a thru-hiker with 2,100+ miles to go, but a thru-hiker all the same. The staff here like to help hikers downsize and organize. Many hikers send home lots of stuff they once felt they needed, but have realized they can do without. Many other hikers call it quits here. In hiker terminology they are now "off the trail." This is not merely a walk in the woods; this is ass-kicking stuff out here.

I am in the outfitter browsing when I see a young guy with a bizarre, close-cropped haircut. He turns around and I recognize him. It's I'm Fine. I cannot believe what I am seeing. Only yesterday he had dreads that he had been working on for nine years. He tells me he cut them off and left them in the shelter on top of Blood Mountain. When I asked him why, he said, "Because I wanted to make my dad proud." This comment from a guy who hiked the entire AT at 17? What could possibly make a dad prouder than that?

The hostel people had cooked up some cheeseburgers and I got the last one. This is my first experience in a hostel. They gave me my bed assignment and down I went to the bunkroom. I opened the door and looked into the eyes of a bunch of tired-looking thru-hikers. I felt immediately at home.

I took the best shower I have had in my life. It felt like hot rain, almost orgasmic. Later, my bunkmates and I were treated to a huge spaghetti dinner, complete with garlic bread and salad. A local church sponsors the food and serves us. The people that served us did so with such pleasure.

This place is full. Any new arrivals will have to tent outside somewhere. I'm feeling glad I pushed on the day prior, so that I had a relatively short walk today assuring me of a bed. Remarkably, the trail runs directly between the outfitter and the hostel. I'll have a hot breakfast tomorrow morning at 7 a.m., and then push on. I want to make Hiawassee, Georgia, by Saturday morning, thirty-seven miles in three days. I need a cell charger and I need to do laundry and resupply. And maybe eat a giant pizza. Only three days in and already food dominates my mind.

The terrain has been rough and rocky. Blood Mountain was 4,400 feet, the highest point in Georgia. I'm forever questioning myself. *Can I actually ever finish this thing?* I am constantly exhausted and famished.

I sat on my bunk for an hour or so after dinner talking with others with the same mission as me: completing a thru-hike of the AT. All seemed proud they had hiked thirty-plus miles. There are some wonderful people here. Some names I remember: Huey, Dewey, and Lewey, brothers from the Netherlands. They are tall and athletic, with broad smiles. They had spent five years planning their journey to America and their AT hike. They are sponsored, and have raised more than $12,000 for charity. They look in great shape and have such a positive air about them. They started about the same time as me, but hike much faster. I would love to spend some hiking days with them, because they feed off each other and are very funny.

There was also Jersey, Due South, Schooner, Megan, and Cass. Due South is a slightly overweight guy who acts like he knows the ins and outs of the trail. Maybe he does. Says he will never use a bear bag. Say what? He said he went to an AT presentation and learned if he just keeps his food in the tent with him, he will be fine. He may be right but I'd never want to take the chance. Cass was in the military for years, and was recently discharged. Others in the hostel did not have trail names yet.

APRIL 1, 8 A.M.

It's hard to sleep when a B-52 is touching down. Due South was the culprit. He kept everyone up all night. Night Moves (young, handsome, laid-back dude) woke up early in the morning and said, almost crying, "I can't take it anymore." He jumped off his bunk, ran to Due South's bed, and begged him to roll over. Due South rolled over and went back to sleep, minus snoring. Simple. I don't think Due South even knew he rolled over. Someone should have done that six hours ago.

Everyone is up, quietly packing. I see everyone else has the same problem as I have when packing. Don't quite know where to put what. What a great group. I find myself wondering if I will see some of these folks way down the trail, if I am lucky enough to get way down the trail. I now know why Due South has no bear bag. A bear would be a fool to approach his tent with the sounds that come from him as he sleeps.

The hot breakfast promised last night turned into cold leftover beans sitting on the table.

APRIL 1 | ROCKY KNOB, 17.1 MILES, 47.8 TOTAL

I am alone in the woods six miles past Low Gap, at Rocky Knob, cooking dinner. Very tired. I feel so good once I get twenty minutes into the hike now, that I scare myself. I was going to stop at Low Gap shelter with the Dutch guys, but felt like walking on. It was too early in the day, and I didn't feel like sitting around in the chilly air. So I filled my water from a nearby stream, and off I went. Time would tell if I traveled too far. For some reason, I just wanted to be alone.

All my kids have called to check on me. I got the messages when I had service. What a good feeling. I love those kids of mine. They tried not to let on, but I do believe they are worried about me.

I had only hiked a mile or so out of Neels Gap when I caught up with Jersey and Magic (a young, thin man with an English accent). They offered me some pot, but I declined. I can't smoke pot and hike. No way. This hike would take me a couple years to finish if I did. Magic asked if it was okay if he smoked, implying I wouldn't approve. I just said, "All good. I started smoking pot before your dad was born." They were already high and just cracked up laughing. I laughed too.

I pitched the tent in a flat clearing and quietly cooked my meal. I'm starting to realize this is all I have to do. Walk, drink, and eat. And keep my sleeping bag dry.

I thought about war often today. Here I am with a full backpack thinking about humping back in 1967 under fire with a full rucksack. Not simply walking up hills, but crawling, scared beyond words, all while receiving incoming fire and suffering casualties. What innocent boys we were.

April 2, 8 A.M.

The rain started at 10 p.m. or so, and continued all night. I lie here dreading having to tear down in the rain once again. This is work. Not in the least bit pleasant. But then again, what the hell, I have all day. *Keep the positive attitude, Naneek.* I am not risking my life anymore with every step. And agonizing over the physicality of this hike will send me off the trail for sure. The daylight brings light rain and fog. Dreary.

Addis Gap

14.3 miles, 62.1 miles total

I made it to Addis Gap today. It was a miserable and exhausting day. Rainy, windy, cold, and foggy. I pitched the tent in driving rain and sleet. Another tent was pitched near me, blowing in the wind. Looked like one of those cheap tents, not made for this kind of weather. I yelled over that I was setting up, hoping to talk with someone through our tents, but got no response.

Just before I arrived, hiking in the fog, wind, and rain with my head down, I was jolted by the sight of a pack of wild boars. Adults and their babies, stampeding across the trail maybe twenty meters in front of me. At first I thought they were bears, but then I saw the snouts. My eyes must have been as big as headlights. I am thankful the noise from my trekking poles frightened them enough to send them in another direction. The marks they made in the earth look like a rototiller came through. My heart was jacked up a notch. Those huge animals could do major damage to a human.

Saw two men going south. Neither had teeth. I thought of the folks in Michigan warning me to be wary of Deliverance people in the woods down south. They'd urged me to pack a weapon and I refused. Both of the toothless guys were talkative, informative, and kind. And not built like your stereotypical hiker. They were big. One was hiking south to meet his wife for their anniversary.

As I crossed GA 75 today, feeling depleted mentally and physically, a robust man with a full, gray beard sat in his van in a small parking lot near the trail. He called to me from a distance, yelling, "You a thru-hiker?" I said that I was and he waved me over and offered cold soda, fruit, cookies, anything he had, plus a chair to rest my weary bod. This was the "trail magic" my friend Peach had told me about. Wonderful!

I had an apple, an orange, and a cold Coke, all of which tasted delicious. That guy rejuvenated me, and he did it at the perfect time, too, just before I began a thousand-foot climb, to be followed by another and then another. All in pouring rain.

As I hiked on, I passed some section hikers heading south. Section hikers are people that hike for days, maybe a couple weeks at a time, then stop, and head home to their jobs. The next year they pick up where they left off. Some do this for years until they complete. There were six of them and they were older like me. Seemed like nice guys, but the hiker bringing up the rear was far behind his companions and was limping badly from a knee injury. He had a full pack. His friends knew he was injured, yet had refused to take on any of the weight in his pack.

> We would never have treated anyone like that in Vietnam. We took care of each other. We were like brothers. If someone was in need, we stepped up.

APRIL 3 | HIAWASSEE, GEORGIA, 5.4 MILES. 67.5 MILES TOTAL

As I tore down my tent this morning in the wind and the rain, I saw that the tent near me was lying on its side, as if the poles had broken. The same tent I'd gotten no response from last night. There was a lump under the remains of the tent that resembled a human. My heart sank. I gulped and slowly walked over, afraid of what I might find. I called out but got no answer. I unzipped the door and slowly lifted the nylon. Nothing but equipment and provisions. I was relieved! Someone must have just left all their equipment, walked to the road, hitched into town, and headed home. They'd probably seen enough of the AT.

I made it to Dicks Creek Gap, ten miles from the North Carolina border, intending to hike on when I saw a fellow hiker setting up his tent. I stopped momentarily to chat. I said, "It's a cold one." He said there was supposed to be snow the next three days. I moonwalked back down to the road and hitched the eleven miles into Hiawassee, GA. This was my first hitchhiking experience in forty years. The radio in the car forecasts snow for the next three days, just like the dude said. I am dropped off at a Holiday Inn Express. I have a plan. Get a room with a Jacuzzi. Buy a six-pack, a *USA Today*, and a pizza. Make some phone calls while soaking my aching body in the tub.

That was a nice fantasy, but I varied my plan a bit. First I bought a new cell phone, because the old one got wet. Then I did laundry, and tended to the blisters on both my little toes, and then I went to an all-you-can eat buffet. Seven pieces of chicken, potatoes, rolls, mac and cheese, and two desserts later, I returned to my room with the newspaper and a six-pack of Bud. I put the beer on ice and immersed myself in the hot tub. For two hours. This is what dreams are made of.

I phoned some friends while soaking, boasting I had hiked seventy miles. *I am the man.* It seemed so far, the equivalent of hiking from my hometown of Traverse City, Michigan, to the neighboring town of Cadillac. Every time I'd made that journey, it had been by car. On the highway.

Alone with my thoughts, I have to admit there have been times on this journey when I've gotten down. Down to a level I have not experienced since Vietnam. I try to stay positive, but my mind keeps twisting and turning, always thinking and wondering if the trail would be easier if I wasn't always alone. Or I could just get out of the cold and quit. I promised I would go a month, and if it were a month right now, I would probably hang it up. I miss Kinsley. Many folks that start on the AT as couples soon find out how difficult it is to be with someone 24/7. I think Kinsley and I could make it.

Today, as every day, my mind thinks of Vietnam as I hike. A wee bit different from this trail. Food was a common obsession, as I always thought of food, then and now. Beyond that it was survival. Intensely missing my sisters, my mom, my dad, my friends. I wished then I could at least speak to them on the phone, but that wasn't to be. Wondering several times a day if I would see another sunrise. Wondering what it would be like to lose a leg, an arm. Wondering if I would lose my mind. Putting all my faith in my brothers in arms. The heat, rain, bugs were nothing compared to life itself. Wondering if I would receive a letter or a package the next resupply. Thinking always to keep my weapon clean, fearful of it jamming. Will we get dug in before dark so I can heat up those shitty C-rations? And of course as time allowed, thinking of the girls back home.

I am noticing that lots of folks cheat on this hike. They blue-blaze (take an easier route) around the mountain instead of white-blazing over it. Blue blazes are marked on the trees the same as white blazes. I have even heard of some people yellow-blazing it (take a car or hitch a road north and get dropped off way up the trail, instead of hiking the trail). I decided early on that if I do this trail, I would do it by following the white blazes. I will be a "pure" thru-hiker. If I quit, I quit.

Due South told me he blue- and yellow-blazed to Hiawassee. He skipped some of the trail. He is already cutting the miles? I say, If you're doing that, why hike at all?

I often wonder how many people I know from back home would be out here if they had the time. Few, if any. Up and down mountains. Cold rain, wind, and sleet. No bed to sleep in. Ten hours of hiking a day.

As difficult as this is, at the end of the day I always feel proud. And I know the weather will get better. Physically, I feel strong and have been putting in some good miles. The knees are a little achy and the feet are sore.

I used my new phone to call Kinsley, T.J., Tommy, Kevin, and Mac. Met a few thru-hikers today: The Birds: Mockingbird, Hummingbird, and Tufted Titmouse. Hummingbird and Mockingbird are tiny women. One of them had black toes from shoes too tight. But they all had great attitudes and smiles. The outfitter from Neels Gap drove to Hiawassee with lots of shoes for her to try on. The Birds say they will leave the day after tomorrow. I wonder if and when they all will truly push on.

APRIL 4, 5, AND 6 | HOLIDAY INN EXPRESS' HOT TUB, 0 MILES

I am in a rut. For four days I have been holed up here, not feeling good about myself. Not feeling good about being here. Not feeling motivated to get back on the trail. Here I am judging everyone else, and yet I have not gotten back on the trail. I need to do that, or get off.

Talked to my good friend Mac, subtly looking for motivation. "You need to get back on the trail." Then I spoke with my son, Jonathon, who said, "Foul weather is part of the journey." I'm all stocked up and ready to go, so that is not the problem. I just feel reluctant. I know I must go on for *me*; being physically hurt is one thing, but I can't be defeated mentally. I won't. I said I would go a month minimum if I stayed physically capable. All I do here is eat, drink beer, read, watch TV, and look out the window. It is so cold out there.

3 NORTH CAROLINA AND TENNESSEE

APRIL 7, 8:00 A.M.

I checked out of the Holiday Inn Express. Watched the Michigan State Spartans lose to North Carolina in the NCAA final last night. Dammit. Now I am about to venture out into the cold to hitch to the trail. I feel determined.

I got a quick ride to Dicks Creek Gap from a meat salesman. As he dropped me off, he said, "Nice day for a hike, a little chilly but once you get going, you should have a beautiful walk."

He had a beautiful well-trained golden retriever, who reminded me so much of my dog, Benham. But Benham has an easy life and wouldn't last two days on the AT, walking all day, every day.

MUSKRAT CREEK SHELTER | 11.8 MILES, 79.3 MILES TOTAL

My most agonizing day on the trail by far, mentally and physically. Colder than shit. Blizzard conditions. The salesman can kiss my buttocks area. Beautiful day for a hike? I was so scared. Two-foot snowdrifts. Wind howling. I couldn't make out the white blazes on trees because the snow was sticking to them. I was way out of my comfort zone. I didn't know if I was on the trail, or walking aimlessly through the woods. I plodded along and every now and then I would think I saw a blaze, wipe the snow off the tree, and sometimes yes, sometimes no. I shivered and shook all day. I thought I was miserable in the rain and sleet. Now I'm paying mightily for those do-nothing days at the hotel.

Why am I thinking about ambush patrol, in the middle of the wilderness in a blizzard? I don't know, but I am. I am recalling digging in for the evening in early November of '67 when our platoon leader told me that I was to take a squad out on ambush patrol (AP). Take six guys, he said, leave the perimeter and walk 1,000 meters or so through the jungle and set up for the night. And if you get

26

the chance, ambush some NVA. It sounded absurd. It sounded like grade-school war games. It sounded like suicide.

We left the perimeter a couple hours before dark. On the way out we passed our LP (listening post). The LP was three guys, set up 50 meters in front of our bunkers. They have a radio and stay in contact with the perimeter about any movement, or lack thereof, of enemy in the area. The three guys pull 10 hours of guard duty in the night, three hours and 20 minutes apiece. The idea being, better to have three guys killed than the whole company.

I thought how easy it would be for our AP to simply set up with the LP. How would anyone know? Certainly our company commander was not coming out there to check on us. We would have 10 people to pull guard so we would actually get a full night's sleep. When the RTO (radio telephone operator) in charge calls the LP or AP during the night, and asks for a situation report, we are ordered not to speak, but simply to break squelch on the radio three times if the situation is negative. So if the AP and the LP were set up together? When the RTO in charge in the perimeter calls the 5-1 LP and asks for a situation report, whoever is on guard could simply break squelch three times. Then when the RTO calls 5-1 AP and asks for same, the same person breaks the squelch three times once again. No one would ever know we were set up together. I actually did that a couple times during my tour, but not this night. This night we walked.

All of us were scared beyond imagination as we tried to get to our night location. Eventually, we came to a clearing. This was our set-up point. We quickly placed claymore mines around the area and dug some half-ass holes with no overhead cover. I called in artillery to surround us in case we did get into trouble. This means giving the artillery battery our location, then asking for a smoke round. If the round is way off, adjust by telling them "right 100 meters," or "drop 50 meters." Then, another smoke, and fine-tune it from there.

After adjustments we were set for the night. And we were terrified. These hills were crawling with NVA.

We would pull 10 hours of guard between the seven of us, 1.5 hours apiece. "Do not fall asleep on guard" was such an obvious rule it didn't need to be stated out loud or written down, but I woke up in the middle of the night to the sound of our radio blurting. It was the RTO in the perimeter, calling 5-1 Alpha Papa, 5-1 Alpha Papa, asking for a situation report. Over and over he asked. I crawled to the radio and found one of our guys totally zonked, headset in his hand. The perimeter had been calling for almost three hours. They thought we'd been ambushed. I was livid. We could have had our throats slit. The guard's sleepy response? "Aw, man, I was tired! Shiiit, we're ok."

At the first sign of daylight, we had permission to pack up and head back to our company. I was relieved. There's comfort in numbers. We made it back without incident, but I cannot begin to explain how harrowing the walk out, the night spent, and the walk back to our company was for all of us. I don't want people to have to go to war, but part of me still wishes people could experience the horror of combat. No one could support war as a means for peace if they actually lived it for a few days.

Surprisingly, thinking of war sometimes makes hiking easier. I think to myself, "How bad can this be?"

At last I heard voices ahead, and I was elated to make it to Muskrat Creek Shelter at Muskrat Gap. There are five other guys here. All are thru-hikers and all are freezing. We tried building a fire, but the wood we gathered had been covered with snow and was cold and wet. The fire smoldered, but never caught. All of these guys are nice and some had big problems. One said his wife just left him. One was AWOL from the military. One was very silent. One quit his job and didn't know what to do. One, Roadrunner, was a retired school administrator. He was a slightly built man with a quick smile. He was shivering more than the others. We posed for a photo and smiled as if we were having fun.

I was in my sleeping bag by 5:30. I had mac and cheese for dinner, but my hands were so cold I could barely hold the spoon. I tried to drink from my water bladder, but the hose was frozen. It was an extremely long night and getting up to pee was torture. It was so difficult getting out of that warm bag. I couldn't find my penis because it had shriveled so much from the cold. My balls were like BBs. I have poor circulation anyway, and my toes would not warm, making it difficult to sleep. The guy next to me had no mat to sleep on and only a light blanket. He said he'd wanted to carry a light pack. He was shaking all night long even though we hunkered in next to one another.

THE BOYS OF THE APPALACHIAN TRAIL.

THE PONIES. (PAGE 78)

APRIL 8, 8 A.M.

Up very early, at the first sign of light. Roadrunner's watch told us the temperature was 19 degrees. I have no desire to eat breakfast, but will force myself. My hands are freezing.

Night Moves trudged out of the woods shivering, showing up just before I left. He was one of the guys I met on Springer Mountain at the start of the trail who'd decided to stay for three days and wait for the sun to break through. He was also the guy who woke up Due South to stop his torturous snoring. He'd been tenting out in the woods, waiting for the snow to stop. None of us could see him from the shelter and had no idea he was there. He said he just stayed in his bag for two days as the snow piled up, camouflaging his tent. He would stay one more day and then hike on.

One by one the hikers finish eating and hit the trail. I am one of the last to leave. I am having a problem functioning because I am shaking so badly. My water bladder is still frozen so I got water from a nearby stream and filtered it into a bottle. As a motivational tool, I told myself that everyone else was in the same boat as me, and off I went.

BETTY CREEK GAP | 16.2 MILES, 95.5 MILES TOTAL

When I made it back to the trail, the snowdrifts were deep. It was clear and cold, cold, cold. The tree branches covered in ice and snow did make the trail so beautiful. The wind had subsided. It was still. Later, the weather warmed. The sun shined. I felt invigorated, strong, and energized.

I hiked with some section hikers for a bit. One guy had previously thru-hiked. He said he finished in four months and thirteen days. Trail name, Nuclear. He is a short, round man, full of trail knowledge. I enjoyed hiking with him for a bit. One by one I hiked past all the other guys who had stayed at the shelter and who had started out before me. I crossed into North Carolina. Goodbye, Georgia. One state down, thirteen to go.

At a road crossing some guy gave me a Snickers bar and told me that I had completed the most difficult sections in the area. He said North Carolina is all switchbacks. It's easier to go back and forth then straight up a mountain so hearing that was a nice morale boost. I hiked to Betty Creek Gap, 16.2 miles. I am 14 miles from Franklin, North Carolina, and a hostel. I look forward to warmth, good food, and supplies.

There will be another chill in the air tonight. I managed to find a flat spot and pitched the tent. I had pasta for dinner, hung the bear bag, brushed my teeth, and wiggled my way into the warmth of my sleeping bag. The body is sore, with both knees and my right foot giving me trouble. I have blisters on the small toes of both feet. The worse part of today's journey was wiping my ass with snow because the rookie ran out of TP. Worse shit ever. Chafed, I became.

APRIL 9 | FRANKLIN, NC, HOSTEL, 12.2 MILES, 107.7 MILES TOTAL

The snow has melted. A gorgeous sunny day is upon me. It is beautifully quiet. I tore the tent down, packed up, and had just finished breakfast when along comes a human. A guy named Eric, from Maine. He looked at me puzzled at first, and then asked if I was with someone, because he had heard voices. "That was me talking to me," I said. He smiled and said he understood. He has been section hiking for four years on the AT during his vacations. This is his last leg. He persevered. We took pictures of each other, then he showed me a stone and told me to hold it. I looked at it quizzically, wondering the significance. He said it was a stone from Mt. Katahdin, the northern terminus of the AT, my destination. That is a place that seems not miles, but years away.

At times today I checked for phone service and finally found it after a few miles and a climb straight up Albert Mountain, elevation 5,220 feet. At one point, I had to throw my poles up to a ledge, because they were hindering my progress. I needed to grasp the rocks with my hands. I cussed out the dude who said I had nothing but switchbacks in front of me. My reward on the mountaintop was a pleasant conversation with Kinsley, but she told me her trail days are now a week later than I expected. I have to adjust to her not arriving until the end of May.

I climbed to the top of a fire tower and took some photos. Today was another good day. Thoughts of quitting had danced through my head these past couple of days, but I pushed through them. At this moment I feel that if my body holds out, I will hold out mentally. I hear of more and more people leaving the trail for various reasons, and most of them are mental. Word travels up and down the trail like a soap opera.

The temperature climbed to 70 today. After a low of 21 yesterday.

The warmth feels good, but both my knees still hurt, especially the left one. The right one has been surgically repaired, leaving me with little range of motion. The right foot feels hot by the third toe. Very irritating. On the bottoms of both feet, blisters formed, but have subsided. Both ankles are sore. I've had two back surgeries, but have experienced no problems in that area so far. Every morning when I start my hike I am stiff and sore. Twenty minutes in, I feel surprisingly normal.

Milestone: Passed the 100-mile mark. I have hiked 100 miles!

When emerging from the woods onto US 64, I was met by some trail angels wearing "Jesus Saves" hats. Beautiful folks. They provided me a can of Coke, a bag of chips, and a chair to sit in.

Highway 64 heads into Franklin, North Carolina, home of a hiker hostel and non-trail food. Two other thru-hikers joined the trail angels and me. A phone call would bring the hostel shuttle, but I preferred to hitch into town. An old preacher named Tommy gave me a ride to the post office, where I picked up a package from Kinsley. A woman named Lynn gave me a ride to the hostel. All along the AT, I have never waited longer than five minutes for a ride. What a wonderful testament to the goodness of people. I just love this. And the country is so beautiful. I like this, today anyway. I ask myself: does this make weathering all of the cold, snowy, miserable days worth it? Maybe.

I got a private room at the hostel, did my laundry, and got my resupply. Everything is ready to go for tomorrow. I like to have my shit wired tight before I partake in pleasure.

I opened up the package from Kinsley with a huge smile on my face. Chili, brownies, spaghetti. I will be eating like a king for a few days.

I had dinner at a place called Cody's with Roadrunner and Speartip, two guys I was stuck in the snow with at Muskrat Gap. What great company. What great food. Bottomless salad, beer, steak, and a potato. Roadrunner is a 64-year-old former high school administrator. Speartip is AWOL from the Army. He was a former medic. His wife left him and took their two children to Japan. He was extremely troubled about it, and seemed like such a nice guy, the type to be a good dad and a good soldier. I can't help but wonder if there is more to the story.

I will exit here at 8:30 a.m. sharp. I hike at 2 mph on a good day now; was 1.5 mph in Georgia. Get up early and go.

APRIL 10 | COLD SPRING SHELTER, 14.6 MILES, 123.5 MILES TOTAL

After devouring my breakfast I waited outside for the shuttle back to the trail. All the thru-hikers are "zeroing" (zero days are when you do nothing) here today because of the pouring rain. I am moving on. I feel determined today. Had a plan and I won't deviate from it. The air feels relatively warm and the shuttle dropped me off exactly where I left the trail. Away I went in the rain, alone.

Spoke with Kinsley on the phone near Siler Bald. She is meeting me on May 15, wherever I am. Company! And a love I miss dearly.

My mind drifted to thoughts of Trail Days, a hiker celebration in mid-May in Damascus, Virginia, 340 miles from here. I thought of all the people back home who suggested I stay in the shelters as opposed to my tent because of bears. I haven't seen one bear. So I will stay in shelters if I want to be around people or desperately need cover from the weather; otherwise I'll be tenting it. The trail seems to be weaving in and out of Tennessee and North Carolina.

I find myself at the Cold Spring Shelter. Rain came down all day, and a miserable and cold rain it was. At Burningtown Gap, 1.2 miles from shelter, there were trail angels: people with grills making burgers, hot dogs, etc. They offer beer. I declined. Too cold. How about hot chocolate? Right on. What great hospitality. Diamond Doug and friends were there, most who had previously thru-hiked. I enjoyed talking to them, but after two great cheeseburgers and the hot chocolate, I had the overpowering urge to get to the shelter and into my bag. I needed warmth. They were talking about how difficult Virginia was going to be. And New York and New Hampshire, too. I needed to stay positive.

Once in the shelter, the rain increased and a horrendous lightning and thunderstorm ensued. Buckets of rain and hail came down, making me feel edgy and scared. An angry drunk came in with his dog, yelling at it that he was going to kick its ass if it didn't behave. He didn't know I was there but when he saw me, he became gentle with the dog. The dude had been drinking whiskey and beer with the trail angels. He just got settled in when two couples showed up just before dark. They got into their bags next to me and proceeded to eat their food while in their bags. A trail no-no. Bears and mice have good noses. These hikers reinforced my reasoning for not sleeping in shelters. My body is sore, but once I get moving in the morning the pain subsides.

APRIL 11, 7 A.M.

I got a fairly good night's sleep, save when I stepped in a pile of mud at 3 a.m. when exiting the shelter to pee. I was just getting back to sleep when I was forced to listen to the woman next to me moan while her man massaged her under her sleeping bag. I felt jealous. I missed Kinsley.

In the morning the rain poured on. I packed up my shit, ate some nuts, drank some Emergen-C, filled up my water, and was on my way. I will undoubtedly feel horny all day, after listening to my shelter neighbors.

SASSAFRAS GAP SHELTER | 9 P.M., 18.4 MILES, 141.9 MILES TOTAL

Up, then down. Up, then down. High, then low. I had to throw my pack up the hill sometimes just in order to climb, and then throw it down to descend. I'm still cussing that dude who gave me the Snickers. I arrived at the Nantahala Outdoor Center about 4 p.m. I thought I had traveled further, but had gone only 11.6 miles. But those were 11.6 tough miles. This is a big kayaking spot in the mountains so the NOC was bustling. I bought myself a couple of treats and headed out. I was tempted to stay, but I wanted to get to the Sassafras Gap Shelter by dark. Lots of folks zero here, but I felt like pushing on. The last 6.9 miles turned out to be exhausting. Climbed what felt like straight up for six miles, then down for one.

I can only try to describe the beauty of the landscape here: the singing birds, the beautiful flowers, the ultra-quiet of the woods. Words don't feel adequate. How could I ever explain this? I passed an older guy, probably my age, who was hiking with his grandson. They were also hiking to the shelter and he was struggling. Darkness had descended when I arrived at the shelter, only to find it packed with hikers. The last thing I wanted to do was pitch my tent and heat and eat my chow in the dark, but even in my weary state, I managed. Then I crawled into my warm sleeping bag and went to bed with a smile on my face. I had cell service and was able to say good night to Kinsley.

April 12 | Easter Sunday, Cable Gap Shelter, 15.2 miles, 157.1 miles total

Today begins with a beautiful, bright, sunny morning. I tear down and eat breakfast. All the others here are doing the same. According to the map, we have some big ups and downs today. I spoke with my sisters Charlee, Eve, and Cindy yesterday morning. They chatted about what they'd be preparing for Easter dinner. Prime rib, ham, and chicken. Here I am in the middle of the woods, feeling almost constantly famished, and they're talking about food! I've learned how to have a conference call with all three of them, and hearing their voices made my day.

I hiked up and up to Cheoah Bald, 5,062 elevation, where all I saw was beauty lying beneath me in every direction.

I look forward to a zero day at Fontana Dam. Let my body rest, catch up on e-mail, relax. Knock on wood (tree), I feel well physically. I fell on my ass yesterday, probably five minutes after boasting to myself about not falling. I wish I could look around and enjoy the scenery more as I walk, but looking down at all the jagged rocks is a must. I have to completely stop to enjoy what lies around me.

I rarely, if ever, had the opportunity to stop and enjoy the beauty around me when I was in Vietnam. The flashbacks are beginning to be slightly less frequent.

The food Kinsley sent was great. I dined on chili last night. I miss Speartip and Road Runner. Maybe we will meet again in Damascus at Trail Days. I am sure I am way out ahead of them. I made it to Cable Gap Shelter as planned, pitched the tent and ate. The shelter is overflowing with people. At least ten tents decorate the forest around the shelter. We had a wonderful conversation around a roaring fire, sharing why each of us was out here, where we were from, and how we felt. We all went to sleep at hiker midnight, which is 9 p.m. No one shared their given name, just their trail name. Splice, Couscous, Mad Chatter, Carpenter, Lemonhead, Soundtrack (Detroit), Roach, Scab, Whupwhup, Ryan and his dog, Pepper.

I tossed and turned all night. The rain kept me awake and just when I thought the flashbacks were fewer, I thought of Tet, the lunar New Year in Vietnam. Tet was when the NVA and Vietcong launched a major surprise offensive throughout South Vietnam. It began at the end of January, 1968. I don't know the official ending, but for us it lasted over a month. We had no idea what was coming.

Our company was located at one of the finest firebases. We were in a very secure area. The terrain was open, a giant field. There was no way anyone could sneak up on us. The firebase had tanks mounted with huge artillery guns that looked like cannons. We felt safe. And, we were treated to the best chow of my entire tour. We even had ice cream.

Then word came down that another firebase was taking fire. Time to go, A Company. I think it was the first day of Tet, January 30th.

We choppered up to the base at the top of a hill and immediately sought bunkers, already dug. I saw GIs in body bags. That was Vietnam. We were eating steak and ice cream one minute, in combat the next.

The NVA were dug in approximately 300 meters from our location. It was a slight uphill to the top, all jungle. Our platoon was somewhere in the middle when we moved out. After what happened next, I'd write home to friends urging them to do whatever it took to not come here.

I was maybe 75 meters outside the firebase, following the pack, when the firing started. Between the AK-47 and M-16 fire, and the mortars, the sound was deafening. I screamed as loud as I could, but couldn't hear myself. We were pinned down, afraid to move.

We had no idea how many NVA were up there or where they were, given the dense jungle. Some of our unit had been hit. As the sound of weapons began to cease, screams for help filled the air. "Medic! Medic!" Some of these screams came from the NVA as they tried to lure our medics to them so they could end their lives. We ended up pulling back. Only to attempt the same mission the next day.

Early the next morning, jets pounded the location with 500-pound bombs making the scene resemble a Hollywood horror flick. But this was real. The F-4 Phantom jets would release their bombs a few hundred meters from our location and bank to the right. The bombs would silently drift over our bunkers before hitting their targets. Gazing up at them gliding over us was surreal. After dropping their ordnance, the jets banked to the right and we could see green tracers zip by the aircraft. It was the NVA, trying to shoot them down, moments before a 500-pound bomb landed amongst them.

It felt like suicide to try to take that hill. We didn't know it at the time but what would come to be known as The Tet offensive was in full swing.

As luck had it, my platoon would be in the middle of our company, which meant roughly 50 guys would be headed up that hill before me: 50 guys x 5 meters between men = 250 meters, almost to the top. I thought, "I may never leave this perimeter," and yet I was still terrified.

After the air strike the morning was quiet as the first platoon left the perimeter, heading toward the top. We stayed in our bunkers, guarding the perimeter while they moved. It didn't take long for the shit to come raining down.

Our platoon never did leave that perimeter. But the men in front walked directly into a U-shaped ambush. Our point-man almost stepped on an enemy machine gun, and that triggered the ambush. Many GIs were killed immediately, many more were wounded. Others came screaming back to the perimeter.

The next day we did it again. This time we sent a squad up the hill. They made it without confrontation. Our squad followed. We brought body bags. I hated it. They were from another platoon, but I knew them. Some had no dog tags. Rumor had it that the families of some of these men received a letter from the North Vietnamese government stating they had killed their sons. Those letters supposedly arrived before the U.S. government knew they were KIA.

1968 | THE BOYS OF THE 1ST PLATOON, A COMPANY, 3RD BATTALION, 12TH INFANTRY, 4TH INFANTRY DIVISION.

We found very few enemy dead. We surmised they had buried their dead and had left the location in the dark of night.

Our point man was not among the dead. He was listed as MIA (missing in action), presumed dead, but we worried he might have become a POW (prisoner of war). It was a sad, sad day.

Days later and back at the firebase, we heard movement down the hill. Whatever it was, it was heading our way. The sun was shining brightly as our point man emerged from the jungle. We were all smiles, but he was not the same person we knew a few days ago. He wore a look of terror. He spoke little. We called a helicopter in and flew him back to the rear. I never saw him again.

APRIL 13 | FONTANA DAM, 5.5 MILES, 162.6 MILES TOTAL

The rains came last night and never let up. I am hitting the trail early. Last night I woke to pee, but I didn't want to exit the tent and get wet, so I hung myself out of the tent and let it go. The pee filtered into a steam of rain and flowed under the tent near me. Damn. I couldn't bring myself to wake the dude up who slept in the tent about my mistake. Back to sleep I went.

This impresses me immensely: no complaining from thru-hikers. Through rain, sleet, snow, wind, blisters, aches, and pains, they are all still happy to be here. Incredible. Everyone knows we are attempting the same mission in the same conditions.

I hiked the 5.5 miles to NC-28, near Fontana Dam. I hooked up with Mad Chatter on the road and we hitched to town together, looking for food supplies and laundry facilities. A guy in a camper stopped for us and we hopped in the back. We didn't know we only had a half-mile walk, nor did we know the guy would pass right by where we needed to go. From the back of his camper, we couldn't see a thing, but after a few miles we got concerned and Mad Chatter asked the driver where we were.

"Why, are yawl scairt or sumthin'?" the driver growled back, in a deep southern voice.

"Stop the truck! Let us out, NOW!" we yelped in unison.

Thankfully, he did, but by then we were five miles past Fontana Dam. There was nothing to do but start walking. Luckily, we got another ride from a great couple so loaded down they had to move their belongings around to make room for us. Mad Chatter and I agreed the dude in the camper was up to no good.

I did my laundry and walked over to a small store. There I met Yuki, a 63-year-old Japanese thru-hiker, and I ate three hot dogs with all the fixings in five minutes. Yuki only knew a little bit of English, but said, "I hike fifteen miles a day. Every day. I come to this country to thru-hike Appalachian Trail."

> Every time I see an Asian I remember the damn war. War turned me into a racist. A sickness was born inside me that year in Southeast Asia that will never truly go away. I think of how many years I have worked on healing this sickness, trying not to hate Asians. I went so far as to take my R&R (rest and recuperation) in Australia, a place where there was nothing but people whose eyes looked like mine. I came to Vietnam without this deep racism, but when I exited I was prejudiced against millions of people. My dad's friends from WWII spoke of Japs and Krauts. Afghanistan and Iraq vets call middle-easterners rag-heads and sand niggers. We called the Vietnamese gooks, chinks, Charlie. War breeds racism.

I ended up getting a room at an inn in Fontana Dam instead of hiking back to a shelter on the trail. I had dinner and relaxed in a soft bed. Spoke with Kinsley prior to turning in. I love hearing her voice.

Thoughts of a zero day are dancing in my head, but I decide to push on. I head into the Smoky Mountains tomorrow, with six days to Hot Springs, North Carolina, if all goes well. Going up a mountain continues to leave me a bit winded, although I am improving. Going down the mountain today was very hard on my old knees. I imagine this pattern will continue.

I miss communication with my children, and I wonder all the time what they are doing, and how they are. I think about Benham, our dog. I hope he is okay and being exercised. Ryan's dog, Pepper, has an ear infection and I hope he won't have to get off the trail.

APRIL 14 | SPENCE FIELD SHELTER AREA, 17.8, 180.4 MILES TOTAL

Had breakfast at the inn with Robo, a 60-something year-old man from Grand Rapids, Michigan. Robo is a large guy with a big gray beard, a deep voice, and a broad smile. He is a pleasure to converse with. He knows about Yesterdog, my friend Bill Lewis's hot dog restaurant in Grand Rapids. "Everyone knows Yesterdog," he said. Out here on the trail Robo is taking it "one day at a time." While we were talking a young couple who looked like hikers walked into the restaurant and took a table not far from us. Both seemed to be staring at Robo. Finally, the guy said, "Hey man, we know you." Robo's eyes lit up. "Nitro? Ziplock?" The three immediately embraced. They had hiked a section of the AT together in 2007.

Into the Great Smoky Mountains I walked on a rainy and mud-ridden day. I felt strong early today, but the weather sapped my energy. I will hole up at this shelter, 1.8 miles from Thunderhead Mountain (5,527 feet). I am cold and wet once again.

The Rugged Shark is here, a scraggly 45-ish dude from Chicago. I guess I am a scraggly 60-ish dude from Traverse City. Shark has a quick smile and great attitude. He likes to talk and he likes to listen. Two brothers are also here, one is hunkered in his sleeping bag, so cold he doesn't want to get out. His brother made his meal and handed it to him and gave him coffee. Not even a thank you from the cold brother and I think, hiking with someone with that kind of attitude would get old in a hurry. The one out of his bag said they were thru-hikers, which surprised me.

Walked by Mollies Ridge Shelter today and it looked like a zoo for humans, caged in to keep the bears out. I took one look at that place and moved on.

I have encountered more "ridge runners" here in the Smokies than anywhere on the trail thus far. These conservation officers check to see if you're registered to enter this section of the trail, and no dogs are allowed. Hikers that have trail dogs must kennel them. There are businesses that do this for a reasonable fee. They meet you at the beginning of this section and have your pet waiting for you at the end of it, seventy or so miles down the trail. I think there are too many rules here in the Smokies. The one I dislike the most is not being allowed to pitch my tent unless it is in sight of the shelter. My goal is to get out of the Smokies as soon as possible.

April 15 | Double Spring Gap Shelter 13.5 miles, 193.9 total

A restless night's sleep. As stellar as my sleeping bag is, I just can't seem to get my feet warm.

I made a wrong turn immediately after I got back on the trail from the shelter. I'd let my mind wander, then realized I hadn't seen a white blaze in a while. I walked at least a mile out of the way. *Pay attention, Naneek. You already have 2,000 miles to go. You don't need to tack on any extra.* Once back on the trail, I trudged all day in the rain, cold, mud, and fog until I made it to this shelter.

Travis and Chad from Florida and California are here. They greeted me like I was a long-lost relative. Two young and handsome nice guys. They were high school friends who stayed in touch and made a pact to hike somewhere once a year. They are on a four-day hike. They asked if they could be on my mailing list so they could follow my progress, so I got both their e-mails. I will stay in touch.

Rugged Shark sauntered in a bit after me. Two things are certain about him: He carries a huge pack and he eats like a horse. I knew I would meet some lifelong friends out here and I feel a real connection with him. Shark mentioned an 86-year-old man on the AT trying to break the record as the oldest thru-hiker. This makes even me feel like a young man.

I saw a deer outside the shelter today. The first real wildlife I have seen. I know I could see much more, but I need to look down constantly to keep from falling on the wet rocks and roots, which are extremely slippery.

I wandered down to the stream to get water, slipped on some rocks and fell, breaking one of my trekking poles. I cursed the forest. Tomorrow morning, I will be summiting a mountain, the highest point on the AT, Clingmans Dome, 6,643 feet, with one pole and no gloves. I forgot them at the motel in Fontana Dam.

APRIL 16 | ICEWATER SPRING SHELTER, 13.8 MILES, 207.7 MILES TOTAL

Sleeping did not go well last night. Again, my feet were cold. Then another thru-hiker came in late and his phone alarm went off, over and over, playing this funny, high-pitched music. Someone woke him and he apologized, fixed the problem, and quickly got back in his bag. Moments later another guy (probably Shark) farted in tune with the alarm. I thought people were asleep, but everyone in the shelter broke out laughing.

We were all up at 7 a.m., ready to summit Clingmans Dome. I said goodbye to Travis and Chad and told them I would see them in Mexico. These are young guys, but guys I believe I will know for quite some time.

All of today was beautiful. When the sun shines after so many bleak days, I find new energy. I am appreciating the songbirds, the quiet, the views, and the people. Hikers are wonderful folks. Some are extremely focused. Most are extremely friendly. Some are ill prepared. Witness: no sleeping bag. Or no tent. Or no pad to sleep on. Little water. Little food. All to keep their pack weight down. I think this is stupid and selfish because they know other hikers will feel sorry for them and give them what they need.

A guy I passed on the trail was carrying one pack on his back and a pack on his front. He is a slight man, who wears a big grin on his face. I have no idea how long he will last with his present two-pack strategy.

I summited the highest peak on the AT, and passed two hundred miles. Yes! That's like walking from Traverse City past Lansing. Lots of folks are here at the shelter tonight, and I am deciding to hunker down with them because I am exhausted. Going to bed early.

Less than 2,000 miles to go.

APRIL 17 | COSBY KNOB SHELTER, 19.3 MILES. 228 MILES TOTAL

Another gorgeous day hiking through the Smoky Mountains. Incredible. The sun is shining down on me. I hiked strong today. Felt good.

Some trail names that I remember thus far: Bam Bam, Hot Feet, Butter Toes, Larry, Moe and Curly, (formerly Huey, Dewey, and Lewey), Up and At'Em, Incognito, Two Pack, Concrete Joe, Curious George, Soundtrack, Scab, Roach, Just Mike, I'm Fine, Wheels, Jesse's Girl, Due South, Pirate, Privy, Wrath, Rugged Shark, Ryan and Pepper (dog), Mad Chatter, Yuki, None, Honey Dew, Road Runner, Spear Tip, Bonesy, Bust, Creep.

I arrived at the shelter late, but there was still plenty of light out. I find lots of folks here. I entered the shelter and said hi, but got little response from the occupants. Some were reading, some were eating, so perhaps they are too tired to acknowledge me. I found a spot away from the shelter, pitched my tent, and made some chow. Bam Bam, a young dude with long curly brown hair, sauntered down to my tent site and introduced himself. He had started his thru-hike on March 5, more than three weeks before me. After a few minutes of chatter, he asked me if I wanted to get high. I nodded yes, but wanted to get my shit tightly wired before partaking. After I was done setting up, I partook in his tiny bit of marijuana. Funny – a 20-year-old approaching a 62-year-old and asking him if he wanted to smoke some pot. He said it was the last of his stash and that was a good thing. If he had more, he would be on this trail for a year. He had a three-week head start on me, plus four decades, and I'd caught up with him. He was averaging five miles a day, I was averaging almost twelve.

The Stooges are here. We agree to meet in Hot Springs and have dinner and some beers. Yuki is also here. He said he plans to complete his hike by mid-August.

APRIL 18 | GROUNDHOG CREEK SHELTER, 17.6 MILES, 243.8 MILES TOTAL

The two little toes on my right foot throbbed all day. I soaked them in a stream for a half hour or so. Maybe I will see a doctor in Hot Springs, if possible. I feel somewhat worried. I forbid new injuries.

Trail magic today. Two cans of Coke, two hard-boiled eggs, and a chair at a two-track I crossed, courtesy of Schooner's (hadn't seen him in two weeks) parents. Nice. Yuki was there. "I have heard a lot of negative things about Americans over the years," he said to me, "but I love Americans. You are good people." He spoke with a huge smile on his face. Yuki is probably 5'6", 130 lbs. He has a big pack and hikes slowly and methodically, fifteen miles a day.

Later, more trail magic. I happen upon two cheap white coolers, with rocks on top for weight. Looked like a mirage, because I was a huffin' and a puffin' when I spotted them. I opened them to find cold soda, cookies, and sandwiches. Someone had come up a side trail from somewhere and left them. I have nobody to thank.

I never saw trail magic in Vietnam.

I had a plan tonight. Get my water, cook dinner and eat, brush the teeth and get in my bag. No tent. Doing the shelter thing. Read and sleep. I have slogged thirty-seven miles in two days. My feet need a rest. Hopefully, I will make it to Hot Springs Monday and soak my feet and body. The thought of a hot tub is almost orgasmic.

As I lay here in my sleeping bag I feel so humbled by this experience and the people. I feel wonderful. I was going to read, but the plans changed. Concrete Joe made a wonderful fire and we all talked about lots of stuff--volleyball, gymnastics, parenting, intimacy, relationships. All contributed to the conversation. A woman with no trail name is here. Gail. She appears to be my age or older and is thru-hiking alone. She has a wonderful hammock setup, but refuses a trail name.

I was restless once again in the night (there were also mice). I always seem to toss and turn. Is it the adrenaline? The anticipation of the next day? Or what I've come to label, "war thinking"?

I often think of the war when I doze. No nightmares yet, but I'm now thinking of Vietnam almost every night. Tonight I remembered nightly guard duty in the bush. When we had three grunts to a bunker, our shift would be two hours on, wake the guy next to you, four hours off to try to sleep, then get awakened for a final

1 hour and 20 minutes, then wake the guy next to you, then try to get your final 2 hours and 40 minutes of sleep. Ten hours total. So each person gets 6 hours and 40 minutes of sleep, if you are lucky enough to go right to sleep. When we had the luxury of four to a hole we did 1½ hours on, sleep for 4½, then one hour on, sleep for three.

While on guard we sit on the bunker in the middle of the night and listen for the enemy. If a stick cracked or a branch fell my heart raced and I broke into a sweat. When morning came, we packed up our shit for another run at an enemy we didn't want to find. I don't have to go searching for the enemy here on the AT. Or pull guard duty. And yet, I still find myself sleeping with one eye open. The memories are still so clear even after all these years.

APRIL 19 | HOT SPRINGS, 26.2 MILES, 271.8 MILES TOTAL

I am the first to arise when staying in this shelter for the first time on this journey. I am planning on a 14-mile day if my foot holds up. As I quietly pack I see people hunkered down in the shelter in the warmth of their bags. No movement. Wonderful.

In the war I was afraid of the quiet because of what was to follow. I take a deep, deep breath, and tell myself I am okay. No enemy. Relax. This is the good hike.

Oh, my God, I walked a marathon with a full pack. How proud am I? Foot felt great all day. Steady light rain, but not too cold. I am damp and fatigued. 26.2 miles! Wow. I just felt good all day, and those hot springs were a carrot for this weary body. I shouldn't have traveled so far, but I was feeling it. I was walking in a rain forest, so beautiful and green and lush. Some big ups and downs. Also a lot of ridge walking. I was thinking I was going to have a tough day, but I got a second wind and just trucked. A 14-mile day that was supposed to be followed by a 12.2 day turned into a marathon.

Events of the day: Trail magic cookies at a road. Walking by the shelter where I was going to stay (Walnut Mountain) at 1:20 p.m. and meeting Ninja. Hiking to the top of Bluff Mountain (4,686 feet) and meeting Tall Grass and Coffee Bean, a son and mother from Wisconsin. Tall Grass is a lean young man with longer hair and scraggly growth on his face. Coffee

Bean is a beautiful, yet frail-looking woman. They were eating in the cold rain, with big smiles on their faces. And I met six section hikers and chatted with them for a while. The knees began hurting at twenty miles, especially on descents.

Vietnam was with me all of the day. The rain. The terrain. I am thankful for being alive. Stopped and took a deep breath more than once after searching the forest for movement and realizing there are no bullets here. No shrapnel. No firefights.

Thank you, Denny Leach. I am indebted to you forever. I met Denny on my first day in the bush. He was one of the few who were kind and understanding. He related to my fear and taught me how to survive. He taught me how to take care of myself, how to cook my wretched C-rations, how to cut a field of fire, when to smoke and when not to smoke a cigarette. He taught me the importance of staying aware of what is happening around me and the importance of following my gut. He taught me the importance of camaraderie. He taught me the importance of treating every brother out here with respect and dignity, because I will need them one day, as they will need me.

On December 3, 1967 we were about to go up Hill 943 for the second time. A film crew had choppered out a few days prior to film a documentary for CBS television. They planned on being with us for a few weeks to get the footage they needed.

We were anxious and edgy this day because we'd lost a man the day before to a freak shrapnel incident. A minute piece of metal from a bomb had traveled several hundred meters through the jungle and hit him in the jugular. A cameraman had his camera inches from the wound, filming the blood. I felt like shooting the photographer, he seemed so insensitive. This was our brother.

As we anxiously awaited word to move out a thunderous blast exploded in the trees inside our perimeter. Everyone dove into the nearest bunker. One of the guys, Archie, dove in the same hole that I did, screaming, "I'm hit, I'm hit!" A piece of shrapnel had got him in the wrist. The wound was tiny but it spurted blood. Together we worked on the wound, but could hear moans from nearby. Both of us knew others must have been hit. I looked back and saw a body lying on the jungle floor, quivering in pain. The artillery battery had made a mistake and set one of its guns on the wrong azimuth, resulting in a short round that wounded many.

I left my bunker and crawled to the wounded body. It was Denny. He had a stick in his mouth, biting hard into it to keep from screaming and giving away our position. The lower half of his leg was attached by threads and facing the wrong way. The bone was severed. I screamed for a medic, but they were busy with other wounded. I tried to comfort Denny, tried to be strong for him. Finally a medic arrived and administered morphine, then frantically worked on the leg, trying to clean it with the hopes of saving it. I retrieved branches to use as splints as the medic tried to put the leg back where it should be, taping it in place. Then he put the splints around the leg and heavily taped them, hoping if and when Denny got to a hospital, the leg could be saved. In what seemed liked hours later, a "dust off" medivac helicopter arrived. We carried Denny and placed him in the bird. Other wounded filled the helicopter, with Denny being the most severe. That was the last time I saw my mentor.

I did get one letter from him. He was in Japan at an Army hospital. He had lost the leg. He said he was okay with the loss, but concerned his girlfriend would end their relationship. He signed it, "Long John Silver."

Many other brothers were wounded that day.

Two men in the film crew were wounded. I heard later the lieutenant in charge of the artillery battery that dropped the round on us was relieved of his duty. He was reassigned back to base camp, where he would escort movie stars, athletes, and dignitaries to various hospitals and events.

After getting the wounded on the chopper safely, we reached the summit of the hill unopposed.

All of the men wounded or dead were the result of friendly fire. Hill 943 was a CBS special report that aired in June of 1968, one month before I came home.

I stayed dry throughout my day in the pouring rain, clad in my rain gear. I now reside at a spa. The carrot that was dangling in front of me for miles and miles is now a reality. As I write this I sit soaking my aching old body in a hot tub with a cold beer in my hand. My feet hurt, especially the toes. But 271.8 miles are behind me.

I will meet Kinsley a week from tomorrow. My pace will slow because she is a rookie and will need to get those trail legs under her.

I plan on zeroing for a couple days. I will try to heal, soak, relax, soak, read, eat good food, soak, write, watch some TV, soak. Did I say drink beer?

I'll catch up on the news, see how the Tigers and the Pistons are doing. My head dropped when I heard about the death of "The Bird," Mark Fidrych. His truck fell on him as he worked on it. What a terrible way to go out.

I walked from Fontana Dam to Hot Springs: 107 miles, in six days, averaging 17.8 per day. *Slow down, Naneek.*

I thought all day on the trail, as usual, and remembered talking to the Stooges about hiking for charity. Maybe I can get some friends and family, and perhaps their friends and family and whoever else might be interested, to sponsor me on this journey. I will send out an e-mail to all who are following me and ask for a penny a mile. I will hike to establish a scholarship at my hometown institution, Northwestern Michigan College, for a financially needy veteran, or for his or her child to attend college. It will be named the John Lewis Veterans for Peace scholarship, named after one of the most peaceful men I know. And I will hike for the Women's Resource Center to aid victims of domestic violence.

April 20 | Zero miles

Today was uneventful. I went to a local outfitter and got a new trekking pole and some gloves. I went to breakfast and had two separate meals, pancakes and omelets. Hunger is constant. Had myself a long nap. Ate a pizza. Did whatever, whenever. Hot tub. Oh, yes, and got a massage. My body, and especially my feet, are aching. The masseuse didn't do a very good job, didn't get in deep like some massages I've had, but it was nice to be touched.

April 21 | Zero miles

Had a wonderful time last night drinking beer with the Stooges and Plaid Feedbag at the Bridge Street Cafe. Saw Concrete Joe and Curious George, the father and son team, and met their family. Concrete will get off the trail and Curious George will thru-hike. I will miss Concrete Joe, for his personality and for the wonderful fires he creates at shelters. The Stooges and Feedbag were very inquisitive about Vietnam. They said they don't understand why people go to war. Neither do I. As Feedbag left, he thanked me for my service.

I will e-mail everyone back home today and relay my progress and condition. I plan to buy a new bear-hang mechanism, perhaps it will just be Tupperware. I will do some major doctoring of my feet. I will pack up and have everything ready to go for an early-morning departure. I will once again have "my shit wired tight." Feedbag is doing a documentary and has a video camera along. The Stooges are probably legends in the Netherlands. At their going-away gig, the entertainment was the second-place finisher of the Netherlands' version of "American Idol." A barbecue will happen tonight at their cabin at 5 p.m.

10 p.m. - Sitting in the hot tub reflecting on a perfect night. Nothing eventful transpired, other than trail talk and friendship. I love these guys known as the Stooges. They have great attitudes about life and are quite the comedy team. Larry made burgers and hot dogs. Moe and I went searching for the Rugged Shark who was supposed to be in town, but he was nowhere to be seen. Moe stood in the middle of the road in Hot Springs and kept yelling, "Rugged Shark, Rugged Shark," to no avail. Megan and Schooner were at the cookout. Megan drinks Jack Daniels and we all tried to come up with a trail name for her. Schooner did not like the idea of calling her Jack, after Jack Daniel. This was a night worth remembering, just sitting by the fire and talking. Tomorrow all will be back on the trail.

April 22 | Little Laurel Shelter, 19.6 miles, 291.4 miles total

I ate breakfast once again at the Smoky Mountain Diner. This time I had a double order of French toast with a side of ham. I saw a huge woman (at least three hundred fifty pounds) eating breakfast with Bama. She had a pack, but I couldn't imagine her on the trail. Bama had thru-hiked the trail a couple years ago, and was hiking to Damascus, Virginia, for trail days. I later saw the big woman on the trail just out of Hot Springs and she was struggling big time. She was drenched in sweat after barely starting out. My hat was off to her for the determined look she had on her face. She was hiking alone which made me feel worried for her.

I labored early before I got my second wind. Coming off double zeros, a bunch of beers, and a full stomach doesn't help. I would have waited for the Stooges, but I knew they would catch up with me soon enough. Upon arrival at the shelter, I found a flat spot to pitch my tent. Flat spots on the trail are hard to come by, as odd as that may seem. I met two others here, but can't remember their names because I am in bed early, ultra-fatigued. I read a bit from *The Lincoln Lawyer,* a mystery TJ bought me. I miss that guy. I miss my family and friends. I think about them every day. To be blessed with so many people that love me is something I'll never take for granted. I crashed hard until pee call. Getting out of bed is so very difficult for this old body tonight, but I had to make my move. I sort of rolled out of the tent and onto my feet. The body is sore. I was thankful it wasn't cold or rainy.

APRIL 23 | FROZEN KNOB, 18.8 MILES, 310.2 MILES TOTAL

I was up early and ate breakfast at the shelter, shooting the shit with the boys. Took a couple photos and moved out thinking about possibly doing an 18-mile day.

I am into a routine now: Get up before sunrise. Get out of my sleeping bag, but stay in the tent. Pack up all my gear inside the tent including my sleeping bag, thermarest, and stuff bag full of my extra clothes that I use as a pillow and to carry my book and journal. Then out of the tent, and bring all my stuff outside. Zip tent up and tear it down. Pack everything in my pack other than my meds, toothbrush, and breakfast. Relax and eat breakfast. Pack up the rest, brush my teeth, do my medications, saddle up and gone. If there is a water source, I fill up. What used to take me an hour and a half now takes forty minutes. I am becoming a veteran hiker.

In Vietnam, this was the routine if we were not in contact with the enemy: Up at 6, grab a quick bite, tear down the bunker by emptying the sandbags and filling in the hole that was the bunker, bring in the trip flares and claymores, do or not do a malaria pill, pack up my rucksack, make sure my weapon is clean, get instructions on where our destination is this day and move out, allowing five meters between men. Usually we would move between 3,000 and 5,000 meters a day, searching, and eventually taking a "hill" and hope against hope it was NVA free. The higher-highers (media and upper echelon soldiers, none of whom are involved in combat) want bloodshed so they can achieve rank and glory.

The maps are elaborate and we hack our way through the jungle until we achieve our mission. Never take a trail.

If we arrive on the hill with no resistance, everyone goes about their job. Two dig a hole and fill sixty sandbags. (Each troop carries 15 and there are four troops to a bunker.) Ideally the hole is chest deep and ten-feet long, but sometimes the terrain didn't allow such luxury. While two troops dug the hole, the other two would cut overhead cover and clear foliage. Overhead cover was usually three or four trees maybe 9" wide and 12' long. Those trees would be placed on top of the sandbags (three high, two deep) that we'd built up on both ends of the hole we were digging. Then we would lay the rest of the sandbags on top of the trees, giving us overhead cover in case of a mortar attack. Foliage needed to be cleared so we would have an open field of fire in case of enemy attack.

The two troops not digging would also be responsible for strategic placing of trip flares and claymore mines in front of our location. Trip flares are little round canisters equipped with a pin inserted into a handle and fine wire. We'd tie the canister to a small tree and string the wire tight approximately ten meters before tying it off. We'd then pull the pin on the canister until it was almost out, just hanging on, and attach the wire to it. We'd place three of these trip flares in front of our perimeter, so wire was extended the entire width of our field of fire. If an enemy happened through, they'd trip the wire, the pin would pop off, the handle would release, and the canister would light up the perimeter.

The claymore mines are electrical devices that all are required to carry. The mine itself is half-moon shaped, about eight inches long and five inches wide. It is a highly explosive device triggered by a detonator. The mines are placed in front of a tree or stump twenty to thirty meters in front of the bunker. Heavy-duty wire is then strung from the mine to inside our bunker and attached to the detonator. In case of attack, we ignite the mines by squeezing the detonator. Each mine sends hundreds of ball bearings at hundreds of miles an hour into whoever may be in the way, instantly eliminating them.

Nobody complained of the work required for set up, even though we were dog-tired from moving all day. When we finished with security and bunkers, we constructed a hooch, or tent. We cut two forked stripped branches to be used as braces for the long stick that was used as the upper beam, and then we snapped two ponchos together and strung them over the "beam." We pulled the ponchos tight and staked them down. Often times, in the monsoons, we would place our steel pot on each end of the poncho and catch drinking water. If we were fortunate enough to finish our duties before dark, we could heat up our C-rations. If not, we ate them cold. No using heating devices at night. A fire after dark would turn us into targets.

This was the routine of the "grunt." Those of us who actually fought that damn war. We were like pawns out there in the bush.

It was a rough day. Big climbs. Making good time did not happen. The feet hurt. The knees. The back. Not good. I wanted to stop earlier, but I couldn't find a flat spot to pitch my tent. How could I not find a flat spot when I searched for one for more than three miles?

As it turned out, the spot I now find myself in was worth the wait. I could use the words "gorgeous" or "beautiful" all day, every day. I can be physically spent, but the beauty just takes hold of me. After pitching the tent, I cooked and ate dinner in a hurry. There are gnats and mosquitos everywhere.

Just as I have the pack-up routine down now, I have the setup routine down, too. Pitch tent. Get all my inside stuff assembled and ready to go on the outside by the zipper of the tent. In one quick move, unzip, throw it all in, and zip it back up. Bugs are not welcome in my tent house.

I am in bed at 7:30 p.m. I write for a bit, then read, then turn my headlamp out. Sleep time.

Near disaster. I woke up to a horrendous smell around my tent. The smell was coupled with major movement and heavy breathing. I am scared shitless. My pack was right next to me, and I knew I had no food in it. Like a good Boy Scout, I'd hung my food up the trail in a tree. Then I remembered leaving some candy wrappers in my pack. Not a good move. I just lay there waiting, barely breathing. (It reminded me of the many times my sister Charlee and I would lie in bed as kids, just knowing someone was coming up the stairs to get us, except this was real.) Finally, whatever was out there in the dark moved on. I suspect it was a bear. Boars and bears danced through my dreams the rest of the night.

I waltzed past the 300-mile mark today. That's like walking from Traverse City, Michigan, to Toledo, Ohio. I hiked a bit today with Sodfather and his dog.

APRIL 24 | WHISTLING GAP, 16.4 MILES, 326.4 TOTAL

I was up this morning at 7 a.m. and I moved quickly because of the gnats and mosquitos trying for a food-fest courtesy of my body. I needed to take an ultra-quick shit and eat breakfast without getting eaten myself. This put me in a bad mood. I'd intended on relaxing and enjoying a beautiful view with breakfast. Not to be.

I hiked about three miles and then followed the arrow to the Hogback Ridge Shelter. I needed water. When I reached the shelter I realized I had to hike down a ridge, some 500 feet, to find the water source. A lone male hiker was at the shelter lounging around and asked me if I would fill his water bladder for him. I agreed, not knowing how far I had to hike. The little walk to get water ended up being a half hour down and forty minutes back up. When I finally got back to the shelter with the guy's water, he said, "What took you so long, man? I need to get going." That pissed me off, but I tried to remain calm.

I arrived here at 6 p.m. or so. A rough day it was. Mount Bald kicked my ass. I met a guy named Feather Feet on top of the Bald today, along with a couple other hikers. Both had chewed-up feet.

I pounded so much water today. My right foot is so sore. I pitched the tent in the woods once again, away from shelter. I found a flat spot and immediately dropped my pack. Wherever I get tired, I stop if I find a flat spot. I was eating dinner alone in the quiet of the woods when Feather Feet happened by. He set up near me. We chatted a bit. He is fifty-ish, a marathon runner, tall and thin. He, like me, is physically challenged every day, some days more than others. This is a mind game out here, a most difficult mind game. There is no describing the stress on the body. One has to experience this to understand it. And the pictures I take of the scenery could never do justice to what I see with my eyes. No way.

I love the simplicity of this life. I love eating out in the woods, although I need to be more creative with the food I make, as my meals are getting boring. I wish I remembered the creativity and recipes I used in Vietnam. I could make some good chow with those dreaded C-rations.

APRIL 25 | IRWIN, TENNESSEE, 13 MILES, 339.4 TOTAL

I take the tent down per usual. Go to a stream and filter my water. Eat breakfast. Feather Feet quietly does the same and is back on the trail before me. I will probably never see him again, unless he does a zero. That's the way it goes out here. I watched the sun rise through the trees. The quiet, except for the chirping of birds, brings a smile to my face.

Descriptive words to relay home: grueling, brutal, beautiful, hunger, physical, challenging, endless thinking, water source, mountains, feet, knees, trail magic, two m.p.h., elevation, ridge lines, switchbacks, downhills, rocks, roots, rain, sleet, snow, loneliness, family.

I've seen one thru-hiker my age to this point, as most I meet are much younger. I've found that it helps to stop two times daily to take my socks off and air out my feet. . Let them breathe. Have I shaved? No. I look like a mountain man. At first I liked it, but now my beard is at the itchy stage so it may have to go. Pack? 35-40 lbs. Mostly water and food. I have lost weight. I'm down to 173 from 195. Most of the hikers I see have been section hikers. Irwin is on my mind, as is Kinsley. I was supposed to get there on the 27th, but have logged some big days. Once I get my rhythm and there is still daylight, I find my thinking to be, *why not keep moving?*

I gave lots of thought today to my accumulated aches and injuries.

In September of '67, while on a combat assault of a hill, I twisted my leg jumping from a chopper. We'd been choppering in to a makeshift landing zone (LZ). The upper echelon of officers were actually hoping for contact with the enemy, but none of us grunts wanted contact. And we didn't appreciate our lives being played with like a game of *Risk*. On this particular day there was no contact, but we never know going in. The chopper would buzz in and hover for seconds about three feet off the ground and we were to jump out and run for cover, hoping not to get our head blown off by the NVA. That was how I twisted my knee. I thought I would be okay in the morning, but it was extremely swollen. I was pleased, although I kept those thoughts to myself. This could mean I could get out of the bush! This could mean I could go to the hospital! This injury could save my life!

My platoon leader looked at it and said, "He'll be okay. Let's get ready to move." The company medic said otherwise, and I was airlifted back to base camp and taken by jeep to the hospital. Ah, American nurses. Hot chow every day. A real bed. Flushing toilets. TV, radio, and hot showers. Heaven!

The shower area had mirrors. I had not seen myself in a couple of months and the reflection I confronted was staggeringly horrible. I had jungle rot between my lip and my nose and all down my neck. My face was gaunt and I was terribly thin.

I showered quickly, dressed in my robe, and sought out a nurse. "Look at me!" I said. "Will this ever leave my face or am I scarred for life?" She smiled and calmed me down, explaining that if I took a couple showers a day and washed the sores, they would disappear.

She put me on the scale. I weighed 128 lbs; I was 185 when I left infantry training at Fort Polk, Louisiana. I'd lost 57 pounds in two months. Stress, humping, C-rations, and missing home had taken their toll on my body.

I spent ten days in the hospital. One day, while dozing, I was awakened by a fuss around the foot of my bed. Through half-open eyes, I saw a handsome man in freshly pressed fatigues. He extended his hand. "Are you PFC Keenan?" he asked. I sat up and said, "Yes, sir," thinking he was a general or something. He said, "Hi Tim, I'm Charlton Heston." We spoke briefly and he finished with, "I am going back to the states soon. If there is anyone you want me to contact and tell them you are okay, I will be happy to do so." I declined. None of my family knew I was in the hospital. But thinking back later, my sisters or my mom would have been thrilled to speak with Mr. Heston; after all, he was the star of Ben Hur.

X-rays proved negative on the knee. The swelling subsided. I was sent back out to the bush on my 21st birthday. No celebrating. The jungle rot was gone, but I was a gloomy soldier that day.

Another beautiful view on the AT, this time from Temple Hill, overlooking the Nolichucky River and Irwin, Tennessee. I headed down the mountain and arrived in Irwin at 4 p.m. I stopped at Jonnie's hostel for a quick beer and hitched a ride to the Holiday Inn Express. I could catch up on my computer updates to friends and family and relax. I could have stayed at Jonnie's, but felt like being by myself. I did meet a young guy at the hostel named Pork Chop, from my hometown of Traverse City. He is a sweet guy with long blond dreads and a quick, engaging smile. I watched him pack his food at the hostel. A healthy eater.

I've been averaging a little over twelve miles a day. I must stick to this average if I am to finish the trail in six months. Zero days backed me up a bit, especially the string of them in Hiawassee, but zero I will while waiting for Kinsley.

April 26 | Irwin, Tennessee, Zero

I walked to the local barbershop and got a haircut from an old veteran barber. In conversation, he said he was going to retire in eight years, at which time he will be 88. This guy is so laid back. He said, "If I see a hair, I cut it." This barber told me a story of years ago when the town hung an elephant. "The year was 1916. The crime? The elephant was guilty of murder." And he was not joking. He also spoke of the horrific methadone problem here in Irwin, saying, "Many young people have died from over-doses recently."

My feet are a major problem. No feeling. I already had limited feeling in my left foot from the back surgery. Now I cannot feel the last three toes on my right foot. No blisters though. I shaved my scraggily face, did a little shopping at Goodwill, then walked back to the motel and checked my e-mails. How easy it is walking with no pack. I ate some luscious pizza while watching sports on TV. Like R&R, or base camp in Vietnam, little luxuries gratify me.

I am hiking the AT! When I started this journey, I had no idea I'd be able to get this far. And yet, now I would recommend this extreme hike to all ex-soldiers with PTSD. Reflection is part of the cure. Forgiveness is part of the cure. Both can be found on the AT.

APRIL 27 | IRWIN, TENNESSEE, ANOTHER ZERO DAY

Kinsley arrives this afternoon! I am extremely excited to see her face. I haven't seen her in a month and I miss her so. Initially she'd said she might visit me somewhere on the trail. Then the plan was to hike a hundred miles or so. Now she plans on hiking 1,800 miles, all the way to the northern terminus. I'm both happy and worried about this. I hope she and I can hike without hassles. There will be some, but I hope they are minimal. This will be the ultimate test of friendship and togetherness.

I looked out the window of my room and saw Kinsley and her cousin pull up directly below. I had a hop in my step as I bounded down the stairs to greet them. I was introduced to cousin Claire, whom I had heard so much about, a beautiful young woman with blonde hair and a radiant smile. After the women freshened up, we all went to dinner that night in Johnson City, Tennessee, at a German restaurant. Holding Kinsley in my arms was a beautiful feeling. I had so longed for her.

Missing Kinsley for a month got me thinking about R&R. In Vietnam we were allotted one R&R per year. Six days if we went to Australia or Hawaii, five days if we went to Bangkok, Tokyo, or wherever else. How sweet of the Army. One R&R for a year of hell. And they would fly us there at no cost. Whoopee!

The guys that were married or had girlfriends went to Hawaii. We were not allowed to go home for R&R. This was against those

Army rules, because they surmised going home might mean we would never come back.

I don't remember names, but I do remember stories. One guy met his wife in Hawaii. He'd been in Vietnam for seven months. She showed up to meet him five months pregnant. Devastation.

Another guy, Tom, was also supposed to meet his wife in Hawaii. He left our company in the bush and made his way back to base camp via helicopters and convoys. He cleaned himself up, caught a plane to Cam Ranh Bay, and off to Hawaii he went. He anxiously waited at the airport. He had a beautiful hotel room on the ocean and he anticipated a wonderful reunion. When the plane arrived, she did not appear. She was flying in from the West Coast so he figured she missed the plane and would be on the next one. Same results. Tom waited and waited. He phoned her again and again. No answer. He called home and spoke with his parents and her parents, but did not get a definitive answer. Eventually, he went to his hotel. Tom ended up staying in Hawaii by himself for six days. When he got back to the company area in base camp, he had mail waiting. There was a letter from his wife informing him she was not showing up in Hawaii. The reason? To punish him for not writing more often. When Tom came back out to the company he was a basket case. He was eventually sent back to base camp because he was a danger to himself and others out in the bush. We needed people to be focused. All of us felt miserable for Tom.

APRIL 28 | IRWIN, TN, THIRD ZERO

Yet another zero with Kinsley. Cousin Claire hit the road for home. Prior to her leaving, the three of us tried to come up with a trail name for Kinsley. As we discussed different planet names, either Claire or I suggested Cosmos. The name would stick.

Kins and I planned out our journey for the next day, supplied ourselves, and got our packs squared away. I feel like I have been off the trail for days. I have. I walk big miles, but take too many zero days consecutively. That will change from this day forth. At this pace, I won't finish until mid-October, at the earliest. I was averaging more than twelve miles a day when I arrived here, and now that average has dropped to 10.9 and I'm going to have to slow my pace for Kinsley. I do believe she will be a strong hiker. When hiking back home with her I couldn't keep up.

I have heard so many horror stories about hiking with a partner. "You're too slow." "You're too fast." "You're in a bad mood." And on and on. Time will tell how we do.

APRIL 29 | BEAUTY SPOT GAP, 10.9 MILES, 350.7 MILES TOTAL

Directly after breakfast we are on our way. We hiked two miles down the road to the hostel and trail. We ran into Twopack, so named because of the pack in the front, pack in the back. I said, "Twopack, this is my new hiking partner, Cosmos." He smiled. He liked the name. Kinsley looked at me strangely, but I think she liked her new name, too. All new names take getting used to. Cosmos got on the scales at the hostel and weighed in at 142.5 lbs. Twopack laughed and said, "You weigh more than me." Cosmos simply smiled at him. She is a beautiful woman, medium height (5'6" or so) with a well-kept physique and smooth tanned skin. She has gorgeous large green eyes that are riveting. And she sports a wonderful new, shortly styled hairdo, cut just for this journey. I look forward to getting to know the ins and outs of her mind.

Off into the woods we ventured at 7:45 a.m. We hiked briskly the 4.2 miles to Curly Gap Shelter. We should have stopped right there at 10:30, but we moved on. I assured her we would find a nice spot in the woods. She had told me she prefers camping to the shelters. Perfect. We ended up going 10.9 miles to Beauty Spot Gap, and then rain came. We must make decisions together and we couldn't find a flat spot to pitch our two-person tent (my tent went home with Claire) and I'm already realizing we are different people and things won't be quite as simple as hiking alone. But I do believe the good of having a partner will far outweigh the bad.

I know Cosmos and I will have some wonderful experiences together. She is, in fact, a strong hiker. She will have to get used to me disrupting her in the middle of the night to pee. It is difficult for me to quietly exit the tent in the middle of the night when I am so sore.

APRIL 30 | JUST PAST LITTLE BALD KNOB, 8 MILES, 358.7 MILES TOTAL

Hiked to near an old logging road near Bald Knob and settled in about 3 p.m. We have walked 18.8 miles in the last two days. We had some big climbs, most notably over Unaka Mountain, elevation 5,180 feet. Cosmos said she felt good, but thought it best to stop until she gets her "trail legs." She is a strong hiker, but I know her body will experience problems she has not seen in her lifetime. She picked some leeks on the trail and we had them in our dinner. I can see I am out of the dinner-making business, which is fine with me. She is taking charge and cooks better tasting food than I ever could. I feel like I ate in a restaurant. Probably gain some of that weight back. I notice Cosmos sees things (plants, insects, critters) on the trail that I pass by without notice. Now I'm starting to see them. Bonus.

I love this woman's attitude. She is not afraid to say exactly what is on her mind and we need that mentality for the trail. It reminds me of Vietnam, when we would say anything and do anything to keep our morale up. Cosmos will keep me going.

MAY 1 | JUST PAST LITTLE ROCK KNOB, 9.6 MILES, 368.3 MILES TOTAL

Had a good hike today. Cosmos pitched the tent and made dinner. Then she showed me how to make a fire. I had hiked thirty days alone. I used to do everything for myself. Now, all of a sudden, I don't have any responsibilities. Cosmos seems to be taking charge of everything. I know she is far more experienced in the outdoors than me, because she has been camping all her life, but I still need to make some decisions. For her and for me. We had a good discussion about that tonight. As we get to know each other more and more, we will see each other's faults. We will see each other's emotions run high and low. This is the ultimate test in patience and compromise in a relationship. Who we are mentally, physically, and emotionally will become clear to both of us. Together twenty-four hours a day. Stinky, ornery, happy, physically hurting, thinking, impatient, patient, understanding, stubborn, nurturing and not so nurturing. I notice this journal is going from trail talk to relationship talk. Hmmm.

MAY 2 | OVERMOUNTAIN SHELTER, 10.7 MILES. 379 MILES TOTAL

More rain. Every day that Cosmos has been on the trail she has seen rain. Not major downpours, but rain nevertheless. Today was great hiking weather. There was light rain, no mud, and mild temperatures. The Overmountain Shelter is a sight to behold. A big red barn that could sleep a hundred-plus in a pinch. The shelter overlooks expanses of mountains and valleys. Tonight there is a slight fog hanging over the valley. There are at least twenty hikers here: Pyrofly, and his nephew, Good and Plenty (age 12), Twopack, Bonesy, and Lucky Star, to name a few. Good and Plenty is hiking twenty-plus miles with his uncle; then his parents are picking him up at a road crossing. Good and Plenty had all the ingredients to make s'mores. Though most of the folks here are section hikers, that was a real treat for the thru-hikers! We made a fire, had the time to shoot the shit with everyone regarding their experiences out here, and there was plenty of room for everyone to get a good night's sleep.

Our plan will be to go 9.2 miles tomorrow to Elk Park, then resupply, do laundry, eat, and zero. Rest Cosmos' body. She is starting to hurt. She is hiking strong, but has a weak leg right now. This is what happens out here. An ache here, then that ache is replaced by an ache somewhere else that overpowers the original ache.

We are slowing way down. This is difficult for me. I have no idea the extent of her pain, but I know I have aching toes and aching knees and I just keep plodding along. I feel the conflict within myself. Part of me wants to be the perfect nurturing hiking partner, and the other part wants to walk every day from sunrise to sunset. I like to do the miles, but I know I need to find a middle ground. Sometimes I walk ahead and sit and wait and when Cosmos catches up she feels bad. This is what previous thru-hikers warned me about: Sometimes your partner slows you down, or vice versa and it can wear on you mentally. I want to avoid that. I want to have fun. I want Cosmos to have fun.

I thought today of a young soldier in our platoon humping the bush near Dak To. He was fairly new in country, having been with us only a month or so. He was a big man, maybe 6'3," 240 lbs. He reminded me of Lurch from the Adams Family, but his name was Frank. Anyway, we were moving through the jungle searching for the enemy we did not want to find. There were many bomb craters to maneuver through this day, the result of "arch lights" (B-52 air strikes of dozens of 1,000 lb. bombs). Friendly troops could not be within miles of these strikes for fear of friendly casualties. The craters rendered the ground soft and made it difficult to navigate and we had to move quickly through these craters because we were exposed. Frank was having a bad day. Finally he simply dropped and started crying, almost howling, "I can't take this anymore." He was in the open. It was imperative he get in the tree line, but he refused to move, saying, "Leave me, leave me. I've led my life. Leave me." Our platoon leader, Terry, pleaded with him to get up and move. He offered to help him with his pack, but Frank refused. "I'm not moving," he said. Terry called him a coward. Frank responded, "I am not a coward," through sobs. "I took 15 credits one semester in college!" And he rolled over and cried.

All the soldiers, myself included, who were trying to get him to move were exposed, too, sitting ducks ripe for ambush. Explaining this to Frank did nothing. He still wanted us to leave him. Finally, a guy in our platoon, Tex, told us all to move on and he would handle it. And so we moved, not having far to go to our night location. We arrived and were digging in and setting up for the night when Tex and Frank came walking in. Frank had a bruise on his face, but nobody asked questions. He was here. He was safe.

Going over Roan Mountain, elevation 6,285 feet, sucked. Rain and fog limited visibility and made the rocks and roots extremely slippery. The vista, which was supposed to be spectacular, was not. We could see nothing but white fog. Saw Bonesy and Butter Toes on the trail, she in her black dress, her legs covered with insect bites. She seemed to be struggling.

Next was a beautiful, but difficult climb from Carvers Gap, Tennessee. Fog rolled in and out, I fell a couple times, and Cosmos hiked strongly and way ahead of me. We stopped at Stan Murray Shelter for a break where we met Dutch, from Petoskey, Michigan. He is in the final leg of section hiking the entire trail. He is sixty-something. What an accomplishment! Birch was also at the shelter. She's a short strong woman with grey hair who appears to be in her sixties. She is doing a 980-mile section hike to complete the trail.

In Deep stopped for lunch along with two others, and Dutch expressed his irritation with some "ditzy" young women on the trail. He also does not approve of guys who sleep in, hike until late at night, then arrive at a shelter and make all kinds of noise while everyone else is trying to sleep. Yet another reason I rarely sleep in shelters.

The fog and rain rolled in at about 5 p.m. The mountains were no longer visible. Cosmos and I found a spot on the top floor of the barn. Just rolled out our thermarests and bags and went to sleep, listening to other peoples' conversations. The setting was peaceful; it sounds like lots of folks will be sleeping in.

May 3 | Elk Park, North Carolina, 8.8 miles, 387.8 miles total

Today I almost fell off a mountain and killed myself. I fell off a rock and slipped over the edge. I hit my head and shoulder on a boulder, but my pack stopped me from rolling straight down the mountain. I hurt my shoulder and leg and ripped my rain jacket, but otherwise I'm okay.

The day had begun normally, but Cosmos is hurting badly. She needs a rest. So do I, both mentally and physically, though we did encounter some incredible trail magic a half-mile from the highway.

We were hiking along, wondering exactly where we were, when we came upon Apple Mountain Shelter. It was mid-afternoon so the shelter was empty. As we walked toward it, we observed two chairs and a cooler. "Probably full of cold beer," I joked to Cosmos. I had never seen any chairs in shelters on the trail before, and I sat down out of principle. Chairs feel better than the rocks or stumps I had been sitting on for five weeks. A little white cooler sat right between the chairs. We opened it up, and lo and behold, four Budweisers on ice.

Pyrofly and In Deep came walking through. We offered them each a cold beer from the cooler. Until they felt the cold cans in their hands, they thought we were joking. We relaxed together, sipped a cold one, and then off we went.

Pyrofly is so-named because he says he always starts late and flies by everyone. Probably one of those guys Dutch was talking about that sleeps in, hikes into the night, and wakes everyone up at the shelters as he arrives well after sunset (hiker midnight). Pyrofly is always all smiles.

After finishing the beer Cosmos and I made our way to the highway and met Pyro's aunt and uncle. They treated us to some Gatorade, after which we started walking with our thumbs out, hitchhiking towards Elk Park, North Carolina. We were anticipating a relaxing zero day tomorrow. We'd walked maybe three quarters of a mile when we saw a car coming down a two track. The driver turned out to be Katie, a section hiker who'd spent the night sleeping near us at the Overmountain Shelter. We were so excited about a bed and hot shower and Katie drove us straight to the motel in Elk Park. The place was closed for remodeling. Bummer. We didn't know what to do at that point, since this was the only motel in town. More trail magic, as Katie said not to worry, she knew the area, and ended up driving us at least fifteen miles out of her way to another motel in Banner Elk, North Carolina. Katie waited for us to check in, and then we said our thank yous and good byes to this latest trail angel. Cosmo and I splurged and got a room with a hot tub.

The nearest store was about a mile up the road. Sometimes I wish I had a car. We'd been walking all day, and now we'd have to walk another mile to get a newspaper, munchies, and some beer. I volunteered to go, so Cosmos could rest. I assembled our munchies, paper, and beer at the store and attempted to pay by credit card, only to find out the store didn't accept credit cards. I emptied my pockets of cash and came up $1.50 short. I was going to put something back, but the cashier dug deeply into her purse and came up with six quarters. I was astonished. This was a small town where everyone seemed to have very limited income. What goodness.

After soaking in the hot tub and absorbing beers and munchies while catching up on the news, we went to dinner at the restaurant in the hotel. We met the cook, who came out to greet us. His name was Matt and he'd heard we were thru-hikers. We were the only ones there and he and the waitress, Mary El, treated us like royalty. They offered to give us a ride back to the AT whenever we needed it. Good thing, because we had no idea where we were in relation to the trail.

After dinner I made another mile trek up to the store to pay the woman back the $1.50 and get some ice cream. I put the ice cream on the counter and gave her a $20 bill. I don't think she recognized me because one, I didn't stink, two, I had shaved and showered, and three, I had a different shirt on. She gave me my change and I gave it all back to her. "This money is for you for being such a wonderful person. For helping a perfect stranger, a smelly stranger at that, to buy some provisions." She was reluctant to take the money but finally agreed saying, "Thank you, honey, God bless," with tears welling in her eyes. I'll admit I had no intention of giving her all the change from that twenty bucks, but it sure felt good to do it.

I walked back to the room with a smile on my face and Cosmos and I devoured the ice cream, brushed our teeth, and turned in for the night.

The last thing I do before I close my eyes is write in this journal. I am determined to have a full account of this journey. At times I am so fatigued I want to skip a night, but I continue.

MAY 4 | BANNER ELK, NORTH CAROLINA, ZERO

I was up early to soak in the hot tub and read *USA Today*, trying to catch up on what's going on in the world. As always, the news is mostly bad. We ate a huge breakfast while I silently hoped this zero works for Cosmos and her leg becomes trail ready. We went to the grocery store to resupply, which was a three-mile hike uphill. I felt relaxed while we were shopping, because I know Cosmos knows exactly what we need. She eats healthy, a bonus for me. We decided to hitch from the grocery store and were picked up by two women who took us a total of two blocks. Then we walked back to the motel, downhill.

Heidi, a friend from work, called my cell phone. She's pregnant! That beautiful woman has been trying so hard and for so long to have a baby. She and husband, Josh, tried every trick medicine could offer to no avail. And just when they were about to put their hopes of pregnancy aside and adopt instead, boom, pregnant. That news made my day.

Cosmos is worried about her left "pin" (that's what my dad used to call women's legs. At a young age I realized he only used the term when the pins were nice ones). Cosmos' pin is not working properly; it's extremely weak, but she says it doesn't hurt much.

While Cosmos rested, I got caught up on computer stuff. Oh, these zero days. I must have been on the computer three hours. I had to answer e-mails and update my adventure for the folks back home.

We ate dinner at a Vietnamese restaurant across the street. It was the first time I had eaten at such a place in my life.

> I have avoided all contact with anything related to Vietnam. I am trying so hard to expel the demons and the racism that goes with it. I don't feel the intensity as much as when I first came home all those years ago, but being around Vietnamese people still evokes eerie emotions. Here in this restaurant the Vietnamese seem like good folk. No, they are good folk. But I still see the enemy. Still. I try to ward off those evil feelings and focus on the beauty of Cosmos.

MAY 5 | JUST PAST MOUNTAINEER FALLS SHELTER, 10.4 MILES, 398.2 MILES TOTAL

Matt and Mary El gave us a ride to the exact spot where we'd come off the AT two days earlier. These acts of goodwill are what make this hike special. We began our hike and Cosmos' leg started bothering her almost immediately, but she hiked on. Again, the rain fell all day. The creek water was yellow so we used the filter and tabs. I joked that maybe there was a bear upriver. We met Jersey Girl on the trail today. For her sixtieth birthday and retirement present, she informed her husband she was going to hike the AT. Now that is a woman!

She had just gotten back on the trail after going home for nineteen days because she thought she had a stress fracture. Her doctor told her she had arthritis and to get back on the trail, so here she is.

The rain was coming down so hard I could barely see my hand in front of my face. We got off the trail and followed a blue blaze to a shelter, hoping the rains would subside. We found a hiker at the shelter who seemed extremely distressed. He just stared out into the woods with seriousness written all over him. I asked what his trail name was and he responded, "Doesn't matter." That became his trail name. We felt a bit uncomfortable leaving when the skies cleared, because Jersey Girl was going to spend the night, but Doesn't Matter seemed harmless, so we hiked on.

We camped on some rocks next to a creek. We looked and looked for a flat spot, but this was the best we could do. We set up in the rain once again. I had a hard time figuring out a place to hang the bear bag, eventually ending up a few hundred meters from our spot.

At nightfall, as is becoming our custom, I read Cosmos and myself to sleep.

Today's rain reminded me of months of weather in Vietnam. Torrential. It made traveling very difficult with the mud and rocks. We moved in all elements, every day. Rarely did we spend two nights in a row at the same location. Always we were seeking out the enemy. Trying to engage them in war. In the times of rain, it was imperative we cleaned our weapons daily, lest they jam in a time of need from rust or corrosion. Few things can cause panic like a jammed weapon in a firefight.

MAY 6 | DENNIS COVE HOSTEL, 14.8 MILES, 413 MILES TOTAL

What a tough day it was, with a hard rain falling continuously. We walked west off the trail to a hostel where they were supposed to have groceries and pizza. They have an open bunkhouse, but nobody was here. People that live in the area said the owner was in school and sometimes didn't get home until 10 p.m. So the store remained closed until then. We hung our tent and other wet equipment over the railings to dry. The tent is so damn heavy when wet.

I played basketball with some girls that lived nearby. Why was I playing basketball after such a grueling day? Because I have game!

We waited for what seemed like forever for someone to show up and open the store. Finally, the dude shows. He had been studying at the library. I went in his store and introduced myself and said something like, "Two of those. Three of those. Three of those"—soda, pizza, and candy. We watched a couple movies in the bunkhouse/kitchen/dining room as we ate. When I get in civilization like this, I almost forget I am on the trail. Even after such a difficult hike.

The news on TV said a guy who killed his wife and two others outside a playhouse in Athens, Georgia, is on the AT somewhere, trying to escape. He was a professor at the University of Georgia. I do not want to encounter this dude.

Cosmos' leg continues to trouble her. But, she had a classic quote today as she emerged from the woods: "I just took the best shit of my life." I love this woman. *She would have been a great infantry soldier.* I so love to look into her eyes, and it ain't so bad hiking behind her, either. I hope she can work through the pain. Something is always sore and hurting on me, too. Everyone on the trail has something bothering them, one hundred percent of the time. I am thinking professional or college athletes get the best doctors' care for their injuries. We thru-hikers just keep moving, rarely complaining.

I have completed 400 miles.

Today I wondered how many miles I had hiked on my tour in the war. Maybe 500? Grueling miles, indeed. We never took a trail. Whoever was walking point that day was armed with a machete and just started hacking as we moved through dense jungle, heading towards a location given to us by the "higher, higher": Colonels and generals who didn't do the fighting. The reason we didn't take a trail is trails were ripe for ambush. But not taking a trail took time. Consequently, it would take all day to get to our night location. But if the enemy was there to thwart us? We would alter our plans for the evening, set up for the night somewhere, and try to take the hill in the morning. This would make for a harrowing couple days. Imagine setting up for the evening and thinking all night that some will die tomorrow, maybe me. Some will get wounded, maybe me.

The "higher, higher" could care less. They thirst for us to be in contact.

MAY 7 | HOSTEL IN HAMPTON, TENNESSEE, 8.8 MILES, 421.8 TOTAL

Our plan is to go almost nine miles today to the hostel, and then do two long hikes, if possible, to Damascus, Virginia.

I spend too much time thinking about this, but I am having an overall wonderful time with Cosmos. The good far outweighs the bad. We have our edgy moments, and this is what I expected. She is cramping (period) and we must slow down. I can't measure her pain. I love having her with me, yet sometimes I act like a jerk. The weather continues to pummel us and I know more rain will come today. I don't mind walking in the rain, but I like moving quickly so I don't chill.

This is a big test. Adapting to being with someone I love 24/7 in extremely trying conditions and sometimes having differing views. This is good for me. A life test, indeed.

Cosmos needs tampons. I screwed up and left our first-aid kit containing tampons at a previous hostel. And then I remembered the water purification tabs are also in the kit. And I had already ruined the filter by not maintaining it properly. I needed to clean it every so often, but shirked my duty and the thing is shot. I didn't mind making mistakes when they affected only me, but when they affect someone who is counting on me? I do not like. I may have that aloof attitude that, "everything will work out," but I hate to negatively affect others. Hate it. *The PTSD from the war comes into play. The thought is that everything will be fine; we are not going to be ambushed. There are no snipers. No booby traps.* But this kind of attitude when someone is counting on me has got to go.

Hallelujah! No rain while hiking today. It did rain later in the evening, but the sun shined down on us today, making for a beautiful hike. The fog hangs in the mountains. Today feels like spring.

Since Cosmos' arrival, and her way of pointing things out to me, I am trying to be more aware of the beauty on the trail. Flowers, buds, plants, trees, bugs. Although I like to peel off the miles, more and more I find myself trying to notice the beauty that surrounds me. Interesting phenomenon: The woods are quiet, and then I hear the wind blowing hard in the distance, heading my way. And then it blows over the tops of the trees and is gone. Awesome. It never gets old.

My legs feel strong, but downhills are killer on my knees. My feet seem to be doing better. Perhaps because my toes are numb.

After an all-day hike, we came down a hill to a clearing and a road. There in front of us is a park, with a lake. The lake has high water from all the rain and the outdoor grills and picnic tables are in standing water. On one of the tables, almost totally submerged, sit pale-skinned, waving thru-hikers: Splice, Couscous, I'm Happy, and Twopack. We went swimming and talked, took photos, got dressed, and hitched into town to the hostel. A pickup truck with a cap over the bed pulled over almost immediately. We go to jump in the back only to see it full of other thru-hikers who were getting a ride into town to resupply. They made room for us, and to the store we went. We shopped, had a couple of crackers and a cold pop.

The driver dropped us off at the hostel in town. We got cleaned up and went to dinner. We drank some beers at a local biker bar. Then home early to turn in. I went into the TV room to check it out only to see Cass sitting on the couch. I had not seen her since Neels Gap, over 300 miles back. She must have passed me when I did the zeros in Irwin. I had a great night with Cosmos. She'd called her mom and was a bit giddy.

I am very sore today. Big climbs and big downhills.

MAY 8 | JUST PAST VANDEVENTER SHELTER, 12.4 MILES, 434.9 MILES TOTAL

Driving rain. We got an early morning ride to the AT from the hostel owner. He is a wonderful funny man. The day started off with us hiking in knee-deep water. We took our shoes and socks off, but they got wet later. When will I learn to just leave them on and get wet? The sun came out in the early evening. The terrain is beautiful and the forest is lush green. When it rains and rains, I am learning to appreciate the sun.

The lush, green foliage and the depth of the forest brought me back to one of the days I was walking point. I was hacking my way through vine after solid vine with my machete, trying to get us to our night location and hoping for no contact with the NVA. I was struggling when I noticed a small piece of paper hanging in one of the trees. A leaflet...and another leaflet...and another. How could there be litter out here in the jungle where nobody had ever been? I reached out and snatched one. On one side of the paper was an African-American man being beaten with billy clubs by police. In the USA. On the other side half of the page was an image of an African-American GI in the prone position under fire in Vietnam with a look of horror on his face. The other half said something like, "What are you doing here fighting a white man's war, nigger? You can't even get into college in America. You can't get a decent job in America. Yet you are over here fighting a war for the white man, who calls you nigger. Your real fight is on your native land. Go home now."

I reached for another leaflet. This one had a picture of a steel pot lying on the ground with a hole blown through it and a daisy protruding. On the other side? A song of sorts that went something like this: "Hey, hey LBJ, how many kids did you kill today? 400,000 GIs have served in Vietnam, with 180,000 killed or maimed. Honeywell, Dow Chemical, and other companies are hauling it in while they are hauling you guys out. Get out now before you are pushing up daisies too."

It was supposed to be propaganda, but the other guys and I could only shake our heads at how true it was. The general reaction was, "Show us how to get out of here and we will go." Did the NVA really think we like it here? Do they think these leaflets can possibly drop our morale lower than it already is? I for one just shook it off. Both leaflets were right on, but my goal was to stay alive and keep the faith.

When Cosmos and I got to our night location, I started putting up the tent. Apparently I put some stakes in the wrong spot because Cosmos abruptly moved them. An argument ensued. Things got ugly. All of our frustrations surfaced until she promised that I only had to put up with her for twenty-eight more miles and she would be gone, off the trail.

We usually have so much fun together, but there have been times when we get on each other's nerves. She can be so abrasive. I can be overly sensitive and abrasive. We can both be defensive and now we've come to a stalemate. She says she can do nothing right. I feel the same. I am afraid to cook, set up the tent, get water, whatever, for fear I will fuck it up. And now I am fucking up. I didn't clean the water filter, so it was destroyed and ruined. I forgot the first aid kit with her tampons and the pills to purify our water. I lost my hat, etc., etc.

I either can't or don't know how to make this work. We love hiking together, making love, laughing, joking around, and kidding each other. I told Cosmos I don't want her to leave the trail. Maybe we should split up. She or I could hike a bit ahead for a few days. We will see what develops between us. The hiking and nights are so much better when we get along.

There are very few couples on the trail. Now I know why.

MAY 9 | ABINGDON GAP SHELTER, 17.9 MILES, 452.8 MILES TOTAL

Saw Mad Chatter at the store yesterday and forgot to write that down. Last time I saw him was at Fontana Dam when the dude in the pickup said to us, "You ain't scairt, are yuh?" That was miles and miles ago. What a nice reunion.

After we arrived at the shelter and got the tent squared away, I hiked eight hundred feet down to a creek to get water, and then the same eight hundred feet back up, a major trek after a long day. I was gone forever, or so it seemed.

Cosmos is sore. She struggled today, but she passed one hundred miles. Awesome. We have 10.2 miles to Damascus, home of "Trail Days." Trail Days doesn't start until May 14, so we will probably push on and hitchhike back for the event.

> I filled our water bladders and sat by the stream for a bit. Mother's Day is coming up. Back in 1968, a friend in Vietnam, Jim Phillips, was getting ready to go on R&R in Australia. Before he left he asked me if I wanted him to wire flowers to my mom on Mother's Day. I jumped on that and received a letter from my mom two weeks later, thanking me for the flowers and the wonderful note attached. Over the years, every time my mom told that story she would get emotional. Thank you, Jim Phillips.

It rained again today. Surprise. But the sun will shine on us eventually. It always does. We get rewarded for our struggles with something wonderful, or so we tell ourselves. Cosmos and I said nary a word about yesterday's blowout. The day was good. Another form of sunlight.

We met Ranger, Bushman, Otter, and Flatlander at the shelter. There were also some teenagers from town here for the evening. They took up part of the shelter.

A major storm swept in after dinner. Driving rain and wind. I thought the tent might blow down. I was concerned about Bushman, as he is in his hammock.

4 Virginia

Upon rising I went straight to see how Bushman was doing. He was tearing down while whistling. I was impressed he had stayed totally dry. The hammock had wrapped him up like a cocoon.

The hike to Damascus was enjoyable. We arrived about 3:30 p.m. Virginia--I have hiked into my fourth state. The rest of this state and ten more to go before I reach the end of the AT. Virginia is the big one, with over 500 miles of trail. I remember way back when, when I'm Fine told me things would be easier once I got to Virginia. Well, here I am. This is supposed to be a beautiful state, with rolling hills, though I do not know how the terrain and the vistas could be any more beautiful than what I have already seen.

We saw Bushman, Otter, and another hiker before we got into town. They were just sitting on the edge of town, resting. We did the same. The other hiker was a section hiker. Cosmos named him Whittler because he does sections at a time. He loved that name.

All the hostels were full, so we opted for a bed and breakfast, The Apple Tree. Deb and Les are the proprietors. Deb is so sweet. She is an older woman with gray hair. Reminds me of my grandma, although I must say she is my age. She did our laundry and gave us a cold soda. This is my first experience at a B&B. We had a TV, a good bed, a phone, and Internet access. Deb initially thought Cosmos was my daughter and wanted us in separate beds. Cosmos told her we had been sharing the same tent all this time, so one bed is good. She didn't look pleased, but gave us the one bed. Later, when we were sorting our food, I had my robe on (laundry was being done), sitting on the bed. Cosmos was naked on the sofa, sorting through what food we had left. Deb surprised us by opening the door. When she saw Cosmos sitting on the sofa, she turned her head away and said softly to me, "Please, let her put the robe on." And she shut the door. Cosmos and I stifled our laughter.

We went to a small restaurant named Fatties for dinner. I had a big hamburger and three ice-cold beers. Then we walked around town for a bit, checking things out, and headed back to the Apple Tree. We relaxed and went to bed early, but not until after I ordered and then consumed an entire pizza. I am always hungry.

I like the Bushman. We probably won't see much of him in the days and weeks to come. He is ahead of us on the trail and he puts in big miles. I should have gotten his e-mail, or any contact information. I have made this mistake too many times.

MAY 11 | BEAR TREE GAP, 11.7 MILES, 474.7 MILES TOTAL

What a wonderful breakfast Deb made. Four other lodgers shared the table with us, one a former thru-hiker, and all were great company. I used the Internet to update friends and family back home. We had our packs ready before breakfast, so as soon as we finished, off we went. We stopped at a salon on the way out of town because Cosmos wanted to get a haircut.

The stylist's name was Myrtle. The guy who was getting his hair cut when we walked in hopped out of his chair when Myrtle was finished, looked at himself in the mirror, and said, "It's okay. I can wear a hat for a few days." Cosmos ended up asking for her head to be shaved, military style. And so it was. And she looked gorgeous.

As we hiked out of town, someone yelled from a truck, "Don't leave town." They wanted us to stay for Trail Days, but our plan was to hike up the trail and hitch back in. No way could we sit still for four days worth of zeros. We found the trail and disappeared into the woods.

After eleven-plus miles, we found a beautiful area to camp adjacent to a stream that filtered into a stunning pond. I had packed out a couple of beers, and Cosmos cooked dinner. We ate at sunset. I wonder how many times I will say Cosmos is a great cook. She is so creative even with such limited supplies. When I cooked for myself, I enjoyed it, but not like this. Cosmos was pleasantly surprised when I brought out a beer for her.

We have not discussed her leaving the trail. After our argument, Damascus was going to be the end for her, but I don't bring it up.

Instead, I should start making a count of the number of bugs I inhale. More than once a day I'll inhale one as I walk, then I cough and gag for the next half hour. I try to breathe through my nose, but I can't do that when I'm huffing and puffing. I should count how many spider webs I walk through every single day, too.

MAY 12 | THOMAS KNOB SHELTER, 16.3 MILES, 491 MILES TOTAL

We arrived here at 6:15 p.m. after a very difficult day. The top of the mountain seemed to remain far in the distance.

We saw several deer today. And a wild pony was hanging out by the shelter. I had heard and read about these ponies; they are supposed to be wild, but are friendly.

My stomach growls constantly. Thud (Zach from Back Country Outfitters in my hometown) told me I would always be hungry on the trail, and I'd need to get used to it. He was right, but I am not getting "used to it." Seems like most of my days are spent thinking about eating, about my children, my friends, Cosmos, or Vietnam.

Some days, like today, I can do nothing but take a deep breath while absorbing my thoughts of war. I am okay. Cosmos has no knowledge of my anxiety as I refuse to share much of it with her. When I do, I keep it light. I never get emotional out here regarding the war. I don't know if that's right or wrong. Jets flew low today over the trail.

I had flashbacks of strafing F4 Phantoms and a firefight. Of Sergeant Andretti getting killed. Of Top, who was the company first sergeant, getting killed. Of a horror that doesn't leave me, even on the AT. It was February 26, 1968, somewhere near Dak To, Vietnam. We had orders to conduct a helicopter combat assault into an area that was supposed to be infiltrated by NVA elements. Rarely do we make contact on combat assaults. If the NVA hear us coming, they get moving off into the jungle. This day I was on the third bird in. I was on the outside looking down (there are no doors on these helicopters) and as we descended I saw NVA scurrying through the jungle, occasionally stopping and, from behind trees, firing their AK-47s at troops already on the ground. They were everywhere. Oh Lordy, how I wanted the pilot to turn this thing around and take me home.

But we descended and hit the ground running, looking for cover. The chopper banked and headed back to get more troops.

More and more birds flew in until we had our entire company on the ground. We moved cautiously. One guy, Buddy, was actually hit in his rucksack by AK fire. Later, when we unpacked for the night, he found the bullet had gone through a couple cans of C-rations. At least those C-rations are good for something, we laughed. A couple months prior, when Buddy was still green, he'd said, "When are we going to see some shit, man?" The veterans just rolled their eyes, never wanting to hear that kind of bullshit. When the time did come, he vomited and cried in his bunker.

Miraculously, we got out of this day with no casualties. We climbed to the top of a little knoll and dug in for the night, not knowing what was to come. I, for one, was grateful the NVA had disappeared into the jungle. We did notice the sophisticated trench lines around this "hill." The NVA had been here for some time.

The next morning brought soothing sunlight and a warm breeze. Everyone was up and about, eating breakfast, packing up, etc. Sergeant Andretti was our acting platoon leader, as our regular leader was on R&R. He and I ate breakfast together, sitting on the ground. Sergeant Andretti was a big Hawaiian with dark islander skin. I was his RTO (radio-telephone operator), so I always stayed by his side. He talked of his upcoming R&R in Hawaii. He would meet his entire family there, including his son, who played football for the University of Texas, and his grandmother, who was getting on in years. He seemed at ease. He was a patient man who had the respect of anyone he came in contact with. His men, me included, loved him.

Let me interject a tidbit of info. Wherever we are as infantry soldiers, our weapons and ammunition are always within arm's reach of us. Always. One never wants to bustle around looking for his rifle and ammunition when a firefight is happening, or is about to happen.

As we talked, someone a dozen feet away on the perimeter said, "I hear movement." When someone says those words, action is immediate. Everyone drops whatever they are doing and either crawls, runs, or lunges into the nearest bunker.

I grabbed my radio, M-16, and ammunition and crawled and dove into the nearest bunker. Just as I landed, all hell broke loose. Rocket grenades and AK fire filled the air. We returned fire, not exactly knowing where the NVA were. (War is not like the movies, where someone fires his weapon while standing up and screaming.) We raised our weapons above our heads from inside the bunker and fired down the hill. As we laid down this base of fire, the enemy took cover.

The firing subsided after a couple minutes of extreme intensity. This is their strategy. They try to catch us off guard and give it everything they have for a couple minutes, then wait until we become uncomfortable crouched in the bunker. When we get fidgety, thinking maybe this is over, and emerge from the hole, they hit us again full bore.

As soon as the firing subsided, I called on my radio to both bunkers in our platoon, asking for 5-1, Sergeant Andretti (his call sign was 5-1, mine 5-1 Charlie). I thought he was right behind me, but now he was not at any of our bunkers. I feared the worst.

I asked our guys to lay down a base of fire to keep the NVA at bay, if they were still there. When the firing began I quickly exited the bunker and crawled up to where 5-1 and I had been about to eat our breakfast. There was 5-1, lying on his back in a half-dug hole, his face gray. He had a severe head wound from what could have been a rifle grenade and was unconscious. I ripped off some of his shirt and put pressure on his wound, talking to him, wanting him to open his eyes. I screamed for a medic. No response. More screaming as I kept talking to 5-1, still no medic. I tried to get him to drink some water, but that was not happening, so I put some on his face and tried to clean him. I felt so inept as I tried to save 5-1.

Finally, I crawled frantically to the command bunker to find the company medic, who I thought had to be in the bunker with Captain Foye. When I arrived, I looked into the bunker and saw Captain Foye (6 was his call sign), his RTOs, the forward observer (a first lieutenant), his RTO, our first sergeant, Top, who had just come out a couple days prior from base camp, and the command medic (Doc). All looked scared shitless. Captain Foye always had my respect. I looked him in the eye and forcibly said, "I need a medic now, 5-1 has a bad head wound." I looked at Doc and he appeared so scared I didn't know how he could function, or if he could function.

Moments passed that seemed like minutes, but nobody said or did anything. So I screamed at them, looking at Doc and saying, "Get out of that hole and follow me to 5-1, now!" Finally he moved. It was as if a light went on and the look of terror disappeared from his face. He seemed calm and ready to do work as he grabbed his medical bag and followed me as I crawled to 5-1's location. When we arrived 5-1 was still unconscious. Doc immediately took charge of the situation, getting plasma going while checking his wound closely. Sergeant Andretti was breathing cleanly. He appeared to be regaining color. Captain Foye had called in a dust off, so things were looking up.

It had now been thirty minutes since the surprise attack on our perimeter, and remembering the strategy they used on us, we should have been wary and alert. Instead, people were now outside their bunkers, talking, helping each other out, and tending to those who were wounded. We could hear the chopper in the distance, and Captain Foye asked me or someone to throw a smoke grenade out in front of our bunker so the chopper could see our location and at least get near the ground so we could load Sergeant Andretti and some other wounded onto a helicopter, get them out of here, and get them the help that they needed. A red smoke was popped.

Joe, one of Captain Foye's RTOs, was just outside of the perimeter in front of our bunkers, directing the chopper in. As the chopper circled and swayed the pilot spotted the smoke and descended toward our area. I could see the eyes of both the pilot and co-pilot. Suddenly, a look of terror swept onto the faces of those two. And then I saw tracers (green ones) from AK fire hit the chopper, which banked, almost crashed, and peeled off, heading out of the area.

Initially everyone dove for cover, some into bunkers, some behind trees, some lying prone on the ground, trying to be invisible. I dove behind a tree. It was chaos, with people screaming and crying out. After about a minute, the onslaught stopped once again as we returned fire with M-16s and grenades. Oh Lord! I looked out from behind the tree and immediately saw Top. He was kind of sitting up against a fallen tree with a strange look on his face. I crawled to him, saying, "You okay, Top?" He looked at me and said quietly, "I'm hit." The entire front of his fatigues were brown with blood. He died in seconds.

Joe, the RTO, was shot twice in the head and three times in the body. He fell in a heap. Miraculously, he lived, regaining consciousness on a runway in Japan in route to a hospital, attended by nurses and doctors. Sergeant Andretti was hit again, the plasma bottle shattered, and he died moments later.

Others were wounded. One guy, Anderson, got the tip of his thumb shot off. Just the very tip. A million dollar wound. He will get out of the bush, he will get out of the Army, he will go home, he will get a purple heart, and he will receive a lifetime pension. Made the rest of us wish it was our thumb that had been hit.

Back in our bunkers after that attack, we called in airstrikes and eventually the F4 Phantoms were dropping napalm within 50 meters of our perimeter. Napalm creates hot, fiery, rolling balls of destruction that fry anyone in the area. Their ability to bring it in so close to our location rested with the sighter plane, a little piper cub whose pilot shot white phosphorus into the jungle that was to be the target of the jets. I was amazed by the ability of those pilots, bringing in those explosives so close to us, and in the middle of a jungle. It was deadly stuff that probably saved our lives.

The other side of the perimeter was not so fortunate. They were getting hit as well. They had also called in airstrikes. Not napalm, but heavy ammo strafing from the nose of the jet. They brought the serious stuff in too close and the deadly fire hit one of our own bunkers, killing two and wounding several. One of the guys from the fourth platoon lost it emotionally and mentally, started screaming and ran down the hill and into a trenchline. As he rounded a corner with his weapon on automatic, he came face to face with a startled NVA. Both opened fire at one another, but neither got hit. I think that brought our guy back to reality and he ran back into the perimeter, unscathed, but crazy looking.

How young we were. And yet, I became an old man at 21. Little did we know it at the time, but we all would suffer for the rest of our lives. We will never be able to forget. And the families of the boys killed and wounded. What of them? And the families of those that will suffer psychologically? What of them? And what of the consciences of the politicians that keep us here? What of them? And all the civilians and families here in Vietnam we have damaged. What of them? The list goes on.

The politicians and "higher highers" were using us. Why? For what? To take another hill? Shame on them.

We stayed there through the night. We were hyper-alert all night long. We would throw up illumination rounds from time to time to light up the area and look for anything. We were scared. Occasionally, we would hear movement to our front, we'd alert the rest of the perimeter, and loft a grenade toward the movement. Then we would hear moaning. Eerie. And sickening. The last thing we wanted was any NVA inside our perimeter in the dark. That could mean throats slit and total chaos because we wouldn't know who's who.

I don't think I was ever so happy to see the morning light. It had been a harrowing couple days. Early in the a.m. 6 called and asked for an enemy body count. How was I to know? I guessed 10 dead NVA. There was silence on the radio, as 6 was speechless. I trusted he didn't like my figure. One of the guys laughingly suggested I tell him a hugely exaggerated figure. I did. *"Two hundred," I said, and received an immediate response. "Roger 5-1- Charlie." This is how these war "games" work? Embellish the body count to make it look in our favor, and send it home, overdramatizing, making it look like we had kicked ass?*

Six called once again, saying he was sending over 5-4 (4th platoon leader) to take over as our new platoon leader. 5-4 happened to be Lt. Mike Lawton, who was wounded on Hill 943 in December, but was back with his company after rehabbing.

We were still in our bunkers when I heard, "Keenan, lay down a base of fire, I'm coming down." So we did. Our new platoon leader crawled and fell into our bunker, breathing a sigh of relief. He was minus his protective headgear. He quickly said, "My steel pot popped off somewhere back there. Go get it for me, will you?" I looked at the guy next to me and we both simply smiled, or we may have laughed out loud. "Nice try," I said, "but you need to get that yourself. We'll lay down another base of fire for you." He laughed, said something like, "Doesn't hurt to ask." We laid down another base of fire, and off he went. And he came back in a flash with no problems.

The next day we brought in another dust-off to take out the wounded and the bodies. No problems this time getting them out, as Charlie had moved on. Placing Top and Sergeant Andretti in body bags was gut-wrenching, but there was never time to grieve. Joe was unconscious when we loaded him on the chopper, but still alive.

I recall our platoon going on a small reconnaissance of the area, looking for bodies. Near the bottom of the hill we came across a severely wounded NVA. He was shot up badly. He lay there with horror in his eyes. I had hate in my mind. We were going to shoot him and put him out of his misery, and enjoy it, but ended up leaving him. I made radio contact with 6. He said, "Let him suffer and die for what he did to us. Killing him is too easy." And so we let him suffer.

I hike on.

I pitched our tent at sunset once again, in a gorgeous area looking down the mountain. When we stop at shelters they are always full of section- or day-hikers, often young people, be it students from University of Pittsburgh or high schoolers from Ohio. They get college credit for hiking and studying at the same time. They hike a half day, then paint, draw, or write the other half. I think students should get a minimum of 30 credit hours for thru hiking the AT. This is education.

The trail was beautiful once again today. The temperature has been very cold in the evening with a steady fog during the day. I devoured dinner tonight. The people at the shelter said there were lots of mice. When there are no mice, it's due to snakes. Pineapple had a snake fall on him from overhead in the middle of the night at a shelter. Freaky! We encounter no problems with either mice or snakes, because we tent.

MAY 13 | NEAR BIG WILSON CREEK, 6.3 MILES, 497.3 MILES TOTAL

Up early. The weather was cold, rainy, misty, and windy when we ate breakfast and pulled up stakes, but the skies cleared later in the day. We are into the routine of saying little to each other, just packing up our shit. We just look at each other and nod when we have our packs on, ready to go. Then, off we trudge.

As I crested a knoll I was treated to a beautiful sight – several wild ponies. I expected them to run off as we approached, but we were able to touch and pet them. What a way to start a day. They are so very friendly. Cosmos' eyes welled with tears when she saw them. She so loves all animals and critters, the flowers and the trees. One of the things I love about her is her emotional attachment to nature.

When we found a flat spot, the same routine: I pitch the tent and arrange our sleeping gear. She makes dinner. I get water. We eat, brush our teeth, pee, and get in bed. I write in my journal, read out loud to her for a bit, and we both fall into a deep slumber.

MAY 14 | DICKEY GAP, TROUTDALE, 14.9 MILES, 512.2 MILES TOTAL

We were up and out early, looking to end the day near a road so we could hitch back to Damascus for Trail Days, yet also log some serious miles. I moved past the 500-mile mark. I feel exuberant.

This was a big day for us. Our plan worked and we hiked almost 15 miles before hitching back to Damascus. If someone would have told me I would be on the AT on May 14 a couple of years ago, I would have laughed. More than half of the people who started this trek about the same time I did have quit. Physically, I am feeling good…if I discount my feet, ankles, hair, teeth, fingers, and knees.

A man named Jack York picked us up and drove us a few miles and dropped us at a diner. Cosmos and I look at each other for only a moment, nod, and know what to do: chow down. After stuffing ourselves, we hitched again and got a great ride in the back of a pickup all the way to Damascus. Before the AT, I hadn't hitchhiked in forty years. Now it has become routine. We were supposed to look for a place near town called "Tent City." This was an area for thru-hikers to camp, but we ran into Phantom Cupcake and he showed us a neat little spot to pitch our tent, right next to a smooth-running river. Perfecto. He said Tent City is hectic and we would never be able to sleep. Wise advice.

I am worried about Cosmos' knee. She's not her normal self. I want to shake the stigma of me being, in her opinion, "the least nurturing man I have ever met in my life." We got a laugh out of that, but I know I am preoccupied with myself and my ailments, and don't pay enough mind to hers.

We ate dinner at Fatties, then went to the only bar in town, Dot's Bar, where all the hikers were hanging. The Stooges hitched from almost 100 miles up the trail to get back here. I wasn't sure I'd ever see them again so I was elated. They are funny men, brothers in their late twenties and early thirties, who feed off one another. I look forward to zeroing with them and having big fun. The Birds are here, too. I have not seen them since Hiawassee, more than four hundred miles ago. I am disappointed Rugged Shark did not show. He had said that if we got separated, he would find me here.

From time to time I gazed up at the TV and watched the Red Wings in a playoff game at the bar. I was amazed at how many of the hikers were rabid hockey fans.

Trail Days brought me back to April 1968. R&R. The 4th Division allotted one 6-day R&R a year. I waited until I was "short" (under 90 days to go) before I took mine. Six days in Australia. I was called out of the field sometime in April, near the time Martin Luther King was assassinated. I didn't realize this at the time, but Vietnam had turned me into an angry racist. I chose Australia over other places because it would be minus people with slant eyes. I thought that was normal. Racism is another effect of war you don't read about in the newspaper or see on television.

Our platoon had a little contest going. Who could be gone from the company on R&R the longest? I planned on setting the record. A chopper was sent out to retrieve me from the field and the first stop was Dak To, a semi-base camp. When I exited the chopper, an old friend, Phillips, was there to greet me. Phillips meant to our platoon what Radar O'Riley meant to the MASH unit in Korea. He had a jeep and loaded me up. It was late in the day so I was to leave early the next morning for base camp near Pleiku. Phillips took me to his super bunker. The place had a stereo, bunk beds, a card table, pot, snacks, and above all, a garbage can full of beer on ice. Ice! I'd forgotten what ice looked like. I dreamed of ice and cold, of snow and winter, of having a cold beer more times than I could count.

Phillips and I partied until the wee hours. Cards, pot, snacks, and beer. I won more than $500 that night, which would pay for my R&R. I was up early the next day to catch the first bird to base camp. Keep this in mind: I had not seen a woman since September, almost seven months ago. Our unit never went into villages. Anyone we saw was enemy.

Once in base camp, I showered, picked up a change of clothes, and off I went to the PX to see what these GIs stationed here had at their disposal in their day-to-day living. I browsed about for a bit and soon found myself at the barbershop. I treated myself to a haircut, shave, manicure, head massage, and hand massage. From there I went to the back room for a sauna. After a cold shower, I was led into a room by one of the Vietnamese women who worked on the base. Then I was treated to an hour massage, complete with her walking around on my back. All of this for two bucks!

The GIs stationed here not only had this luxury on a daily basis, they were receiving combat pay equal to mine. None of them had any idea what the war we were fighting was really like. And yet, they would eventually become Vietnam veterans, and most civilians in the states would just assume they were in combat, like I thought all World War II veterans were in combat.

The next morning I jumped the first cargo plane to Cam Ranh Bay, the most secure spot in Vietnam. When I arrived I was stunned: American women on the beaches. Live bands. The latest movies on a big screen outdoors. Water skiing. Fried chicken and hamburgers. I walked around wide-eyed, surrounded by thousands of service people, all drawing combat pay equal to mine. It didn't feel right.

That night I had dinner with some GIs I'd just met. One of them started telling the story of Hill 1338. He was in A Company 3rd of the 12th Infantry but had no idea I, too, had been a member of A Company, 3rd of the 12th Infantry, and was a participant in that horror-filled battle. He had everyone captivated with his story, as he told it well. Tears welled in his eyes as he spoke. When he was near conclusion I asked what platoon he was in. He meekly responded, saying he was in the 1st. I responded, "I am in the 1st platoon of A Company, 3rd of the 12th Infantry and I don't remember you." His jaw dropped and off he went, tail between legs. I wondered at the time if other GIs would be doing that kind of thing when they got home, telling stories to their families and friends as if they were participants.

The next day I boarded the big bird to Sydney. I became friends with my neighbors on the plane, Jim Seibert, who had been wounded badly, but was recovering, as well as a big guy across the aisle. We decided to stay in the same hotel and hang out. The stay in Sydney was uneventful save for a few highlights.

The big guy fell in love on day two of this six-day R&R. He banged on my door late one evening until he woke me up. I groggily answered and he proceeded to show off a tattoo that covered his chest. The art was a gigantic heart full of beautiful colors with an arrow through it. His name was below, her name on top. I was stunned. He was getting married, he said. As it turned out, he couldn't get the blood test in time and had to wait, vowing to return. The love affair might have been fleeting, but that tattoo was forever.

I was drinking a cup of tea in a coffee shop, reading the local newspaper one morning, when a beautiful young woman walked by, and gave me an incredibly sexy glance. I stopped reading, mouth open, not believing what had just happened. Moments later she reappeared, looking at me over the tops of her sunglasses. All I could do was stare in disbelief. She was tall, maybe 5'10," short blonde hair, a slim figure with nice breasts, a lovely behind and stunningly long legs. Wow. This is exactly what we fantasize about as we sit in and around our bunkers and dream. She sauntered to my table, asking if she could join me. I said, "Sure," with a big smile on my face, having no idea how to make conversation. As it turned out, she did all the work and was fantastic at making me feel comfortable. I don't remember her name, but I'll call her "Shontell." After we conversed for twenty minutes or so, she asked me what I was doing later. "Nothing," said I. She said she had to work that evening, but if I wanted I could meet her after work and we could spend some time together. My heart was beating out of my chest. I said, "Okay." She gave me directions and off she went, leaving me staring at her with mouth open as she strolled from the coffee shop. I was in luck!

I asked the waitress for my check, unaware she had been watching my interaction with Shontell. She said to me, "Are you aware of who that is?" I said, "No, but she sure is beautiful." The waitress responded, "He is beautiful, isn't he," with a slight grin on her face. I didn't immediately get what she meant because I was still in la-la land. And then it hit me. "He is beautiful?" I quizzed the waitress and she told me where Shontell worked. At a burlesque show a few blocks away. I slumped in my chair, shaking my head. Damn. And then I thought: What if I would have met Shontell as planned??

Later, I did meet a woman downtown. Her name was Vicki Olson and she was a beauty. We spent time together chatting, going to the beach, and kissing, but nothing major happened. At least, not the major I wanted to happen. I wrote to her for a time after I got back in the states. I always told her I would make my way back to Australia to see her, but I never did. Many GIs made that same promise to women they'd met on R&R, but then once we got our feet planted back in America, those promises were quickly forgotten.

We left Sydney after six days and headed back to Cam Ranh Bay. I dreaded being back out in the bush, and was determined to sham (be away from our unit) as long as I could. I was determined to extend my R&R to a new platoon record. I simply hung around Cam Ranh for two weeks, sleeping in different places. For a while I stayed at the Air Force barracks in exchange for telling gnarly

A PLACE CALLED VC VALLEY.

war stories. I stayed for a while at the barracks of soldiers going on R&R, and no one ever questioned me at either place. Maybe I could have stayed there for the rest of my tour, but eventually I felt guilty. I knew I was doing the wrong thing and perhaps could even be prosecuted as being AWOL.

So I got on a transport plane to Pleiku and base camp, then joined a convoy to Dak To, and eventually hopped on a chopper back to the bush. I had been gone 28 days on a six-day R&R. The first thing 6 (Captain Foye, company commander) said to me was, "Keenan, you back already?"

MAY 15 | DAMASCUS, TRAIL DAYS, ZERO

I am up before sunrise. The rains fell last night, and it was comforting to know I did not have to get up, tear down, and hike. Cosmos is walking very slowly and feeling dejected by her condition. She saw a doctor at Trail Days. The doc said the same thing all medical people say: "Rest will help." I want to say, "Doc, how do you expect us to rest when we have over fifteen hundred miles to go?"

I stopped by the outfitter in town, just browsing, looking for something I could use on the trail that was lightweight. I overheard two guys talking about Aquamira, a chemical used to treat water. I entered into the conversation. Both of these guys swear by this stuff. I spoke to Cosmos about it, and we decided to give it a try for a couple weeks. Simply mix a few drops from two small bottles, let them sit for a few minutes, then pour them into a water bladder. Easy.

The churches in Damascus are a big part of Trail Days. There are tents full of doctors and volunteers. They see all the hikers that sign up, hear their symptoms, and give them a prognosis. One church sponsors foot washing and massage. After a man washed and massaged my feet, he gave me a pair of smart wool socks. All free. I felt euphoric, closing my eyes and relaxing. A trailer full of nurses is on site as they test blood pressure and other vitals. There were showers offered, followed by clean, soft towels. And the sponsoring Baptist church had tablefuls of assorted gifts to choose from. I am glad to be here. The church people are wonderful folks that don't preach but rather, "do what Jesus would do."

Later in the day we power-ate our brunch, and then took a nap by the river. We went to Tent City in the evening. There are many manufacturers of trail equipment here, including shoes. If a hiker's equipment is faulty, they replace it at no cost. They want their equipment used on the trail. They want hikers to be pleased with their product, because the word spreads up and down the trail as if in a small town.

We found the Stooges' campsite at Tent City, and partied with them—Couscous, Whup Whup, I'm Happy, Splice, Soundtrack, KBar, and other hikers. We drank a bunch of beer. Whoever was in charge of Tent City created a huge bonfire. Many people, me included, danced around it while listening to the beat of drums played by relatives and friends of hikers. A crazy, wonderful night it was. A night to savor. This place is teeming with people, including former thru-hikers back for the celebration. I look forward to the fly-fishing tournament tomorrow, which takes place a few feet from where we rest.

MAY 16 | DAMASCUS, TRAIL DAYS, ANOTHER ZERO

The fly-fishers were out at 5:30 a.m. They were so quiet I didn't even know they were in the river until I came out of the tent to pee. Watching them fish was quite relaxing. I originally thought it was a big money event, but found out later the winner took home just $100.

We sought out a restaurant and consumed massive quantities of blueberry pancakes. I saw and talked to Night Moves, whom I hadn't seen since he emerged from his tent in the snow near Hiawassee, Georgia.

I decided to go to a doctor for the numbness in my feet and toes. I have lost one toenail and am in the process of losing two others. I have little concern about losing the toenails, but the numbness has been around for over a month. The doc said what I expected: "You need to rest if you want to get the feeling back in your feet and toes." He said it could take days. This is easy to say to someone who is not on a mission. For me? No can do. I will take an extended rest when I complete the AT, if I am so fortunate. My left leg is also numb, partially from surgery years ago, but it's worse now. The nerves make the side of my leg itch constantly. Every time I take off my pack I am itching like hell.

We all participated in the hiker parade, the biggest event in Damascus. Almost all the spectators had water guns, water balloons, or hoses. Hikers from "The Class of '09" led the parade, followed by hikers from '08, '07, and so on. Big fun! I couldn't keep the smile off my face as I walked the parade route with so many hikers and former hikers. I had goose bumps and even tears several times during this huge celebration. The Stooges had created a dance step for the class of 2009 to act out throughout the parade. So funny. Saw Deb (of the Apple Tree B&B) on her porch when we were walking in the parade. I yelled at her, "Deb, Deb!" She spotted me and waved, and I saw tears rolling down her cheeks. I thought about her saying only two days ago, "Let her put the robe on," referring to Cosmos, and I laughed out loud.

After the parade I stopped by the outfitter again and a young guy approached me and said he was happy I was still on the trail, that he thought I would be gone by now. I looked at him closely, and realized it was I'm Fine. I hadn't seen him since Neels Gap, right after he cut off his dreads on Blood Mountain. I will always remember this young guy. He gave me inspiration with his hiking technique way back when. He said to relax and enjoy. Take the good with the bad. That I have done. He is my Denny Leach (mentor in Vietnam) of the trail.

MAY 17 | PARTNERSHIP SHELTER, 14.5 MILES, 526.7 TOTAL

We were up early, tearing down and packing in the rain (of course). The AT seemed to be saying, "Welcome back to hiking reality after all the fun you have had." It was bittersweet tearing down and moving on. I know I will never see most of these folks again.

We had breakfast at Cowboys and left Damascus looking for a ride to Troutdale, trying to get back to the exact spot where we left off.

Our wait took five minutes. Mr. Nice Guy (trail name) and his girlfriend picked us up and went well out of their way to get us where we needed to go. He had thru-hiked the previous year and gave us a bunch of freeze-dried food he had leftover. Mr. Nice Guy is a perfect trail name for him.

Cosmos and I saw a few cows today. Of course she had to stop and feed and converse with them. We saw an old school bus in the woods near a meadow that reminded us both of Jon Krakauer's *Into the Wild*.

We arrived at the shelter in the daylight, knowing this is the only shelter on the trail where one can order pizza. I walked down a side trail and used a phone at a closed ranger station to order two larges. This shelter is a landmark for hikers. They scramble and do extra miles to get here for the pizza. Since we'd just been at Trail Days we shouldn't have cared about food that much, but we did. We had to get that pizza. Cosmos started a fire, and then she and I ate two large pizzas, drank soda pop, and talked to others who had gathered: Bushman, Rusty, Firebug, Phantom Cupcake, That's What She Said. We had a relaxing evening, sitting around the fire in the chilly night air, and eventually crawled into our bags and drifted off.

MAY 18 | RELAX INN, ATKINS, 11.6 MILES, 538.3 MILES TOTAL

I wake and lie with eyes open for a couple minutes, then rise. Pack up my stuff inside the tent before I unzip and quickly exit. When Cosmos emerges, we tear down the tent and pack everything away. Eat breakfast, brush teeth, fill up on water if need be, and away we go. On the trail by 7:30 a.m.

Cosmos and I rarely hike the entire day together now. So far, I am hiking at a much faster pace than she is. We are still feeling each other out, and this seems to be working for us, but there are still questions: *Should I go first, hike a few miles, then wait? Or should I slow my pace?* When I wait, I read, think, eat candy, get water, so I don't mind waiting, though Cosmos thinks I do. I sometimes wish I could simply slow my pace, but I've tried that and it makes me mentally fatigued. I like to hike at my pace.

I am hoping that Cosmos will learn to cope with the pain she feels. We all have it, and I know that I don't know her pain, that I can't gauge her pain. Maybe if I was hurting as much as she is, I wouldn't be able to go on. But something is always aching on this body. Both my knees hurt horribly yesterday. Today they feel fine and my feet hurt instead.

I finished the Michael Connelly book, *The Lincoln Lawyer,* today and I left it at the Chatfield Shelter. Someone else may want to read it.

No rain yet today. A week ago my rain pants started ripping at the seams. I will probably either send them home or take them to an outfitter on the trail to be repaired.

We ended up at the Relax Inn in Atkins, Virginia. What a dive this place is. We probably should have gone on, but Cosmos was hurting and the tent needs drying out. That thing felt like it weighed a ton today. We have our stuff draped all over our motel room.

Ate at a little diner up the road, and then hitchhiked to the post office, looking for goodies from a friend from back home. This post office was the address Cosmos and I gave him, but there was nothing waiting for us. I felt huge disappointment. Reminded me of Vietnam when I was looking forward to getting a package and it didn't arrive.

I spoke with my son, Colin. Inspired by my journey, he is going to try to bike across the country and will be leaving from Chicago in a couple weeks. He has a trailer and I will let him use my bike. He has no idea how big a journey he is undertaking or the pain he will feel. It is a journey I hope he can finish. The education will be priceless. Bike your own journey, Colin. Don't rush it.

MAY 19 | LYNN CAMP MOUNTAIN, 15.9 MILES, 554.2 MILES TOTAL

We ate breakfast early at a gas station alongside the road. What a beautiful day. If I were just beginning this journey, today's hike would have kicked my ass, but not so now. Met Stickman, a self-proclaimed hiking bum. He has a high-rise apartment in Chicago but loves to stay on the trail.

We camped at the top of a small mountain. Cosmos made an excellent dinner. Chili. She made a ton, but we pounded it down.

Rugged Shark is three days ahead according to the trail register at the last shelter. Seems more than likely I won't see him again until I visit him in Chicago. We would be in close proximity if he had gone to Trail Days, but right now he is hiking big miles, as are the Stooge's. They are also way up ahead. I won't see them again until I visit them in Holland, or if they come to Mexico to visit when I am there for the winter. I had spoken to them about Sayulita, a little surfing town in Mexico, where I have a casa. Visions of catching them dance in my head, but I would much rather hike with Cosmos than do the big miles that would require.

I enjoy reading the trail registers at each shelter. Early on, three days meant I had hiked thirty miles, max. Now three days usually means fifty or sixty miles. The registers are always good reading material. I can gauge the location of all the hikers I have met along the way. If I don't see their name in the register they are either behind me or off the trail.

Cosmos had another classic trail quote today. As we were hiking downhill, with her behind me, I heard her pole bang against a tree. Startled, I turned to ask what was wrong. With a somewhat angry look on her face she said, "All I smell is my crotch and ass." My laughter shook the mountain.

MAY 20 | JENKINS SHELTER, 17.1 MILES, 571.3 MILES TOTAL

My one-time best friend Frank would have been sixty-three today if he didn't screw up his life with alcohol. What a friend he was, writing more letters to me when I was in Vietnam than my mother. And that's saying a bunch.

Another great day of hiking. We toured through a beautiful salmon and violet rhododendron thicket. We literally walked through a tunnel of flowers. What a sweet aroma.

We met a guy named Tick today. I could think of better trail names, but he started on April 2 in Harpers Ferry, West Virginia, and is southbound to where I began in Springer Mountain, Georgia. Then he'll fly to Maine and hike back southbound from Katahdin to Harpers Ferry. This is called flip-flopping.

We set up near Firebug and Muffin Man, next to a beautiful, rippling stream. Falling asleep listening to water soothes me.

My headlamp went on the blink. Damn.

MAY 21 | JUST PAST HELVEYS MILL SHELTER, 21.7 MILES, 592 MILES TOTAL

I woke up early to the wonderful sounds of the stream.

Cosmos left early, a half hour before me. I tore down the tent and meditated by the stream for a few minutes before I headed out. Word was that this is supposed to be an easy hiking day, but I have heard this before. In fact, I have heard this many times. Most of the time, the "easy hike" that people speak of is actually far from the truth.

I felt like a million bucks today. What a joyful walk in the woods. This is what I had thought the entire AT was going to be like. The first twelve miles were the easiest miles I have walked since I began this journey. I had phone service, so I spoke with a variety of friends. I surprised them and it made my day to hear their voices. I was walking on dirt today, not jagged rocks, with few ups and downs.

The only downer was water being hard to come by. I knew long ago not to pass a water source by, even if I still had some. Cosmos waited for me a few miles down the trail and we hiked together for a bit, looking for water. The source we found was well off the trail. I hiked down to fill up and ended up going an extra mile and a half, but it was well worth it. We hiked another couple miles after I got the water and then took a short break, thinking about stopping. We rested for a bit, looked at each other, and our eyes said, "Okay, another couple miles."

After another three-plus miles, Cosmos found a sweet little camp spot on the top of a knoll. She is so good at finding these beautiful spots in the woods. After hiking the first 350 miles alone, the thought of ever hiking without Cosmos leaves me with an empty feeling. I have grown accustomed to her, I love her attitude, and I love her.

For some reason those last miles took a toll on my body. I am completely spent. Cosmos ordered me to sit down. She put up the tent and made dinner, as I did nothing. I could barely move.

I remembered these days in Vietnam. We would bust our ass trying to make a location, stressed out about making contact. We were moving all of the day while on keen alert. No sightseeing. No vistas. Pure physical, emotional, and mental stress. Ninety percent of the time when we reached our night location we were exhausted beyond imagination. There was no Cosmos there to tell me to sit down. Oh, yeah, I can just imagine it: "Hey Keenan, you just relax. I know you're tired. We'll dig the hole, fill the sandbags, cut a field of fire, cut down overhead cover, put out the trip flares, place the claymores. Then we will cook your chow. And don't worry about guard tonight. We have you covered. You take it easy."

Ha. Right.

We saw Couscous, the Blonde Sisters, and Jed, their new trail dog. Other hikers walked by as we were setting up near the trail. There was Sis, Salty Dog, MoFo, and Floater. Salty Dog was packing a pizza he'd bought in town when he hitched into Bland, Virginia. He often blue blazes off the trail to a road, hitches in, and gets the food he is craving. He likes to eat and drink like a king in the woods.

There was trail magic today. First we came across a cooler filled with ice-cold Gatorade and next week's weather report. Later we found ice water in big jugs, strategically placed near the trail. Local churches often do this. I have noticed that many people on the trail read the New Testament. My bible has become my thru-hiker's handbook.

5/22 | DISMAL CREEK FALLS, 11.5 MILES, 603.5 TOTAL

We were surrounded by millipedes last night. Creepy little things that somewhat resemble a caterpillar. Cosmos hung her pack up with the bear bag, and told me to do the same. I did not. She brought her boots in the tent. I did not. Then she woke me in the middle of the night somewhat freaking out because she could hear the millipedes crawling around outside our tent. I rolled over and went back to sleep. Then when I opened my eyes this morning they were everywhere, seemingly consuming the tent. We tore down amongst them. Gross. I was about to put my boots on, had some second thoughts, turned them upside down and shook them. Dozens of millipedes fell out. Cosmos left before me to get away from them. I hurriedly emptied my boots, and got the hell out of there. I am headed for the next shelter and a water source.

I hiked the five miles to the Jenny Knob Shelter and Cosmos was waiting. We met a young guy named Poppins and two other dudes with a dog. After I got my water, Poppins asked if I cared if they smoked some pot. I said no, "If I can participate." Cosmos said no, she was not going to get high on the trail. After indulging, I hiked out. My pace slowed considerably. I was last in our group of five by almost an hour.

Climbing is difficult for me when I'm stoned, but the scenery and the beauty intensified. I crossed streams where rhododendrons abounded, and finally made it to Kimberling Creek (which was more like a river) and walked across a wonderful suspension bridge, some sixty feet long. There sat Cosmos, Poppins, the others guys and their dog. Waiting for me. I made a pact with myself today: no more smoking pot on the trail.

We were treated to trail magic shortly after crossing the creek. Team Dude (five guys hiking the trail together) had coolers filled with ice-cold Budweisers. I simply could not resist. Cosmos had a Bud and a cigarette. Team Dude was just lying around drinking beer, smoking cigarettes, and bullshitting. They are thru-hikers. If they do this often, they won't last.

One guy was telling a vulgar story about pissing his sleeping bag. The team was nice enough, but I would not want to join them.

We walked to a restaurant/store a half-mile down a road that was near the creek. I was starving, and rumor had it the store had cheeseburgers. I ordered and ate a double cheeseburger, fries, two Dr. Peppers and shared a half-gallon of ice cream with Cosmos. I packed in a 24 oz. beer and chips and cheese for tonight and off we hiked the two miles to Dismal Creek Falls. We took a blue blaze trail off the AT to the falls and found a camp spot on a rock along the beautiful Dismal Creek. There is a waterfall with a swimming hole here. We swam, splashed around, and washed alongside Firebug, Muffin Man, and Poppins. Wonderful. I was a bit behind Cosmos and Poppins when we hiked in the two miles, and as I walked I could constantly smell cheese. Not flowers, but cheese. I thought my nose was fooling me, but when I arrived at the creek I soon realized Poppins had packed in a Philly cheesesteak sandwich.

Poppins is slight of build, maybe 5'9," with dark, curly brown hair and a full beard. Quite handsome and very laid back. Later, I found out he had established a new record at Trail Days for consumption of food. He ate a 5 lb. burger at Fatties, with a large bowl of pickles on the side. If any customer consumes the largest burger, they may name it whatever they wish. There is now a burger at Fatties called "Poppins 5 lb. Fatties Burger." He made history.

I drank the beer and ate my dinner. Floater happened in. He is a 65-year-old therapist from New Orleans. He walks and talks so very, very slowly. I talked with him for over an hour before turning in. He immediately became one of my favorites on trail. He said to me in his slow southern manner, "Are you sharing a tent with Cosmos?" I said, "Yes." He smirked, shook his head, and walked to his tent.

The fragrance of the flowers on the trail today was the best yet. A beautiful night it is. No need for a rainfly.

I have now rambled over more than six hundred miles.

MAY 23 | WOODSHOLE HOSTEL, 12 MILES, 615.5 MILES TOTAL

I woke in the early morn and walked down to the falls. I sat quietly, listening. I savored what I am involved in, a nature hike *minus bloodshed, minus stress, minus grieving, minus being worried if I will be alive tomorrow.*

I wandered back to the tent about 6:45 a.m., roused Cosmos, and tore down. We enjoyed breakfast next to the river. I filled up on water, using the Aquamira as treatment. This is the way to go for us. What an easy method of assuring our water is pure. I am sold on this method, as is Cosmos.

What a magical ending to our day's hike of twelve miles. We hiked off the trail and down a little gravel road and landed at the Woodshole Hostel. Seeing no activity, we dropped our packs on the porch of what appeared to be a bunkhouse and looked around. The place was wide open. I saw a scale, hopped on, and weighed in at 163. Two months ago I was 198. I opened the refrigerator and found it full of soda and candy. An oasis. I nestled into a hammock on the front porch for a nap, waking an hour later as the owners pulled in.

Neville and Michael are the proprietors. Neville's grandmother operated this hostel for many years and willed it to her as long as she kept it a hostel. Michael was a thru-hiker and met Neville here two years ago. They will be married in August. Michael seems not to appreciate his situation. He is living with beautiful Neville in a picturesque cabin/hostel in the woods, one revered by all thru-hikers. I shouldn't be quick to judge; perhaps he is having a bad day or they are having a moment.

As we were chatting on the porch, out from the woods comes a slow-moving Floater, covered in sweat. He walks up, sans shirt, looks at Michael, and says very slowly in that southern drawl of his, "Do you have a cold, cold beer?"

The main house was equipped with a hot tub and I took full advantage, soaking my body for an hour, after which Neville gave me a super massage. Other thru-hikers arrived as I basked. One moment I am in the woods, dirty and stinking, the next I am in the lap of luxury. *Reminded me for a moment of going into base camp prior to R&R.*

We had soup, chicken, salad, broccoli and rice, followed by ice cream, for dinner. In attendance were Floater, Poppins, Windbreaker, Brendan, Spencer, Cosmos and I. Before dinner each person at the table gave their name and residence followed by what they were thankful for. I was grateful to be alive. I am also hiking for my children and nephew, Evan. Following dinner Neville showed us old photo albums of her grandmother at this hostel.

Windbreaker showed us pictures of a mother deer with her newborn fawn only minutes old. Hearing him describe the scene made me feel like I was there. Windbreaker carries a banjo and plucks away in his spare time. Where did he get his trail name? He passes gas often and is not shy about it. At shelters, he would simply write in the register: "Windbreaker broke wind here."

We are up at 6 a.m. for breakfast. As we ate, Windbreaker played soft tunes on the banjo outside. We considered doing a zero today, but decided to move on. All the other thru-hikers are doing a zero. I hope Michael realizes the beauty of Neville and doesn't take her or his situation for granted. She is a special woman.

We left about noon after meeting Tufted Titmouse's parents, Lloyd and Nancy. They were to meet the Birds this day at this hostel. As happens so many times on the trail, hikers you think about but haven't seen for many moons are perhaps a day behind. Lloyd gave us a ride to the trailhead. We had an interesting hike, complete with a 2,000-foot downhill finish in a two-mile stretch. We hit a road near the town and ended up walking the mile to town because of limited traffic. When we arrived, I thought I was hallucinating. There before my eyes was a Dairy Queen. Without hesitation we dropped our packs and went inside. I proceeded to eat a double cheeseburger, fries, and a chocolate chip cookie dough-flavored Flurry. Cosmos had a similar order. I constantly marvel at my appetite. I consume mass quantities, yet still have lost thirty-five pounds.

We walked to the Holiday Motor Lodge and got a room. I took a bath with Epsom salts then caught up on my e-mails home. Cosmos and I sent out some photos. I tried to get a *USA Today* to no avail. Believe it or not, many of these townspeople have never heard of *USA Today*. They lead a very simple life, often have no idea what goes on in the world, which sometimes makes me feel envious.

We went to the grocery store, resupplied, and later hit up an Italian restaurant for carryout food for dinner. Then back to our room, where we ate our food while watching a movie on TV. A zero is a possibility tomorrow.

May 25 | Zero

This is Memorial Day. I reflected on those who returned from war with serious physical and mental problems. I thought about Lloyd Slack, a friend I had known since basic training. He was a star athlete from Lowell, near Grand Rapids, my hometown. We went through basic training at Fort Knox, and AIT (advanced individual training) at Fort Polk together. We were to get on the same plane in Grand Rapids en route to Oakland, then Vietnam. Lloyd was there at the airport with his mom and girlfriend.

I remember that day so clearly. My parents had a cookout for my family and my best friends. It was early July, 1967. After eating, my friends and I were in the middle of a rousing game of badminton when my mother walked across the yard and called me to her. She said softly, with her lips trembling. "It's time to get ready, Tim." I handed my racquet to another friend and slowly walked up to my room to shower and put on my uniform. About the time I got dressed, mom knocked on the door, then entered my room. She began weeping silently, and hugged me for an extended period of time. I cried on her shoulder while promising I would come home. She begged me to be careful.

I made my way downstairs and all my friends, my dad, and my sisters were in the kitchen. There was no joy. I loaded my duffel bag into the back of the car and away we went. My friends drove separately. I was sitting in the back seat with my sisters and "If you're going to San Francisco," by Scott MacKenzie, filled the air. San Fran was to be one of my stops on the way to Oakland and GI-ville.

Everyone was out of their comfort zone as we drove. We eventually pulled up to the airport and silence filled the air. I had this eerie feeling I was going to the death chamber. The first person I saw when I entered the airport was Lloyd. He was with his mom and his fiancé. He gave me a comforting smile. And then I heard commotion. There in the airport were dozens of people I knew who'd come to see me off. I started kissing and hugging the women, and hugged and shook hands with the men. The scene was so chaotic I missed my plane! Lloyd was on board, probably wondering what the hell had happened to me. I got rescheduled onto the next flight, leaving a half hour later.

My plane started boarding and I said my final goodbyes. I hugged my sisters. I embraced my mom and told her once again, "I'll see you in a year. I promise you." My dad was the last one to see me. He looked at me with tears streaming down his face and told me he loved me while shaking my hand, not letting go. Finally I boarded, and as I looked out the window of the plane I saw all my friends, who I thought had gone home, on the observation deck waving at me. I cried once again. And I was gone.

I landed in San Francisco early in the morning. I had had a long layover in Detroit; I wish I had ten bucks for every time I thought of walking away and heading to Canada. I could say goodbye USA, goodbye to the Army. That might be easy, but the goodbye I could never handle would be to my family and friends, for I could never return.

In San Francisco I walked around the airport, looking for an Army shuttle to the base I was to report to in Oakland. As I searched I saw a young African-American man walking towards me. As he came into view I recognized him.

"Aren't you Muhammad Ali?" I asked. He nodded and reached out his hand to shake mine. He asked if I was coming or going and I said, "Going." He said he was sorry to hear that, and wished me all the best. I told him I was proud of him for standing up for his religious convictions. He told me he was in San Francisco to try to obtain a visa to box out of country (which was subsequently denied). I was thrilled to meet him.

I made my way to Oakland and the base. The first person I saw when I entered was Lloyd, clad in fatigues. He smiled that same smile. Maybe it was more of a smirk, because he proceeded to give me shit for missing the flight from Grand Rapids.

Fast forward to Christmastime. We were set up at a firebase somewhere, I don't exactly remember where, as we had pulled back a bit because Bob Hope was coming to base camp. Of course the grunts couldn't see Bob Hope, because we had to remain in the field and protect. Word was that Bob Hope was second only to the President on the NVA's assassination wish list.

There was going to be a Christmas truce. Truce? My first thought was that if we can have a temporary truce, why don't we just truce for the rest of my tour?

Lloyd was in C Company; I was in A, but our companies would go on many missions together, including the one to take Hill 1338. I always checked on his status, and he mine. If C Company was engaged in firefights minus A Company, it was comforting to know he was okay. He felt the same. Both of our companies, although not set up together, were in fairly secure areas, equipped with large bunkers and a large field of fire. Initially, we were in areas where the chance of contact was minuscule.

It was a bright, hot, sunny day, and I was reading my mail when someone said they had heard a sniper had fired into the C Company's perimeter and someone may have gotten hit. I immediately hustled to our command bunker to find out what was happening. 6, our company commander, was monitoring the radio, speaking with someone from C Company, shaking his head. I waited. For some reason I had a bad feeling. I said softly, afraid of the answer, "What's happening in C Company? Everyone OK?" when he was done with the radio contact. "They had sniper fire, one round," 6 said. "One of the guys was making a tape for his fiancé to send home. The sniper's bullet hit him in the left shoulder and pierced his heart. KIA."

I gulped and said, "Do you have a name?"

He said, "Just got his last name. Slack." I felt an arrow in my heart. It couldn't be true. Maybe he had the name wrong. And then I thought of Lloyd lying on the ground, dying. I thought of him thinking about his fiancé with his last breath. I thought of his mom, a single parent with only one child.

And now he was going home. His mom would open the door and find two uniformed soldiers standing there. They would say, "I am sorry to inform you that your son, Lloyd Slack, has died in Vietnam as a result of hostile fire," and she would never be the same.

My dad told me that when I was in Vietnam, whenever the doorbell rang at my house my mom would go down to the basement and cry, petrified that two uniformed soldiers were standing outside.

On the AT I think of Lloyd almost every day.

We went to breakfast at a small diner in town. There sat MoFo and his friends. I took an afternoon nap after Cosmos gave me a fantastic massage. I rested my weary old bones and muscles.

Saw the Birds and their hiking partner, Chachi. They looked a bit worn out.

We had a pizza delivered to our room this night. We had spent the day packing up our resupply and getting things in order for tomorrow. The post office is closed today so we need to visit tomorrow before we depart. We could have packages.

This was an uneventful zero. The way they are supposed to be. Many times our zero days are spent doing laundry, going to the post office, grocery store, outfitter, hardware store. Walking everywhere, of course. There seems to be no time to relax. But since it was Memorial Day, everything was closed, so relax we did.

Our company relaxed during the Christmas truce of 1967. We were set up somewhat closer to base camp during the truce. One night on radio watch I got a call from the command post. I was asked to switch the frequency of my radio because someone wanted to speak with me. Other GIs were asked to do the same and we were patched into a group radio chat. I responded with my call sign, "Five one charlie, over," and heard a woman's beautiful voice, the kind of voice a GI dreamed of. She said, "I wanted to come visit you boys in person, but I was told for security reasons, it's not possible." Some of the GIs asked questions, but I could not. I was in la-la land because the voice belonged to Raquel Welch. She was in base camp with the Bob Hope crew. That night I went to sleep with a smile on my face.

The next day those of us on the radio chat moved about the perimeter, telling the others about our experience. I got to the command post bunker and found Top (company first sergeant) reading Sports Illustrated. I was a sports nut and asked Top if I could have the magazine when he finished and later he dropped it off at my bunker. I just happened to look at the address sticker on the cover to see who the magazine had been sent to originally. "PFC Tim Keenan, A Company, 3rd Battalion, 12th Infantry, 4th Infantry Division."

My parents had told me they were going to send me a subscription over four months ago, but I'd figured they forgot. Actually, it had been sent to me, but GIs had stolen it before it was sent out to the field. I was livid and screamed at Top. He'd been at base camp for most of his tour and I asked him how many issues he'd stolen.

"How could you?" I never got a decent answer to that because there wasn't an acceptable one to give.

MAY 26 | SYMMS GAP MEADOW, 11.9 MILES, 637.8 MILES TOTAL

I was up early and waiting at the post office when it opened. No packages from Traverse City once again.

My sister Charlee's package did arrive, though, and it was full of caramel corn and Snickers candy bars. Awesome. Charlee probably has no idea how much we enjoy what she has sent. I will request more of the same as the caramel corn is light to pack and tastes divine. We devoured it all.

We stopped by the Dairy Queen again on our way out of town. A hard rain had begun to fall and what better place to wait it out? I had a double cheeseburger, fries, and coke. Cosmos had the same except with onion rings and a malt. Floater came floating in, drenched. He had hiked from Woodshole, where he had zeroed for two days. Poppins is still there, doing his third consecutive zero. When I said goodbye to Floater, I knew I would not see him again. We were not going to stop for a few days, and we hike many more daily miles than he does. I wonder how far he will go. Every time I see him on the trail, he looks like he is walking his last step. He takes breaks every fifteen minutes.

The hike was difficult today with one big climb. I am in great shape now, but still seem to struggle mentally. I don't have to stop as much to catch my wind on the way up. And when I do summit, I can keep going without a break. Progress. I feel alive and proud.

We made it to the top and found a flat spot to pitch the tent near a couple of other hikers, Cruiser and Frank, from Germany. Cosmos and I ate grapes and candy for dinner, and had great fun doing it. We laughed out loud for what seemed like hours. We had a wonderful day.

Earlier, after we'd left Pearisburg, I had called Father Randall, an old priest friend from my childhood. He was my mentor and role model growing up and I found out he was in an Oblate Nursing Home in Massachusetts. The nursing home staff would not tell me how he was doing because I wasn't family, but they did say he was okay and that they would deliver the message that I had called. (They said he was out smoking a cigarette and did not like answering his phone. Same old Father Randall!) If there are saints, he is one. He chose to spend his entire life in poverty, while helping others. He was a friend of Mother Teresa. I was sad for a bit. Cosmos was sad with me.

It rained all night. I could hear Frank snoring, even with the hard rain. He is packing four or five bottles of German wine. His pack must weigh sixty pounds. He will learn soon enough.

MAY 27 | WAR SPUR SHELTER, 20.1 MILES, 657.9 MILES TOTAL

No laughter this morning, as we had to tear down in the rain. That made my pack, with the wet tent and all the food and water from resupply, extremely heavy. We had some tough climbs today, but they were beautiful. The fragrance from the spring flowers kept a slight smile on my face all the day. We found shelter with a great water source and pitched the tent. Cosmos again made a wonderful dinner. A long day it was. I am bushed. Couscous, MoFo, Cruiser, Whup Whup, and the blonde sisters are here. With all the rain that fell today, I find my sleeping bag damp, but not wet.

MAY 28 | SARVER HOLLOW SHELTER, 12.2 MILES, 670.1 MILES TOTAL

I am up early writing after a restless night with little sleep, even though I was so very tired. Rain fell all night. When I stuck my head out of the tent, I was surprised to see MoFo and Cruiser gone. We had full intentions of going twenty miles today, but it's not to be. I am exhausted and need to rest. The map said the shelter was .03 miles off the trail, but it seemed like two miles to me. Later, Couscous, the blonde sisters, and Whup Whup joined us at this shelter.

I lost two more toenails. The rain softens them. We caught up with MoFo as he was crossing a deep, fast-moving seasonal stream. He shakily crossed and we followed, having to grab onto a log to keep from getting swept away. I tied my boots to my pack as I forded the stream. Cosmos followed. As I write this, my feet are sore and my right knee is aching. The same pain I could have written about every day for the past six weeks, but today it seems more pronounced. And now I also have what could be a heel spur on the left foot. Damn.

Not a good day today, as I was beaten senseless by the mountains. While reaching one summit, I felt totally spent, exhausted. I stopped many times, feeling close to collapsing, sweating profusely while pounding water. Just when I was at my worst, the rain poured down from the heavens on cue, rejuvenating my mind and body. I opened my arms to the sky, and gave thanks to my mom and dad, just knowing this downpour of uplifting medicine had something to do with them.

I often think how proud they would be of their son. How they would boast about me to anyone who would listen. And of course, how they would worry. They gave me strength during those Vietnam days and they give me strength now.

We stayed inside the shelter tonight, because there was no flat area to be seen. Whup Whup made a roaring fire. Cosmos and I played euchre against Couscous and one of the sisters. They gave us some information on a country restaurant in Catawba named "The Homeplace" that has an all-you-can-eat portion of the menu. We started planning our hike to arrive at that area in early afternoon on a day they are open.

The rains came once again as we prepared to sleep. Major rain complete with hail. The shelter leaked in the exact spot I was trying to sleep. Drip, drip, drip. I needed a good night's sleep and didn't get one.

MAY 29 | PICKLE BRANCH SHELTER, 16.1 MILES, 686.2 MILES TOTAL

We hiked back up to the trail from the shelter over jagged rocks at about 8:00 a.m. After two months out here, in my brilliance, I have figured out that all of these damn mountains must be made of rock. What a discovery! How many more mountains do we have?

After hiking a few miles, I veered off trail some 200 feet to the site of a legendary plane crash: Audie Murphy, the most decorated soldier in World War II, and later an actor, died in an airplane crash at this spot. A large stone monument is dedicated to him.

At 11 a.m., while hiking across a spacious meadow, I spotted a station wagon with its hatch open near the end of the meadow. I immediately think, "Trail magic!" and increased my speed, already tasting the ice-cold soda and other goodies. On the way I caught up to the hiker in front of me, who turned out to be MoFo. He had the same thing on his mind. Eventually, we approached a man standing by his car where the trail crossed a two track. He said his name was Stooge, that he was the husband of Nannygoat, a section hiker who is close to completing the entire trail, having started years ago.

The first thing MoFo said to Stooge was not, "Hello."

It was, "What do you have in the back of your car?"

Stooge, who was there to pick up his wife and didn't know what a trail angel was, opened his cooler. Inside was one lone, but ice-cold, can of Dr. Pepper. MoFo and I shared it and expressed our heartfelt gratitude. "I guess I'll come well supplied next time," Stooge said.

I hiked hard after that, thinking about The Homeplace and their all-you-can-eat menu. I used to get excited about sex. Now, it's food.

The plan for tomorrow is get up early, hike the eleven-plus miles to Highway VA-311, and hitch to the food. Arrival time is planned for early afternoon.

MAY 30 | CATAWBA MOUNTAIN SHELTER, 14.6 MILES, 700.8 MILES TOTAL

We got up early and embarked on what looked like a fairly easy hike according to the map. Well, the map lied. This was a difficult day, especially when one has an "easy hike" mindset. We were nearing the destination, and after a long gradual uphill, we were treated to a vista a short ways off the trail. As I dropped my pack to check out the view, Cosmos had another classic quote: "Please don't make me do what I know I should do."

She was worn out. She always wants to see the awesome vistas, but this time she passed, opting to sit on a rock and wait.

The trail brought us into a parking lot that borders highway VA-311. We sat down for a moment before we hitched. I haven't eaten but a small breakfast today. I am thinking I am going to cause major problems for the cook. A couple guys in the parking lot offered to give us a ride in the back of their pickup. One of them smiled lovingly and said that, together, the two of us looked like "kindred spirits." Us. Cosmos and I. Warm feeling.

After being dropped off, we met another hiker on the outside of the restaurant who said he would save a place for us. We committed to eating dinner with him before we knew MoFo was here, as were Cruiser and Doc. We sat in a different part of the restaurant and didn't see them until we were done eating. And eat we did, especially me. And drank. Two Dr. Peppers, three lemonades, three ice waters, one ice tea, eight pieces of chicken, three slabs of roast beef, two helpings of mashed potatoes and gravy, beans, corn, biscuits. Then, peach cobbler for desert. I was a glutton.

We sat for a few minutes outside the restaurant, then walked to a general store and bought some candy bars, other munchies, and a six-pack of beer to share with the folks at the shelter a mile or so up the trail. It had been less than an hour since I'd pigged out, but I was already hungry again. Hard to believe.

Outside of the store we met a young guy named Justin, a friendly big dude. He was a bull rider who just drove up in his pickup to say hi and chat. He said he likes hikers from the trail. Soon after Justin left, a couple driving the other way on the highway turned around, came back, and gave us a ride a mile or so to the trailhead. Good deeds continue to bless us.

We sluggishly disappeared into the woods, packs heavy with the extra munchies and beer. I have walked more than 700 total miles. I cannot fathom it, but here I am.

The shelter is full of hikers. Couscous, Whup Whup, Gozer, So Happy, Doc, Almond Joy (from Israel, loves George Bush), Next Step, and Creaky are all here. We shared beers and munchies. We slept in the shelter and paid the price. It was a hot, humid, mosquito-infested night. We should have pitched our tent.

We saw Chachi on the trail early today. That boy can move out. He was attempting to do a forty-mile day. Forty miles! He was doing this to pick up a package for the Birds at a mail-drop up ahead. The Birds have a following of men, all good guys who like to hike with the women. And who can blame them? The Birds are attractive, very nice, easy company, fun, and strong hikers all.

MAY 31 | DALEVILLE, 17.8 MILES, 718.6 MILES TOTAL

We hiked out early today. Our original plan was to walk close to Daleville and camp there, but we ended up hiking the 17.8 miles to Highway 220. We passed the beautiful Dragon Tooth on our journey, a picturesque rock overhang overlooking the valley below. The drop appeared to be thousands of feet. I had seen many postcards of hikers sitting on Dragon Tooth with their feet dangling, and now here I was.

We stayed on the Dragon Tooth ridgeline for some time on this gorgeous day. When I have days like this it makes me forget all the horrible weather I have encountered. I felt good, other than the usual hurts.

The terrain flattened out the last five miles or so as we neared town. We even had a slight downhill thrown in. Easy.

Almond Joy hiked with us a bit today. He seemed bothersome to me, but I usually don't care because of the gap between us as we walk. But he was right on the Cosmos' ass, trailing her by no more than three feet. I was behind a bit. She tried to let him pass but he said no, "She was doing fine." This pissed off the strong-hiking Cosmos as she does not cater to tailgating. Eventually, she said she was going to wait for me, just to get rid of this guy. He had said he was getting off the trail permanently in Glasgow and asked if he could eat dinner with us and perhaps share a room in Daleville. I kept my frown to myself.

When we got to Daleville, he was waiting for us and asked where we were going to eat. We told him we were going to get a room. I rarely avoid a fellow hiker, but this guy was annoying. I got bad vibes.

In the last mile or so of today's hike, I saw a tent pitched near the trail, a no-no. As I approached I saw a ridge runner speaking to someone, probably telling the person s/he has to move the tent off the trail. It turned out to be the same dude who was drunk and about to beat his dog at Cold Spring Shelter, almost two months ago. He has been yellow blazing (hitching rides and skipping parts of the trail) and he was drunk once again. I still feel sorry for his dog.

As we approached Daleville, we talked about heading to the Howard Johnson's. We heard rumors other hikers were going to zero there. Good company and food awaited us. The room had a big hot tub. My body needs relaxation.

After cleaning up, we walked a half-mile to the 3 Pigs restaurant. We took seats outside and had a wonderful dinner, then it was back to the room and the hot tub for me. Cosmos hung out at the pool with some other hikers, but I didn't feel like socializing. Instead, I watched the Red Wings go up 2-0 on Pittsburg in the Stanley Cup finals.

I have been out here for more than sixty days. Every day I think about all the damage I am doing to my body. And all the good I am doing to my body. Hiking a minimum of ten hours a day, in all kinds of weather and terrain, will be a lifelong memory only shared by others who undergo this pain and joy. Professional or college athletes play a game or practice, and they are in a hot tub, with a trainer at the finest facilities money can buy. They are pampered so they can perform. We, the thru-hikers, have none of that. We have no one to check us out. No one to tape our ankles. No one to give us pep talks. We are on our own out here. Everyone is hurting. We feed off each other. Support each other. A favorite response to a fellow hiker who is telling stories of their aches and pains: "Are you off the trail?" meaning, "Do you hurt enough that you must leave the trail?" Most of the time the answer is no.

I find it heavenly sleeping in this nice soft bed. And of course cuddling with the warm body of someone I care about deeply.

JUNE 1 | DALEVILLE, ZERO

Today is a zero day with lots to do. I had three oranges, an apple, and a Dr. Pepper before 7 a.m. while I did our laundry. Then it was trying to catch up on my e-mails, followed by a trip to the outfitter where I bought new shoes, a risky move, but with my present boots feeling like I was walking around with cement feet when they got wet, I had to do something. I also purchased a new sleeping bag for the warmer climate, light pants, and some Smartwool socks.

We hitched to the post office, getting a ride in a dump truck. The driver, a big, heavily bearded man, seemed to have his eye on Cosmos and it made her very uncomfortable. I don't blame her. He turned out to be somewhat creepy, staring at Cosmos' legs instead of the road. We were glad to exit.

As we rode in the truck to the post office, I couldn't help thinking back to mail drops in the Central Highlands of Vietnam. Every so often we would get resupplied. This might include our C-rations, water, and mail. Sometime in December we got resupplied and I was the joyful recipient of a tape player and homemade cassette recordings I had requested in early November. As soon as I saw the player I was both excited and dejected. Excited I would be able to hear voices from home, dejected I was going to have to "hump" this extra weight, but more importantly, the voices from home were going to make me even more homesick.

That night I was the fourth guard, so I had six hours before my duty. I got inside our hooch with the two other guys that were to guard our section of the perimeter and I turned my tape player on very low volume. I quietly cried as I heard my young sister Cindy. In her sweet voice she was being a DJ. She was ten. She would say, "This is 'The Letter' by the Box Tops." or, "This is 'Reflections' by the Supremes." Listening to the music was grand. But listening to my little sister's voice was heartbreaking to me. I missed her so, and had that fear I would never see her again. Many times I had thought, "It is only a matter of time." I actually visualized her at my funeral, holding my parents' hands. I tried to shake it, but was overcome, only to be comforted by guys in the hooch whose names now escape me.

We listened to the other tapes that night. One had both my mom and dad speaking. They spoke not of war, but of what was going on back in my old world. Sports, Grand Rapids, friends, church. Both ended their conversations telling me how much they loved me. My mom got emotional at the end, but held on quite well. My sisters, Charlee and Eve, also spoke. They were both loving and nonpolitical in their allotted time, speaking of boyfriends, dogs, children, school, and work.

Hearing my family, their voices, picturing their faces, made my heart swell. I wanted to go home. NOW. But I had six months to go. I wondered if I would return in one piece.

At the post office I sent the old boots home, along with other things I no longer felt a need for. I appreciate my friend Thom letting me send stuff to his house. He will just put it in a corner and save it for me. I received a package from Tom Ellis. Nothing but candy. He just buys a bunch of candy and throws it in a box. The only problem with candy is the weight. He wrote how much inspiration I have been for him. He has quit eating red meat and is walking five miles a day. "If Naneek can walk ten hours a day in all kinds of weather," he wrote me in his letter, "I can at least do five miles." Glad I could help.

We went to a grocery store to resupply and got enough food for three to four days. Glasgow is our next stop. Cosmos got a package mailed to her with cookies and other stuff inside. This has been a classic case of a zero day gone awry. The day turned busy when I should be lying around and relaxing, but we must be prepared when we hit the trail.

We had lunch at the Pig place again. Had a couple beers with the Birds, In Deep, and Chachi on a hot, sunny day. After lunch, I took a little nap before I went to the pool and met some other hikers: Plaid Feedbag, the Birds, Butter Toes, In Deep, Cruiser, and MoFo were all sitting by the pool, trail talking. We shared stories, personal histories, and jokes. I went to bed about 11; Cosmos stayed up even later.

JUNE 2 | WILSON CREEK SHELTER, 11.2 MILES, 729.8 MILES TOTAL

The room was in total disarray with all our belongings, so we were up early to pack. Organizing one's stuff after a zero is difficult.

We eventually had breakfast and I did some last-minute computer work. I had to speak with the phone company about sending me a new phone. My chores took way longer than expected and we didn't get out of town until after noon.

The weather was hot and humid. We passed In Deep along the way. Then we passed MoFo and Cruiser. When we stopped for a break they all passed us, but not before Cosmos gifted them with some big heavy cookies, homemade by her mom.

We tented near the shelter. The Birds were there, as well as Cruiser, MoFo, In Deep, Dr. Bob, Chachi, and a couple section hikers. There was lots of sharing of food and drink. Reminiscent of Vietnam in a good way.

JUNE 3 | JENKINS (?) CREEK, 16.4 MILES, 746.6 MILES TOTAL

We were up and out early, but of course not before MoFo and Cruiser. I got far ahead of Cosmos and passed others (including MoFo) on the trail while hiking at a good pace. My mind was taking me on a ride when I realized I had not seen a white blaze for a while. I kept thinking, "I'll go a little further. I'm sure this is the right way." Feeling increasingly nervous, I finally turned around, doubling back and finding my mistake. I had walked two damn miles out of the way. I finally caught up with Cosmos and MoFo at a road crossing. Both were grinning from ear to ear. One of MoFo's former hiking partners was being his trail angel. She had a spread laid out of cookies, candies, cold soda pop, cheese, and crackers. She also carried most of MoFo's heavy pack in her car. This is called "slackpacking" — carrying just enough for the day and having someone drop your full pack at a designated area at the end of your day's hike — but he is still my hero. A former hospital administrator, MoFo thru-hiked the trail in 1985, and is now doing it again.

By slackpacking you can cover more miles, do it quicker, and save your body. My competitive drive won't let me slack-pack. I want to be as "pure" a hiker as I can be, good or bad, right or wrong.

As I was coming down one of the ridgelines today, sweaty, thirsty, and hungry as always, there sat Stooge with a big grin on his face. He had found a two track and was waiting for Nannygoat, and, as it turned out, me. He got up, gave me a broad smile, reached into his cooler and pulled out an icy cold Dr. Pepper. Oh, how I love this guy.

We finally made Jenkins Creek, which was more like a river than a creek. I had planned on swimming, but quickly changed my mind when I saw snakes in the water. I looked on my map and noticed there was a store 1.3 miles down a road where they sold beer and soda. I said adios to Cosmos and walked to the store packless. Upon arrival I found they didn't sell beer. Damn. I bought a couple of Dr. Peppers and some Gatorade, and headed back. Cosmos had pitched the tent near the river. She worried I had been kidnapped because I had taken so long. I admitted to being a fool for venturing for the beer.

We had a wonderful burrito dinner. Cosmos continues to amaze me with the delicious food she prepares out here in the wild. The weather turned sour and we took cover under the bridge. While we ate, we were treated to the sight of two beavers swimming up river and watched as they became separated. They frantically searched for one another, but ended up on opposite sides of the river. They stood on rocks looking for each other. Then they would swim one way or another in the river. We wanted to cry out, "She is over there," and point out the partner on the other side. They finally spotted one another and swam furiously towards each other. If they could have hugged, they would have. It was a beautiful moment.

The Birds and their male company arrived a bit before we were to eat dinner and decided to hitch into town to a restaurant. They were gone a couple of hours, then showed up with a case of Budweiser. I was in my tent, to call it a night, only to hear Hummingbird say, "We bought some of this beer for you, Naneek." We built a fire and sat about shooting the shit for a few hours, telling stories. At some point everyone was trying to guess Cosmos' real name. Hummingbird actually did. Remarkable.

I turned in after midnight with a slight buzz on. Reading tonight was not an option.

This is a different experience for me. I recommend the hike of the AT, or any long-distance hike for that matter, to anyone who suffers from the aftereffects of war. Although I think often of Vietnam, the people on the trail and the beauty of the trail are making my journey a life-changer. I am relaxing. I also have Cosmos. She helps bring me inner peace.

JUNE 4 | THUNDER HILL, HARRISON GROUND SPRING CAMPSITE, 16.9 MILES, 763.3 TOTAL

Up and out late at 9:30 a.m.; me with a slight headache from prior night's beer. We went over Floyd Mountain and Apple Orchard Mountain (elevation 4,225 feet). We passed the Guillotine, a huge boulder suspended over the AT. I had seen photos of this in books I read prior to beginning this journey, and now here I was. After taking some photos of our own, we hiked out quickly, and arrived at the Thunder Hill Shelter early and contemplated staying. I think Cosmos wanted to stay, but I persuaded her to hike on, just another three miles or so.

We startled a deer today. The mom and newborn fawn were next to the trail. Mom seemed distressed as the fawn was not moving. The mom fled. We were concerned something had happened to the fawn. It was a sad moment. Moms never leave their young, do they? No words were spoken for some time.

It is rainy and cold. We searched for and eventually found a quasi-campsite and pitched the tent in the rain with the precision of a crew at Indianapolis Speedway. We should have stayed at the shelter. My bad. We had a makeshift dinner because of our inability to cook outside in the rain. We just wanted to get into our bags and get warm. I read for a bit and said goodnight. We will try for another seventeen-mile day tomorrow, hoping the rain subsides.

> As I lay quietly in my bag, the rain beating down, I reflected on the letter I had sent my parents at Christmastime from Vietnam. It included the card each member of our battalion had received from the chief of the Kontum Province, where Dak To is located. The card thanked us for helping the South Vietnamese and urged us to be careful and return to our loved ones. The card reminded us that this was the Christmas season and that we would be missing our families. I must say it was a very nice note. I look back at it now and wonder if the reason the card was sent was political. At the time I simply viewed the communication with pleasure.
>
> My parents took the card to church to show the Monsignor at St. Paul the Apostle Church, who read it aloud from the pulpit as part

of his sermon to the congregation. One of the attendees happened to be a reporter from the Grand Rapids Press. He approached my parents after church and asked if he could print the letter along with any photo they had of me from Vietnam. My parents gave the reporter a photo of me on top of a battle-battered hill, Hill 1338. I was dirty and grungy.

The photo and story were in the paper the following week, just before the Tet Offensive. Of course, all of this was unbeknownst to me. When I came home months later, my parents showed me the article. They also showed me a laminated copy sent to them by our then-congressman, eventually the President, Gerald Ford, thanking them for my service.

Then my dad showed me another laminated copy. It was sent by Patten Monument, the maker of headstones. In it was a letter telling my parents how proud they must be, and that the war is heating up right now, so if they need services, they could get a good deal on a headstone. Those aren't the exact words, but that is what they were saying. It was disgusting. The letter was sent to my parents in the middle of the Tet Offensive, when lives were regularly being lost. The letter devastated my dad. He never showed it to my mom until I came home.

I paid Patten Monument Company a visit when I was home on leave. Let me just say I voiced my opinion.

I had trouble falling asleep tonight, remembering the monsoons in the war. The terrifying nights sitting on guard with the rain pouring down, unable to see two feet in front of me. It took me a couple months to realize that if I cannot see, neither can they. I nuzzled close to Cosmos. She has no idea how afraid I sometimes feel.

JUNE 5 | BUENA VISTA (HIKED TO HIGHWAY 501, HITCHED INTO THE CITY), 12 MILES, 775.3 MILES TOTAL

We woke up early to pouring rain. We tried to sleep in, hoping the rain would subside. Finally at 10 a.m. we decided we had to make a move, and took the tent down in a driving rain. We said little as we packed our gear and got the rain cover on the pack without getting everything soaked. As usual after a rain, my pack seems to weigh a ton.

Water poured off the mountains today; there were waterfalls seemingly every ten meters or so. With the waterfalls and the steady rain came a trail that was nothing but muck and puddles. Keeping anything, including the feet, dry was impossible. The strategy was simple: walk through the creeks (no rock hopping), puddles, and anything else that was in our way. Every once in a while we would look at one another and start laughing.

We made our way to Hwy 501 after a beautiful walk across a scenic bridge (built especially for hikers) over the fast-rising and rapid James River. A normal human being may have been distraught with the constant thunderous rain, but we viewed the day as another pleasurable experience. We hitched towards Glasgow. A couple named Francine and Tommy picked us up and gave us a ride to the Budget Inn in Buena Vista, because there were no hostels or motels near the trail in Glasgow. After checking in, I took a hot shower. We hung our tent and damp stuff outside to dry, and I did the laundry while Cosmos showered. Then we walked to town in search of an eatery. The sun shone.

Although we were on the lookout for a "dirty old bar" (this was the kind of place where Cosmos wanted to hang out), we ended up at a nice little Italian restaurant. On the walk back to the motel? We ran into Gezza and Top Shelf. We had seen them several times on the trail, but never really conversed. They are a happy couple with a great attitude on life, upbeat and positive. Both Gezza and Top Shelf seem overweight, yet both are strong hikers with determination. They have round, pleasant faces with sweet smiles. Most overweight hikers I've met have exited the trail by now, but I would be surprised if these two did not complete.

I updated myself on the sports scene back in Michigan. The Tigers lost and the Red Wings are tied 2-2 with Pittsburg in the Stanley Cup finals.

Cruiser told us a trail angel provided an all-you-can-eat breakfast for the thru-hikers who stayed at the Thunder Hill Shelter, the place Cosmos had wanted to stay but I'd talked her out of it. He had brought his grill and provisions to the shelter and made mass quantities of food. When Cosmos learned this, she simply gazed at me with a furrowed brow.

JUNE 6 | BROWN MOUNTAIN CREEK, 19 MILES, 794.3 TOTAL

We rise early and pack all of our stuff, which is now dry. Even after packing four extra cans of Budweiser to surprise someone with tonight, my pack weighs far less than it did yesterday. My phone got wet once again, and is ruined. I double-bagged that thing and had it buried in my raincoat, but with the torrential downpour we experienced, the thing still got wet. Two phones I have now managed to destroy.

We walked across the street to a Burger King for breakfast, then I made my way to the gas station next door and bought a luscious Krispy Kreme.

Gezza had given us a number to call for a ride back to the trail. The driver's name was Leggs, a former thru-hiker who seems to be making a living now off transporting hikers to and from the trailhead–the fee was $20. It was a good ten miles back to the trail, so there were no other options and the ride was well worth it. When we got to the trailhead I was astonished. There stood Hatchet, a thru-hiker we hadn't seen in weeks. We also saw Couscous, I'm Happy, Roach, and Whup Whup. They are strongly considering buying a canoe and "aqua blazing" the James River to Harpers Ferry, 250 miles by trail and also the psychological halfway point.

Hatchet and his hiking partner, Holdout, are using Chachi's car to slack-pack. Hatchet drops off Holdout, who starts her hike northbound, packless, and Hatchet drives to a road (usually a two-track) 25 miles or so north. Then Hatchet gets out, locks both their packs in the car, and hikes southbound towards Holdout. When their paths cross, he hands the keys to Holdout who continues to walk north, while Hatchet keeps walking south to the place where he originally dropped her off. Holdout then hikes to the car and drives back and picks up Hatchet. They've used this procedure for miles and miles. They were actually being thru-day hikers. I am proud to say we are pure thru-hiking.

At the trailhead we saw the Birds. Their friend Sunny Side Up, a strong hiker, is leaving the trail today. I notice, as does Cosmos, the dude has incredibly strong thighs. He was a big-time downhill skier out west. The Birds will miss Sunny Side Up, as he is blessed with a continuously positive attitude. And we will miss the Birds, because we will get way ahead of them and may not see them again. They are doing a couple zero days to hang with Sunny Side Up before he heads home. A story that sticks in my mind: Hummingbird left their tent in the middle of the night to take a "poo" (as she calls it). She then returned to the tent. After some time had elapsed, Mockingbird woke up smelling something, and said: "I smell poo." Turns out Hummingbird had stepped in her own "poo" and brought it back into the tent.

We departed for a big climbing day late in the morning. My right knee has been hurting for three days now. When we made it to the Punchbowl Shelter for an afternoon break, I took off the knee supports I have been wearing since day one, and my problems have ceased. I guess they're now a thing of the past.

We crossed a footbridge and found a flat camping spot next to the river. Picturesque. Cosmos and I had a nice dinner. She bathed in the river. We drank the beers. Cosmos smoked a couple cigs. We had a fulfilling day and night with lots of good interaction. As we ate dinner we explored the idea of a night hike. We had a full moon this evening, so we got everything ready in case we were up to it. We would leave at 3 or 4 a.m. We are excited about the prospect of hiking with the headlamps and moon.

JUNE 7 | THE DUTCH HOUSE B&B, FISH HATCHERY ROAD, 19.1 MILES, 813.4 MILES TOTAL

What a wonderful night. We fell asleep listening to the river flow. We awoke, packed, and left camp at 3:30 a.m., under a beautiful full moon. Cosmos walked point, much to my satisfaction. She knows what she is doing out there in the front. Early on she asked me to direct my headlamp off the trail because she sensed something was looking our way. Right she was. Just over some tall bushes two eyes appeared to be looking directly at me. My heart jumped. Cosmos said, "Keep your light on whatever it is and it won't move." I followed the orders, and the whatever, probably a bear, never moved, but its eyes tracked me. It was difficult keeping my headlamp on the animal while at the same time maneuvering through the rocky terrain. It was at this moment I decided I did not like night hiking.

Walking in the dark had me very scared. I continually flashed onto night guard duty when I always felt like the NVA would get into our perimeter and start slitting throats. As I walk the AT, I am keenly aware of the slightest sound, and my eyes are wide-open looking for anything. When it rained during the monsoons in Vietnam not only was our vision impaired, but we were unable to hear.

Early in my tour, maybe 30 days, during the monsoons, I was on listening post (LP) with a couple others. It was pouring rain. I had the radio and the headset near my ear, waiting for the perimeter to call and ask for a situation report. I would then break squelch on the radio three times to give the "all's well." Never break radio silence when on LP.

As I sat in the dark I could barely see shadows in the trees as the rain pelted me. Midway through my guard, I thought I heard movement. I listened long and hard, and became certain of the movement to my front. I wondered if my mind was playing tricks on me. I had been afraid of the dark since childhood, often imagining things and movements that did not exist. But I was certain I could hear a person walking in the jungle, even if I couldn't see him. My body stiffened. I didn't dare wake anyone for fear they might accidentally alert whoever was to my front. The noise advanced toward me, closer and closer. I could hear footsteps now. Quick footsteps.

I was convinced it was a human prowling around in the jungle in a pouring rain. I wondered how this could be, and I was frightened beyond imagination.

When the movement was maybe ten meters to my left, it slowly passed between the perimeter and me. I didn't dare turn my head. I was barely breathing. The movement stopped, and then started again, advancing towards my rear. I was going to shit my pants. The enemy was six feet behind me, and advancing. I had to make a move. I just had to. Before I did, a hand touched my back, near my rear pocket. I turned, screamed, and slapped at the hand, my M-16 at the ready. My scream woke up the other two guards and the "enemy" scurried up a tree. A MONKEY! A fucking monkey. It must have smelled the candy bar I had in my rear pocket and was coming for it. Dedicated to his mission was he. Scared shitless was me.

The sunrise was beautiful and I welcomed the light. We were hiking easily until about 10 a.m. and then hit a wall. Both of us got very tired, but we pushed on. Again Cosmos wanted to stop, but I was determined to make it to Fish Hatchery Road, where there is supposedly a very cool B&B that serves a free lunch to all thru-hikers. We made it to the road a little after 1:00. 19.1 miles. We had hiked over 38 miles in 24 hours. We went way too far. My bad, once again. I deserved the silent treatment Cosmos inflicted on me.

Much to our chagrin, and unbeknownst to us, in order to get a ride to the B&B we had to walk over a mile off the trail to a parking lot. The owner, Lois, picked us up. By the time we arrived at the B&B I could barely get out of the car. My body ached, and I had never seen Cosmos more tired than she was right then. "All of this for a free fucking lunch," she said. And what a disappointing lunch it was. We were served one slightly burnt grilled cheese and a small bowl of chili. We tried to be gracious, but I could have consumed ten bowls of chili and a loaf of grilled cheese sandwiches. When Lois was leading us to our rooms, she was visibly disappointed when we asked for one room, saying, "We don't have double beds." Cosmos answered, "We've been sharing a tent for four hundred miles. Is there a problem?"

After a hot shower we both hit the bed and didn't move for more than four hours. It was the most amazing nap I have ever taken. Jazzman and Turtle, a married couple, had arrived while we were sleeping. We ate dinner with them and shared trail and personal stories. Turtle has a bad knee and is probably off the trail at the next town. She will get a vehicle and support Jazzman in his quest to finish his hike. Jazzman is trying to fulfill a life-long dream, but must wear a helmet on the trail because of the blood-thinning medication he takes. People who overcome pain and illness to finish thru-hikes astonish me.

I used the computer to catch up on my e-mails. I sent a note to my children: Jonathon, Morganne, Colin and Jake, requesting a Father's Day present. The present would be for all four of them to promise to stay in close touch with their siblings, forever. *Please, do not go an extended period of time without contacting each other.* I couldn't stress enough the importance of savoring the people you love.

The things we as Americans take for granted: Hot shower. Home-cooked food. A toilet to sit on and flush. Getting a glass of water from the faucet. Transportation other than our feet. A non-achy body. And finally, clean underwear. As MoFo said a few days ago, "I have to break down and get some new shorts. These even have skid marks on the outside."

JUNE 8 | TYE RIVER, 9.4 MILES, 821.5 MILES TOTAL

We got up at 6:30 a.m., took a shower, and packed up. We had a wonderful breakfast of sausage, quiche, pancakes, orange juice, bananas, and strawberries, all the while engaging in yet another grand conversation with Jazzman and Turtle. Lois gave us a ride back to the trail as far as she could drive on the two-track. We then walked the mile, uphill, to the trail. Cosmos is badly hurting. She has sore arches, a hurting shoulder, and blisters. I didn't make things better by pushing us so far yesterday. I know she is still upset about my sometimes-manic hiking. Today she is being very quiet.

We hiked 9.4 miles in nine hours, up and over mountains. The downhills killed Cosmos, so we took it slow. We saw a deer playing like a little puppy along the trail. Getting down low, tail just a-wagging, looking at us, then prancing around and darting about. The sight was a pleasant mid-day treat. We stayed at a nice little camp spot by the river. We took the opportunity to bathe, and then pitched our tent. MoFo, Nannygoat, and Stooge had found a store up the road and brought back provisions for chilidogs. We had a good fire, shared our food, and had a long conversation about anything and everything. Hatchet and Holdout joined us. They are going to get off the trail for a week tomorrow to attend a wedding, which means we will probably never see them again.

I feel sad for Cosmos and angry with myself. Although she was acting like nothing was wrong when we were eating dinner, I know she is hurting. I am in hopes tomorrow is a better day, both physically and emotionally.

I pulled two ticks off myself today; both were digging in. I washed the dishes and went to bed. I am sleeping well these days.

JUNE 9 | RUSTY'S HOSTEL, BLUE RIDGE PARKWAY, 15.5 MILES, 838.3 MILES TOTAL

I thought we were up early and we were, but MoFo is already gone. We climbed the Three Ridges summit, going from 997 feet elevation to 3,970 feet in six miles. When we stopped at Maupin Field Shelter to visit a water source, there sat Ryan and Pepper the dog. Pepper had a hurt foot and Ryan was staying at the shelter for a couple days to let Pepper heal. I had not seen these two since before Fontana Damn, some seven hundred miles ago. Such is life on the trail. I love these unexpected surprises.

We ended our hiking day at the Dripping Rock parking area. We then hitched back down the road to Rusty's, a legendary hostel for thru-hikers only. I was having second thoughts about stopping, but pleasing Cosmos kept me going. I thought to myself, "Naneek, this is the least you can do after the pain you caused just two days ago." We had some problems finding the place, but eventually made it. Pirate (a volunteer), Cruiser, and Firebug were already here.

Rusty is a crusty, round older man with a big white beard, long hair, and coveralls. He was a great storyteller. We ate dinner and sat around for hours listening to Pirate and Rusty, trail legends, trade stories from "back in the day." Rusty took our photo and pinned it to the ceiling, along with the photos of other thru-hikers.

The bunkhouse was nice enough, but gnats and bugs ruined my sleep. I was glad to see morning.

JUNE 10 | WAYNESBORO, 14.2 MILES, 852.5 MILES TOTAL

Rusty made his famous blueberry pancakes for breakfast. I savor his goodness and that of so many others I have met on and off the trail that go out of their way to help us. They expect nothing in return. I vow to share whatever goodness I have with people for the rest of my life.

Rusty dropped us off at the Dripping Rock Gap, the same place where we left the trail. Off we went after saying our goodbyes. Cosmos led the way and quickly separated from me. After a few miles she almost ran dead into a ram (long-horned sheep) while ascending a small mountain.

The animal startled her, so she waited for me to catch up. I was pleasantly surprised to gaze at this animal. Another lurked nearby. They both had long, long dreads and unicorn-like horns and were actually cute as they eyeballed us, chewing their cuds. We respected their presence, while snapping a couple photos. They tilted their heads and watched us inquisitively as we disappeared out of their sight.

We hiked easily to a road near Waynesboro, Virginia, and got a ride from a local who called himself Mountain Man. He took us all over town. In fact, he brought me to the UPS office, ten miles up the road, to pick up the phone Alltel was sending here, after he dropped Cosmos off at a Quality Inn. Yet another example of the goodness of trail angels. He gave me his phone number and said to call him if I ever needed to go anywhere. I offered him money for gas, but he said, "Absolutely not."

Speaking of trail angels, the ultimate is Stooge. For example: Cosmos and I were walking across town, heading to a restaurant. I had no cash on me and was so very thirsty and out of the blue, I heard screeching tires and a horn honking. I turned to look, and there was Stooge and Nannygoat. Nannygoat had finished her hike and they were heading home, but Stooge had something for me. Out from his cooler he pulled an ice-cold Dr. Pepper. He said he had one left and had just mentioned to Nannygoat what a "great ending to this experience it would be if he could just see Naneek one more time and give him this Dr. Pepper." And there I was walking across the parking lot!

Cosmos and I went to the Chinese restaurant we had heard so much about on the trail. This place put out a spread like no other and I made no fewer than eight trips to the food bar. The fruit bar in itself was incredible.

I waddled back to the room and fell into bed. I iced my aching knees for an hour before I fell into a deep sleep.

JUNE 11 | WAYNESBORO, ZERO

Up early, as usual. I walked quietly about the room, gathering our laundry, wanting to let Cosmos sleep in, and I headed to the laundromat. When I got back to the room we decided to get things done so we could relax by the pool. First breakfast, then an outfitter, then the post office, then the grocery store for resupply, and finally back to the room. I probably should have called the Mountain Man. I know he would gladly have driven us everywhere. At the post office I received brownies from Jonathon, caramel corn from Charlee, a book (*Buddhism Is Not What You Think*) from Dave Murphy, and cookies from Tom Ellis. Big score today, heavy pack tomorrow.

Eventually, I ended up in a lounge chair next to the pool with a cold beer in hand. We had no idea, but MoFo and Cruiser were staying here, too, so they joined us. As we sat by the pool, the Birds, Chachi, and In Deep strolled up, looking for a room. We all sat around the pool, swimming, laughing, and enjoying each other's company. I hung out for a good bit, then snuck back to the room for a nap.

Someone at the pool had mentioned a sub shop in town that had awesome Philly cheesesteak sandwiches, so MoFo, Cruiser, and I made plans for dinner. Cosmos decided to dine with the Birds and their entourage. The Philly cheeses did not disappoint, and I bought two extra sandwiches to go, for a surprise dinner on the trail tomorrow. Bloated, I returned to the room at hiker midnight, 9 p.m.

I spoke with Jake and Jonathon before bed. What a treat hearing their voices. I miss the kids. I tried to call Colin and Morganne, but ended up leaving messages. I prepped my pack for tomorrow. With all the stuff folks have sent me, and the resupply, it is heavy and I envision a tough day tomorrow. Hiking with a heavy pack and coming off a zero, with food and beer galore, will make things difficult. I finished reading *Ride the River* before I slept.

JUNE 12 | CALF MOUNTAIN SHELTER, 7 MILES, 859.5 MILES TOTAL

Today is my sister Charlee's 66th birthday. I drift back to Vietnam, 1968, when I looked forward to her 25th. I carried a little calendar with me and would cross off the days as they passed. I'd have thirty days to go when she turned twenty-five. I would be "short."

On this day in 1968, we were set up at our firebase, serving as protection for the mortars, command post, and artillery. We were securing this place, and so had limited duty. We were on guard, yet relaxing a bit because rarely does the NVA hit when we are dug in at a firebase, so it was a rather secure place for a grunt.

This is a story with two parts:

First, a close friend, Steve Walker, a guy I went through advanced individual training in mortars with at Ft. Polk, had just returned from R&R in Australia. He was from Berkeley and loved smoking pot. Many of us smoked it from time to time, but the unwritten rule was, never smoke weed if there's danger of enemy contact. Walker was a mortar man with our battalion, much like I was supposed to be, and he was always at the firebase, because that was where artillery and mortars were set up.

He had a plan since he arrived in country: On his way back from his R&R, he would find his way to Saigon or another big city, and secure as much pot as he could fit in his duffel bag. We thought this was bravado, a joke, but when he returned from R&R, he told me he'd "scored" fifty pounds of the stuff. He'd crammed it so tightly into two sandbags, that if you hit one with a closed fist, "You would injure your hand." I was astounded.

He had only a month to go in country. "How are you going to get it through customs?" I asked him.

He said, "I'll worry about that later."

For the second part of this story, picture the night my sister was celebrating her birthday in the states, while the nighttime sky in Vietnam was clear, stars filling the sky. I sat on my bunker on guard duty, thinking of home. It was late, perhaps 2 a.m., when I noticed what looked like a firefight up on a mountaintop in the distance. Miles away I could see green tracers going one way, red tracers the other. (Guns in Vietnam generally had one tracer every 5th round. The U.S.'s M-16 tracers were red, the NVA's AK-47 tracers were green.) The firefight was so distant I could barely hear the noise from the rifles and machine guns, and I watched in disbelief because I knew none of the companies from our battalion were in that direction. And yet, I could feel the horror of whoever was involved as the firing continued on and off through the night.

The next morning we got word that Grizzly, our battalion commander, had volunteered our company to help out the other battalion, which had been overrun by the NVA. Overrun means having the enemy in your perimeter, and having the enemy in the perimeter in the dark of night was always my worst nightmare, right up there with being a POW.

Never did any battalion ever volunteer to help us out. We were always on our own. Grizzly had volunteered us, though he wouldn't be the one choppering into the hot landing zone. He wasn't going to be the one doing the fighting, but he would take the credit. He would get the backslapping and probably a medal, too.

The thought of it pisses me off to this day. Not that the unit that got hit didn't need our help, but just the thought of being volunteered to go into a hostile area by someone who wasn't going into the hostile area himself always weighed heavily on my sense of right and wrong. And now I was going to die on my sister's birthday.

Plus, we were leaving our firebase with only one company securing the perimeter, when it was set up for two companies. Some of the bunkers would have no guards on them this evening. Grizzly was rolling the dice thinking the NVA wouldn't know. He was rolling the dice with lives of young men--boys, really.

Rumor was that the unit atop the mountain had eliminated the NVA from the perimeter, which was good news, but it was a rumor. And I had heard dozens of rumors over the last eleven months and while some turned out to be true, most had not.

Hueys (helicopters) were on the way to pick us up, traveling in groups of three.

I was terrified as I boarded the bird, with only thirty days of my tour to go. Death was waiting. As we descended towards our destination, I noticed dead NVA caught in concertina (barbed) wire on one side of the perimeter. It was a morbid sight, but one I cared little about at the moment. I feared for my life. When the chopper neared the ground I jumped, got prone, and crawled to the nearest bunker faster than I'd thought humanly possible. I fell in, gasping for air, and grateful I was still in one piece.

When I got my bearings I noticed one other guy in the bunker with me, a member of the unit we were helping. He stared at me. My jaw dropped when I looked at him, as did his. "Gary Koets?" I said. "Keenan?" he said. We were in the same homeroom in high school and I hadn't seen him since graduation. We exchanged stories, and it turned out to be a peaceful night, as the NVA had retreated. Perhaps us coming to lend a hand caused them to move on. Who knows?

What I do know is that night, as I sat on guard in that bunker, I saw the same horror from afar as I had the night before, but this time it was our firebase getting overrun. Green and red tracers could be clearly seen. A firefight and we were supposed to be there providing security. Damn! Damn! Damn! Steve Walker was there, just back from R&R, and now he could be dead. My disdain for Grizzly was growing into hatred.

Later we got word they'd been overrun and suffered countless casualties and I couldn't help but worry Walker must be among them.

Another of our companies was first to arrive at the firebase the next morning, and reported the number of casualties, and got the dead and wounded out via medivac. I knew in my heart Walker was gone. Two days later we choppered back to that hill. We buried NVA in large bomb craters. When I asked about Walker I was told the rest of the second part of this story. He had been hit in the arm and shoulder but played dead as the NVA scoured the hill, killing survivors. When one of our companies came to the rescue early the next morning, the NVA had vanished, and they found Walker still alive and sent him on one of the first birds back to the hospital. I was relieved my friend was alive. Sad others weren't so fortunate.

A couple weeks later I received a letter from Walker. He said he was hit bad enough to be discharged from the Army. First, he would be sent to Japan to heal his wounds, and then home. His letter sounded cheerful. And there was a PS: "They sent my duffel bag home to Berkeley, untouched."

His 50 pounds of pot made it home safely.

I walked a bit off the trail to get some water from a creek, and there was Gezza, a big Pittsburg Penguin's hockey fan. The first thing out of his mouth was, "Pittsburg beat Detroit 2-1 to win the Stanley Cup. In Detroit." There was a big smile on his face.

Cosmos is sick this morning. Perhaps a hangover? She was out late with the Birds, Chachi, and In Deep. We ended up not pulling out of Waynesboro until after noon. I weighed my pack at the outfitters before leaving town: 47.9 lbs. Two Philly cheese sandwiches, two twenty-four-ounce beers, and more. Ouch!

After a short hike with the heavy pack, we tented near the shelter. The Birds and others arrived later. I actually had cell service up here. After I finished my sandwich and drank my beer, I spoke with Charlee and Dawn, my ex-wife. I hadn't heard from Colin and found out he was off the road. No more biking. Bad knees were his demise. He should have taken as many zeros as it takes to heal, then continued his mission. The advice to "hike your own hike" also applies to biking. His friends were going at a much faster clip, so instead of just slowing down and doing his own thing, he tried to keep up and now his journey is over. Bummer. That sense of accomplishment would have been so good for him. I look forward to speaking with him. Don't give up your dream, Colin.

Cosmos did not want her Philly cheese that I humped up this mountain, so I asked a guy in the shelter if he wanted it. He acted like I was offering him a million dollars.

JUNE 13 | LOFT MOUNTAIN CAMPGROUND, 20.4 MILES, 879.9 MILES TOTAL

We were out of camp at 7:40 a.m., and were in for an easy day. We are now in Shenandoah National Park. Sometime in the morning I was hiking behind Cosmos, maybe a couple hundred yards. I thought I heard her say good morning to someone, and when I came around the bend, there walking toward me was a naked hiker. Clad only in beard, hat, pack, and boots, he cheerfully wished me good morning.

We needed to register at the campground, a national park. Because I'm a veteran, we paid half price. After pitching our tent, we walked down a side trail to a restaurant. There are many spots to eat in these Shenandoahs and as we walked and talked, we heard someone yell out a car window, "Naneek, Cosmos!" It was a wide-grinning MoFo in a car with friends. He has friends in every port, it seems.

The Birds and their entourage showed up at the restaurant, too. We had dinner with them and learned they were camping near us, so I bought some beer and we made our way back up to our site. Chachi built a fire and we sat around and told stories.

When Chachi found out I'd served in Vietnam he asked me right off, "Did you ever kill anyone?" In Deep intervened, I said it was okay, but then quickly changed the subject.

There are deer everywhere here. They almost seem tame. Here are the animals I have seen thus far on the trail: boar, long-horned sheep, turkeys, rabbits, deer, snakes, squirrels, and lots of birds. No bear yet, unless you count the mystery animal sniffing outside my tent, and the other mystery animal staring at me on our night hike.

As I write this I have such a good and thankful feeling. First and foremost, I have Cosmos with me; second, I am able to do what I am doing at this time in my life, and of course, that I am alive.

JUNE 14 | OLD CEMETERY NEAR ELKTON, 17.4 MILES, 897.5 MILES TOTAL

Off we went in the early morning. Cosmos was out ahead of me today so I was hiking alone, although there seems to be quite a few section hikers in this area. I was enjoying the day, and out of nowhere Cosmos appeared, walking rapidly back towards me, the wrong way on the trail. She had fear in her eyes and my first thought was that a swarm of bees might be chasing her.

"What's going on?" I asked.

She looked me dead in the eye and said, "There's a cougar ahead on the trail."

Cosmos had seen it herself. It was walking on the trail towards her and they had made eye contact. The cougar stopped and Cosmos started backing up slowly until she went around a bend, and then ran back to me. Cosmos had mace. I gulped, got my trusty pepper spray at the ready, and we cautiously moved ahead. Word spread up and down the trail very quickly. When events or sightings happen on the trail, everyone soon knows. Other hikers kept asking Cosmos if she took a picture. It's hard to take a picture when you are scared shitless.

The park people say there are no cougars in the Shenandoahs, because if they spoke the truth it would hurt tourism, but the townsfolk know different.

My knee has been acting up for the last two days, buckling. I am worried. I will not leave this trail unless I cannot walk. We are 115 miles from Harpers Ferry, West Virginia, the psychological halfway point of the AT. It used to be the actual halfway point, but the mileage of the trail changes from year-to-year because of detours, new trails, etc. We plan to hike twenty miles tomorrow. A Harpers Ferry rest looms.

I am worried about my son, Colin. He hasn't called me and won't answer his phone when I call him. All I want to do is encourage him, to tell him not to get discouraged. Any long mission is difficult, but also rewarding.

We set up camp near a cemetery. For some reason, Cosmos loves cemeteries. Cruiser happened by and pitched his tent *in* the cemetery, between two graves. The Birds and their entourage walked by as we settled in.

JUNE 15 | ROCK SPRING HUT, 20.3 MILES, 917.8 MILES TOTAL

We got up and began hiking early once again. Stopped twice today to eat, once for lunch at a campsite, and later when Cruiser talked us into walking a half mile off the trail to Big Meadows Wayside, a restaurant and store in the national park for another lunch. "A cheeseburger and fries and a large hot fudge sundae, please." My diet was getting repetitious.

I bought six beers at the store and packed them out to the tent site 4.4 miles away along with some caramel corn. I was out ahead of Cosmos and when she arrived at the place we would pitch our tent she told me she had seen a bear. She was beaming. I think to myself: *Everyone has seen a bear except me.*

The shelter was jammed and all the good tent sites were taken, so we ended up pitching our tent on slanted ground. Cruiser, Cosmos, and I sat on a log and ate the caramel corn and drank the beer as the sun was setting.

Someone on the trail had been stung by a couple of bees today, and it made me remember a moment of panic early on in my tour.

I had been in country less than a month and hadn't seen any enemy. We were moving in an open field and I had little fear at this point. Our squad was in the middle of the company, so there were maybe fifty guys in front of me, each one five meters apart from the other. We were in a marshy area, walking in ankle-deep water, through reeds. We were to be in this open terrain for about 500 meters. Suddenly, guys way out front of us started running in different directions, screaming. We kept moving, confused, not hearing any gunfire. One by one, in rapid succession like dominoes, guys were running and screaming. I had no idea what was happening until I got stung. Then got stung again. And again. Then I started running through the marsh along with the others. We had walked into an ambush of ornery bees, it seemed like there were millions of them, and they brought us to our knees. Some men had even dropped their weapons in the water. Some of them had their bodies swell beyond recognition.

The bees retreated and we set up for the night near the marsh. Medivac helicopters had to get at least three guys out who had reactions to the stings and another helicopter flew in a resupply of M-16s and ammo for those who had lost their weapons to an unexpected enemy.

The deer are everywhere and they are friendly and inquisitive. Cosmos and I watched two fawns play alongside the trail today. Momma was nearby. They were kicking their heels, cutting back and forth over the trail. One was very young, the other probably a year old. They were having so much fun. Before turning in I asked Cosmos if we could leave really early in the morning to increase our chances of seeing a bear. She readily agreed.

I have walked over nine hundred miles.

JUNE 16 | PINEY BRANCH TRAIL, 23.9 MILES, 941.7 MILES TOTAL

We got up well before daybreak, leaving the shelter about 6:15 a.m. after trying to sleep on a slanted hill. My goal this day was to see a bear and find some breakfast. We no sooner made our way back to the white blazes of the AT when a bear bolted across the trail, maybe five meters in front of me. My heart raced. I was awed. A few minutes later, with Cosmos in the lead, out a hundred yards or so, I came around a bend in the trail. She was standing there, pointing into the bush by the trail. She slowly walked on. I was a bit wary, but hiked up to where she was and was greeted by a thunderous noise in the bush next to the trail, followed by a huge bear bolting. Startled the shit out of me. We ended up counting five bears before the grand finale later in the day.

We hiked 4.6 miles in the early morning to a blue blaze trail that led to a restaurant we had heard about from other hikers. Once again we had food on our minds. Cosmos and I ordered four different breakfasts: eggs benedict, French toast, sausage, a fruit plate, two huge cinnamon rolls, and a smoothie. Jazzman and Turtle were settled one table over. This restaurant, like others on the trail, is very kind to thru-hikers, but also has a designated spot in a corner for us to sit. We stink.

We hiked out with bloated stomachs, walked six plus miles to Byrd's Nest #3 Shelter, took a break, and ate some lunch. As we were eating, Chachi appeared out of nowhere, huffing and puffing. Last night, the Birds and he had pitched their tents and headed down to a lodge to hear some music and drink a couple beers. He was in a hurry, so he quickly pitched his tent and threw his pack inside. The pack contained his food. Later, when walking back to the tent in the dark, he noticed a coffee wrapper on the trail and thought, "That looks like my brand." Then the mistake dawned and he sprinted up the trail to his site, only to find his tent totaled. Ripped up, his backpack twenty meters from the tent, sleeping bag clawed. BEAR. He knows he should have hung his food, but he took the chance and paid the price. He was now hiking ahead to an outfitter to buy new gear. An expensive mistake.

We saw Jazzman and Turtle on the trail later in the day. Jazzman had a forlorn look on his face as he rested on a rock. Turtle explained his medical condition. The reason he is on blood thinners is he has problems with clotting in his legs. He knows his condition isn't the best. He knows he must leave the trail, which is a thru-hiker's nightmare. I feel so badly for him. He so wanted to at least make it to Harpers Ferry, the halfway point. They made it to a road and hitched to the nearest doctor. Turtle has a bad knee, so their original plan had been for her to fly home, get a car, and follow

Jazzman on the rest of his hike. Now it was not to be. They had planned this hike for years, and I felt a real sense of loss after saying goodbye to them. And yet, they will still be able to say they hiked more than 900 miles of the AT. Something to hang their hat on for sure.

We saw the Birds on the trail today. We don't usually see them until nightfall. Their dad is joining them tomorrow for ten days. I hope he is in good shape because these women can hike and they have their trail legs under them. Dad is in for a major journey and a major awakening. When he gets a taste of this trail, his pride in what his daughters are accomplishing will reach a whole new level.

Toward the end of our day I was ahead of Cosmos a few hundred yards. We were trying to get to a snack bar (off the trail a few meters) before it closed. Ice cream. We were hiking hard. I came up a moderate hill and in front of me, on a large fallen tree in the woods, was a teeny bear cub, maybe two-feet long, just standing on the tree looking at me. I stopped and looked for momma. She rose in the bushes near me and my heart raced. She was huge. I backed up a couple steps. She looked around, then looked me in the eye, as if to say: "Okay, just no closer." Then she went back to rooting around in the bushes. So I stood there watching the cub. Then another cub the same size climbed up on the log. Then another. They were so cute. Cosmos was behind me and I wanted her to see this so badly. Finally I saw her coming down the trail and motioned her, shhh. She hiked up to my location excitedly. Happy tears welled in her eyes as we watched the cubs play for a few wonderful minutes. They played peek-a-boo with us as they climbed a tree. I love these moments more for Cosmos than I do for myself.

We made it to the diner, Elkwallow Wayside Store and Grill. Elated was I. I dropped my pack and went to the door to enter. LOCKED! CLOSED! NO! We had hiked more than twenty-two miles to get here. There were a couple workers in the diner who saw me, so I banged on the door. I got the attention of one and said pleadingly, "Please, we were counting on a Mountain Blackberry Shake." The burners on the stove were all turned off, so no grill food, but they couldn't turn us totally away. They let us in to buy ice cream, Gatorade, popcorn, and chocolate milk. Minutes after we sat down at a little picnic table to feed, a light rain started falling as Cruiser and some section hikers arrived. Everyone was frantically searching for a place to tent because of the upcoming weather.

We stowed the popcorn and chocolate milk and hiked on, but soon major pouring rain came. We crazily looked for a flat area to camp, because darkness was near. Finally, Cosmos spotted an area off the trail in the woods. Like I said before, she would have been a good infantry soldier. All told, we went 23.9 miles. We tried to pitch the tent without getting it wet inside and were semi-successful. We were both soaked. Neither of us said a word, just took care of business. I hung the bear bag as Cosmos got in the tent. I took off my clothes and stood naked in the rain and darkness of night, shivering, miserable.

> I thought about the Vietnam monsoons. I was always wet. Always worried about the enemy and what the next moment would bring. Never taking the wet boots off. Pulling guard duty sitting on a bunker in the jungle with the rain hammering down, not being able to see the hand in front of my face, and not being able to hear because the rain drowned out any sound movement. Scared. Lonely. Stressed and on edge, thinking of home.

I took a deep breath and tried to relax. Cosmos said, from inside the tent, "What the hell are you doing out there?" I said, "Standing in the rain, trying to figure out how to get into the tent without getting my bag wet." Finally, I just said to myself, "Fuck it," peed, and got in the tent. Cosmos dried me off. A nice touch.

JUNE 17 | FRONT ROYAL, 17.9 MILES, 959.6 MILES TOTAL

As the rain poured down, we lay in the tent trying to come up with a game plan for today. Should we just lie here and wait for the rain to subside? We knew instinctively it was not going to. Okay. We needed to get the tent down, try to pack up, and attempt to keep our sleeping bags dry.

Eventually it was 3, 2, 1 go! We made the move, exiting the tent into a blur of rain. After tearing down and packing to the best of our ability, we both stood there and ate our breakfast in the downpour, laughing. Then we moved out, Cosmos in the lead. She hiked at a blistering pace in the rain and mud as we were determined to get to Front Royal today. We, and our equipment, needed to dry out. My pack weighed a ton and a hot shower was on my mind all day as we hiked. In seven hours we did 17.9 miles through mud, rocks, rain, and wind. Cosmos was on a mission and taking point (Vietnam terminology) to a new level. I did my best to keep up, with zero breaks and zero water stops. We eventually made Highway 522, a four-mile hitch to Front Royal. Soaking wet, we tried to hitch a ride. I said to Cosmos, "Who would pick us up? Look at us." Right about then a small pickup skidded and fishtailed to the side of the road. An old timer who'd lived in Front Royal all his life was the angel. A scraggly beard graced the creased face of this friendly man. He spoke of the weather and inquired about our thru-hiking for a bit. Then he said, "There are cougars in those mountains. Don't let anyone fool ya."

He dropped us at the Quality Inn. As we checked in, Moe and Larry of the Stooges strolled into the lobby along with their girlfriends from the Netherlands. I had not seen them in hundreds of miles. Curly had issues with shin splints and had to stop hiking for a few days so they'd slowed their pace, hoping their brother would heal and catch up. I never thought I would see them again in this country. Perhaps the reason Curly is off the trail for a bit is because they were hiking too many miles too quickly. They had made the mistake of purchasing a plane ticket to return home in August, thus allowing them limited time to rest.

I took four, consecutive hot baths in the tub: soak, drain, wash, drain, shave, drain, soak, and drain. Cosmos did the laundry. We hung our tent, bags, pack, and everything else to dry. I ate a donut and drank a beer while Cosmos bathed.

We walked to town, ate dinner, and shopped for groceries. Later, we met up with the two Stooges and their girlfriends at the Lucky Star Lounge, a nice place with good music. We saw the Birds and met their dad. He was excited and eager to hike with his daughters. They are not as far as we are on the trail, but hitched up here to go to a movie. I believe they are slowing their pace for their dad.

Once back in the room I reflected on the hike today. A blur it was. Humping like crazy in a driving rain, and ending with us having dinner with friends in a good restaurant. I will sleep well.

June 18 | Dicks Dome Shelter, 15.2 miles, 974.8 miles total

Up early. Damn. A zero is so tempting today. The first order of business was eating breakfast and catching up on my e-mails. Then off to the post office. I received a great package from Sandy Bannon, full of healthy stuff. Then it was back to the room to pack up all our dry belongings. Instead of hitching to the trailhead, we taxied and when we got to the trail, Cosmos said, "I don't wanna go," half joking, half serious. The jovial taxi driver then started singing, "Please Mr. Custer, I don't wanna go. No, Mr. Custer, please don't make me go," as he laughed. He sent us back on the trail with smiles on our faces.

We hiked rapidly and without delay, mostly uphill. We got to our night location at a decent hour, hit the water source, and pitched our tent. The two Stooges, Larry and Moe, are here with their girlfriends. The girlfriends are troupers. One of them wanted to go on, but Larry wisely had the whole crew stop for the evening. I love these guys. I miss their brother.

JUNE 19 | NEAR A STREAM JUST PAST PIGEON HOLLOW, 21.1 MILES, 995.9 MILES TOTAL

Hiked out early. Today was a tough one. I had anticipated it would be easier than yesterday, but hiking is like life; mild mood swings can make for a challenge. We make life what it is. If I want to be miserable, I can pull it off. I don't consciously think to be miserable, but just the attitude of the day can dictate the results. I got miserable today, as far as hiking goes. I cannot count the number of times I swore, as we had a continuous jagged rocky terrain. Years ago my friend, TJ, talked me into participating in Chicago's "Hustle up the Hancock Building." Walking up 95 floors, over who knows how many steps. It seemed hard then, but I could do that backwards right now, and with a full pack.

We met a positive and pleasant thru-hiker named Rael a couple of days ago at a shelter. He hikes shirtless and constantly, even on the uphills, sings while hiking. We hiked today in an area called the Roller Coaster and the ups and downs were killing me. Cosmos waited for me on the trail near the Bear's Den Hostel. When I caught up, I just threw off my pack and sat down. I was spent.

Just as I was regaining my strength, Rael came hiking up, a huffin' and a-puffin' and a-singin'. After he got his wind back, he said to us, "This is my third thru-hike, and I have never seen anything like the Naneek and Cosmos relationship." Smiles graced our faces. We sat for a bit, thinking about going to the Bear's Den when Cruiser hiked up. He talked us (me) into hiking another two miles to a road and then going down a side road to the Horseshoe Curve Restaurant and bar, a third-generation mom and pop place with sandwiches, burgers, fries, and beer. No credit cards. He convinced me when he said he would buy us a beer. I think Cosmos wanted to go to the hostel, but she was good either way. She looked like she could do another 10 miles.

We found the road, VA 679, and walked downhill to the Horseshoe. A quaint, vintage mom and pop it was. I had the burger, fries, beer, and a great salad. We had a good conversation as we dined. Learning what other thru-hikers are up to in their personal lives and why they attempt such a challenge as the AT always fascinates me.

We hiked on full stomachs up the road back to the AT and immediately started looking for a flat spot to make camp. We ended up doing an additional three miles and found a tent site just past Pigeon Hollow, bordering a stream. Cruiser hiked on. The stars were glistening tonight as we settled into our tent. Just before I closed my eyes for the evening, a hiker walked up near our home away from home and introduced himself, talking to us through the tent's canvas. He said he was Lone Wolf, a thru-hiker. He asked us if he could read a couple poems he had written that day. "Please do," was our immediate response and he recited two wonderful poems, one about creepy crawly things on the trail, and the other about the rocks on the trail. Both the poems were satisfying and made the end to the day perfect--we, in our tent, after a hard day, and Lone Wolf outside reciting poetry. Life can't get any better than this.

Harpers Ferry tomorrow. Hard to believe.

5 | WEST VIRGINIA

JUNE 20
QUALITY INN, HARPERS FERRY POTOMAC RIVER,
17.5 MILES, 1,013.5 MILES TOTAL

I hate getting up in the middle of the night to pee. And I do so a minimum of once nightly, sometimes twice. A drag to get this old man out of the bag, put on the headlamp, unzip the tent, put on shoes, zip the tent pack up so bugs don't fly in, hike a little bit away from the tent in the dark, pee, fart, and find my way back to tent, unzip the tent, try to climb back into the tent without disturbing Cosmos, take off shoes, get back into bag, zip up bag, take off headlamp, and try to get back to sleep. Not an easy task for a sore old body. Triple difficult if it's raining. This particular night as I tried to get comfortable and get back to sleep, Cosmos asked, "Do you have to fart every time you get out to pee? That's what wakes me up." Laughter in the middle of the night.

Early. Out at 7 a.m. and hiked hard today over very rocky terrain (I say that too often, but it's true). The rocks are about a foot long, very jagged and unstable. I roll my ankles daily.

Cosmos waited for me at one point. She had a befuddled look on her face and as I approached, she pointed to an oversized black bag lying alongside the trail and told me that she knew, someday in her life, she would come across a dead body. I smiled deviously and said, "Why don't you open it"? She reluctantly agreed, and opened the bag very slowly, prodding with her trekking pole. All she found was an old, raggedy tent.

We saw a crew of scouts (actually have seen that several times) coming up the mountain. Later, we saw a group of football players doing the team-bonding thing. The coach said he does this every year with the team. They all looked haggard as they stopped for a break mid-mountain. This old man blew by.

We made it. HARPERS FERRY! The psychological halfway point, whatever that means. We crossed the Potomac River, a la George Washington, but we did it by bridge. We are in West Virginia, my fifth state. Yeah! Out of Virginia after five hundred-plus miles. While crossing, white-water rafts sprinkled the river below. How joyful I feel at this point! I have now walked more than 1,000 miles.

We followed the trail to the AT conservancy and signed in. The staff took our pictures to put with the rest of the class of 2009. I am the #411 thru-hiker this year to pass this point. A ranger informed me that in 2008 only a little over three hundred thru-hikers actually completed the entire trail.

I spoke with my sisters today as I hiked. The woman who gave my nephew, Evan, 16, the methadone that killed him was indicted today by a grand jury in New York. She is in jail.

We trudged to the Comfort Inn, and were told there were "no rooms at the inn." The manager of the place told us where the Quality Inn was located, over a mile away, down a busy road. A mile is easy if we had a vehicle, but our heads dropped. She then said, "Come on, I'll give you a ride over there." The goodwill continues.

We got a room, took a shower, and downstairs I went to do laundry. As I rode the elevator, I saw a sign that advertised free shuttles to a horse track and casino. The shuttle leaves every half hour. After a mini nap, we went down to the bar and had a couple of beers and a snack to discuss the horse issue.

Shuttle we did. We hiked almost eighteen miles on the AT today and now, here we are cheering on #7 horse at the track along with thousands of other racing fanatics. Cosmos had never been to a race before. She was very emotional at how beautiful the horses were and how hard they worked. I made a few bets and lost. Cosmos bet once and won. Her horse's name? Trust.

We had a great dinner at the track, blew $20 on the slots, and shuttled back to the hotel and a big soft bed. We plan a zero tomorrow, but will check out downtown Harpers Ferry.

JUNE 21 | HARPERS FERRY, SUNDAY, FATHER'S DAY, ZERO

I am awake early, just lying in bed, reflecting on my life as a dad and remembering my dad. Both he and my mom worked their asses off to provide for our family. He would be so proud of me right now.

I watch my Cosmos sleep. She is so peaceful. She is so beautiful. One would never believe the language that comes out of that mouth sometimes. She sometimes leaves me aghast and smiling. I call her the homecoming queen, because nobody knows the real Cosmos but me.

One night in Vietnam I had a dream about a woman. It was a great dream until I awakened being poked and prodded and hearing the words "your turn for guard." "Dammit, leave me alone, I have something beautiful happening here," I thought. I think her name was Mary, and she had the cutest face, and lovely soft skin. Her smile was radiant. We were so happy together. That is, until my buddy woke me up telling me it's my turn for guard.

I thought about her every day for a while.

One day as we were moving, a brilliant idea entered my brain. All of us searched for ways to get out of the bush. Some men even "accidentally" shot themselves in the foot and most tried to get malaria. I saw a creative opportunity. The next time I had a chance to write letters, I would write one to "Dear Abby," who was always in the "Stars and Stripes," a soldier newspaper that came out every so often.

And write the letter I did. I told Abby I had the dream and I described it to her. And of course I told her I was in the infantry. Then I exaggerated a bit. I wrote that I cannot do my job out here in the bush, because my mind is preoccupied with Mary. "I love Mary. I cannot stop thinking about her and I am now a danger to myself and my fellow soldiers because I can't keep my mind focused. I'm going to either get myself killed or wounded or get someone else killed, or both. Please help me." I signed it something like, "Love Struck in Vietnam."

I gave the letter to a helicopter door gunner to mail, trusting he would do so. And I waited. And I waited. I had fantasies of getting out of the bush early. I am thinking big. Abby will get in contact with the upper echelon of the army, make a recommendation to them to get this love-struck dude out of the field before someone gets hurt, and back to base camp I will go.

I gave it up after a few weeks wait, giving no more thought to the letter, when one day I received a few letters from home. As I sifted through them, I found one of the letters from Abigail Van Buren. DEAR ABBY! Awesome! I anxiously opened it, hoping for the best. I don't recall her exact words, but she basically said, "Dear Love Struck, I empathize with your problems, but am so happy you had this dream. Use Mary as incentive to focus and make it back to your hometown and family. You will find Mary. You will find each other. And what a story you can tell her. Good Luck." I said to myself, "Thanks, Abby. Thanks a lot."

I sent out all my trail update e-mails and answered all the personal ones. I asked everyone on my list not to send me forwarded e-mails. I have no time for such things. Send me personal notes or nothing.

After breakfast a staff member gave us a ride into Harpers Ferry. We strolled around this very historic town, a place where the Civil War raged. The town is like a movie set, with the people working in the shops dressed like those Civil War days. I remembered hiking yesterday, frustrated and swearing because the rocks were so hard on my feet up in the hills coming into this town. General Lee's troops were walking barefoot up in the hills in the winter on those same rocks. And they were in a war. I thought once again that, as bad as I may have it, there are always others suffering far worse.

Then I thought about how bad I had it in Vietnam. Losing 53 pounds in 60 days. Digging a hole every night to climb into if need be. Eating C-rations on a daily basis. Getting water from a puddle on occasion. Moving every day in the heat. Moving in the pouring rain. Jungle rot, nasty sores that break out on our bodies, unable to heal because we cannot stay clean. Rarely getting a change of clothes. Sleeping on the damp ground every night. Thinking about when I would die or get wounded.

The doc was charged with doling out malaria pills. He would give us a little white one on a daily basis, and every Monday a big orange one. Many, probably the majority of us, never swallowed the pill, choosing to maybe get bitten by the right mosquito, which would result in getting out of the field and going to a clean hospital with showers and American nurses. The average time out of the field was something like thirty days for malaria. There was a possibility that when a guy got released from the hospital, he might land a base camp job, out of the bush. People back in the "world" may shake their heads at the thought of trying to get malaria, but there were benefits. The main one? Your life wouldn't be at stake every moment of every day. You would be safe. One needed a temperature of 103 or above to get out of the field. Then the diagnosis was probably malaria. Anything less than 103 was dubbed "FUO," fever of unknown origin.

More than once I had a high temp, but never high enough. My fevers always subsided. Until I got home, that is. There, I was diagnosed twice with malaria. I had two different varieties, and the doctor at Fitzsimmons Army Hospital in Denver told me I had the largest spleen he had ever felt. Evidently, I had been walking around with malaria for months in the war, unbeknownst to me or any of the medical personnel.

As always, we visited the outfitter, then a restaurant. There, Cosmos, looking at me with sad eyes, said, "Happy Dad's Day," apologizing for not remembering earlier. We saw Cruiser cutting through town. He was headed out of town because he wasn't feeling well. Hikers are like animals, I suppose. Cruiser felt more comfortable in the woods alone than in town where there might be a doctor.

We asked around and eventually were given a ride back to the motel by a conservation officer. A swim in the pool was followed by switching on the TV, watching U.S. Open golf, and taking a wonderful long nap, curled up together.

6 Maryland

Up early as usual. Zero days disappear in a hurry. Tufted Titmouse says, "Getting back on the trail after a zero is like leaving Grandma's house."

We had breakfast and used the computer one last time before departure. We then packed up our gear and headed to the lobby to beg someone for a ride. We didn't wait long before a friendly couple we had met at the horse track dropped us off at the post office. I received two packages from Tricia (Indy girl) and Cosmos got one from her mom. We had just resupplied, so our packs were heavy. I gave away some of my stuff, including a bunch of Slim Jims Tricia had sent. I gifted them to Wolfpack and Spicoli, who were excited and grateful, as they'd received nothing from home.

Stopping by the AT office, we ran into the Birds and their dad. He looked like a tired, beaten-up man. He had now hiked for five days with his daughters. They looked fresh because they had slowed down for him. He now realizes the magnitude of this journey and just how remarkable his daughters are.

We headed for the trail, but not before one last dose of ice cream.

We arrived late at the shelter because of the tardy start. We pitched the tent in a little nearby valley. As we prepared dinner by the shelter, we struck up a conversation with a couple of older guys staying there. Both were well into their 70s. "Been doing this for years," they said. "This is how we stay young." They thought we were section or day hikers and were impressed when they learned we had walked more than 1,000 miles.

We turned in late, 10 p.m. We are now in Maryland, my sixth state. Eight more to go. Some hikers do the four-state challenge. They leave the border of Virginia at midnight, walk into West Virginia, then Maryland, then into Pennsylvania. A little over forty miles in twenty-four hours. Doable, but it is not for me.

JUNE 23 | NEAR ENSIGN COWALL SHELTER, 18.6 MILES, 1,047.5 MILES TOTAL

The usual. Up early and out. We hiked easy today for the most part, the highlight was meeting a beautiful hiking family with trail names: One Lucky Man, Veggie Mom, Beep Beep (three years old), and Flower in Her Hair (five years old). The family is hiking from Port Clinton, Pennsylvania, to Front Royal. 250 miles! With two young children! My heroes, indeed. They all seem so happy to be here.

We stopped short of our goal of 21 miles. I got sick. I tried to deny the illness, but when I shit my pants not once, but twice, the jig was up. I had to venture way downstream to clean myself up. My stomach is upset and I'm hoping that feeling better is a sunrise away. I am in the tent and in my bag at 6 p.m. Cosmos is taking care of my chores out there.

7 PENNSYLVANIA

JUNE 24, CALEDONIA STATE PARK, 25.2 MILES,
1,072.7 MILES TOTAL

I felt a little queasy this morning, but not bad enough to stop me from moving forth on the trail. As the day progressed, my health improved. Who knows what went wrong. I've been told everyone shits their pants at least once on the trail. Me? Twice in thirty minutes.

We are in Pennsylvania, state #7, with seven more to go. My mentor back home, Peach, had told me Pennsylvania was her worst state, due to the rocks and the rattlesnakes.

I was blessed with an amazing experience today. Cosmos was far ahead of me and I was struggling on an uphill when my nostrils breathed in a familiar scent. My mom! That scent only my mom has. I stopped and sniffed my sweet mother's aroma. Mom is with me! She has been gone from this world for more than two years, yet she still watches over me. I smiled and hiked on, a hop in my step. A few miles down the trail, she joined me once again, as her aroma filled the air. Then, after another couple miles, again. Three times I smelled her soothing fragrance. What special moments.

I remembered when we divided up all her clothes after she died. All the kids and grandkids wanted a piece of her clothing, so they could smell her one last time. My son Jake didn't wash her sweatshirt for a long time, maybe never. I truly believe she helped me get over my sickness today. She helped me up that hill. Yesterday when I went to bed, I would never have dreamed I could hike twenty-five miles the next day. Later, when I caught up with Cosmos I asked her if she smelled an unusual fragrance anywhere out there today, but she said she hadn't. So. . . thank you, dear mother.

As we checked the map on a break, we saw there was camping, a snack bar, and a swimming pool at the state park a few miles ahead. We hiked hard. I was feeling really good, so Cosmos suggested I hike ahead so, in case the park closed, I could order something from the snack bar for her. I was flying down the trail but as luck would have it, after a twenty-five-plus mile hike, the snack bar had closed ten minutes earlier. Damn.

I phoned Tricia (Indy girl) to thank her for the packages she had sent to Harpers Ferry. She said, "How did you like the Slim Jims?" I'm thinking, "The ones I gave to Spicoli and Wolfpack?" but I didn't say it. I said they were great, thinking to myself, "How good can a Slim Jim be?" She said, "Then you got the one that had three joints rolled up in it?" I hope Spicoli and Wolfpack enjoyed them.

We got a campsite and were determined to swim in this huge, Olympic-style pool the next day. Meanwhile, I ordered pizza, ginger ale, salad, and dessert from a pizza place near the park. They delivered. We pitched the tent minus the rainfly, and devoured the chow. We showered, played some cards, and star-watched ourselves to sleep.

Beautiful day.

JUNE 25 | WOODROW ROAD (JUST SHORT OF TOMS RUN SHELTER, THE OFFICIAL HALFWAY POINT), 14.9 MILES, 1,087.6 MILES TOTAL

I called my ex-wife, Dawn, this morning. We had a pleasant and an unpleasant conversation. Financial stuff. Kid stuff. Property stuff.

After the conversation, Cosmos and I went to the pool and had a great swim, then we kicked back and ate cheeseburgers. I met a guy in the pool who was enthralled we were hiking the entire AT, and that we had already come more than 1,000 miles. After a dose of ice cream, we put on our socks and boots and headed into the woods. We hiked 14.9 miles in about five hours, landing at a flat area and tent site near Woodrow Road. The original plan had been for a ten-mile day, but the terrain was trouble-free. We want to get to Duncannon, Pennsylvania by Saturday for an annual hiker celebration.

Pennsylvania has the nicest shelters so far, although, we never stayed in one. They are adorned with flowers, are well landscaped, and homey. My feet feel like stumps, similar to how they feel after playing volleyball on the beach in the early spring or late fall in Northern Michigan as the sun sets and the sand is cold. As soon as you walk off the sand onto solid ground, you feel like your feet are stumps.

JUNE 26 | BOILING SPRINGS, 24 MILES, 1,111.6 MILES TOTAL

We are up early and hike 4.6 miles to the Pine Grove Furnace Store, home of the half-gallon ice cream challenge. If you are hiking from Georgia to Maine the tradition is to buy a half-gallon of ice cream at this store and eat it as fast as you can. Katz and another guy were taking the challenge. Matt from Washington, D.C. was there, but did not do the challenge. Cosmos bought the ice cream (cookies and cream) but neither of us participated in the challenge. Nine a.m.? Come on, I am going to eat a half gallon of ice cream at nine in the morning and hike on? I don't think so. If it was later in the day, I would participate, but not with twenty miles to go. I did have two hot dogs for breakfast and a bit of the ice cream. In conversation with Katz I found out he will attend grad school at Michigan State in the fall, majoring in nuclear physics. I love the people on this trail.

I stopped for a couple pictures at the halfway point: 1,089.1 on the trail. Bittersweet. Here I am, halfway to Katahdin, I've been hiking for almost three months, and I am only halfway? I have 1,089.1 miles to go? I won't dwell on that thought for long.

We did some grazing in the bushes today. Blackberries. Nice and ripe. We hiked across PA 34 and upon further study of the map, realized there was a store a half-mile up the road. We decided to hike to it. I bought a newspaper, a roast beef sandwich, Birch beer, Gatorade, and Hawaiian punch. We found a picnic table nearby, sat in the sun, and traded sections of the newspaper while we ate. Headlines report Michael Jackson and Farah Fawcett died within the past week. I'm sad they are gone; yet men, women, and children are dying daily in U.S. wars and that isn't on the front page.

We filled our stomachs and hiked the twelve miles to Boiling Springs. Finding no place to pitch the tent, we located a B&B, Gelinas. We ate at the high-class and pricey Boiling Springs Tavern in town. The smell from our bodies was strong, but we fine-dined and liked it. Cosmos and I will find a ride to the outfitter tomorrow so she can get new shoes. She has had a blowout.

1,100 miles completed.

June 27 | Duncannon, Hiker Feed and Olympic Event, 0 miles

We had an exquisite breakfast at the B&B with four non-hiking folks, who dressed and acted quite conservative. They had lots of questions and were very intrigued by our hike. We then found a ride to Harrisburg to the outfitter; the waiter at the tavern knew a guy who would give us a ride, if we paid. The dude, name of Mike, was older, surly, and somewhat of an asshole. I paid him $50 to drive us to Harrisburg, then to Duncannon, for the hiker feed, and he refused to stop so I could buy water. Today is the day of the feed, and we are 26 miles from here on our hike; that's why we decided to get a ride, and when the feed ends, hike south back to Boiling

Springs so as to remain "pure" thru-hikers. Then we would hitch a ride back here and go north once again. Sounds like a novel idea.

Cosmos got her new shoes, but I don't think she is satisfied. She had no choice, as her others were falling apart and she has 1,400 miles to go. When we reach Katahdin, she has decided to fly back to Irwin, Tennessee, where she first met me, and later hike the trail south until she completes. At first, such a thought wasn't anywhere in her mind, but she now has that thru-hike fever.

We found the famous Doyle's Tavern and hostel in Duncannon, and signed up for a room. The bed looked like Hill 943, bumpy and dirty. The room was hot, humid, and dirty, with no fan. This is just a trifle better than the ground.

We went to the hiker feed, put on by the town and former hikers. A major feast it was: ham, potato salad, salad, corn, and great desserts. Everyone from this town was a part of the celebration, and they brought their finest food.

We saw Whup Whup. Couscous (an Eagle Scout) is off the trail. So are the blonde sisters, I'm Happy and Roach. Couscous and I'm Happy fell in love on the trail and are now living together in Connecticut. She is not pregnant, so the story goes.

The townsfolk had music set up, including karaoke. Whup Whup sang and had a great voice. If "Hurricane" by Bob Dylan would have been on the set list, I would have been up there, too.

Duncannon also sponsored a hiker Olympics. One event: three chances to throw a trekking pole as far as you can, like a javelin. Another event: shotput a fuel canister. Another, like the hammer throw, is to toss a bag containing twenty-five Snickers bars as far as you can. Whup Whup won this event with a toss of 98 feet. The discus event was throwing a collapsing bowl as far as you can. I finished third in the javelin and won a Patagonia t-shirt. I was surprised I won such a nice prize. A fun event indeed, well worth our trouble to get here. I played a bit of volleyball. I was way off my game, but better than all these hikers who knew nothing about the game. My feet are still very stumpy. I don't anticipate that changing.

Great time, great fun, followed by a party for the ages at Doyle's with live music and plenty of beer. We met lots of new hiker friends. Schooner and Megan (now Ferdy) are here. Schooner can shoot some pool. Others I remember are Fat Kid and Star Trek.

June 28 | Darlington Shelter, 11.4 miles, 1,123.0 miles total

We got a late start out of Duncannon, due to hangover-itis. Then we had slow moving because we ran into, and engaged in conversation with, all the north-bounders we knew: the Stooges, Katz, Shargen, Bill and Bill (father, son), Tag Team (husband, wife), Singing Wind, Mountain Man (not the same one as in Waynesboro, but a 70-year-old man, thru-hiking). All is well. The Tag Team was raving about a place in Boiling Springs called Allenberry's, a resort that treats hikers famously, has great food and nice rooms, all for twenty dollars.

I spoke with my son Jonathon today. He will join us in a couple weeks for a two-day hike.

We tented at the shelter and had dinner, then sat around a fire with Gezza, Top Shelf, Flying Scotsman, and others. The Scotsman was hiking with Spicoli and Wolfpack, the recipients of the Slim Jims. In private, I asked Spicoli how he enjoyed the Slim Jims. He claimed to know nothing of the pot. Hmmm.

Cool scene. The woods are sprinkled with tents. Fewer and fewer people stay in the shelters. Bugs do not bother you in a tent.

June 29 | Boiling Springs, 14.3 miles, 1,137.3 miles total

We had an easy hike back to Boiling Springs and went immediately to the AT conservancy looking for a ride back to Duncannon so we could head north. No luck. The officer said it was a hard hitch because there are so many turns, and it's forty-plus miles. The only option was "our friend" Mike, the asshole who gave us a ride for fifty dollars, and neither of us wants that option.

We decided to heed the Tag Team's advice and walked to Allenberry's, a mile up the road. Upon arriving, the place looked closed, and if not, way out of our league. Was the Tag Team pulling our leg? These are beautiful grounds with picturesque, aged trees throughout and a river flowing through the center of this vast compound. I see a pool and hot tub. We were about to leave, feeling out of our element, when we happened upon an older gentleman who asked if he could help us. He introduced himself as Jerry, the owner. As luck would have it, Jerry said, "We will take care of you. We take care of thru-hikers."

He took us downstairs to an empty dining room and sat us down. This place reminded me of the Jack Nicholson movie, *The Shining*, complete with a long mirrored bar with nobody sitting at it. Jerry then brought us a menu. I was confused because the place was closed. A waitress came out of nowhere, putting on her apron. I ordered a big beer, Caesar salad (turned out to be huge), chicken salad sandwich (could have fed both of us), brie, and hot breakfast cinnamon rolls. Three different people served us. The staff treated us like royalty, yet I know we stunk like thru-hikers. The trail magic never stops.

As we dined, Jerry brought his head maintenance man down to meet us and explained he would give us a ride to Duncannon tomorrow morning. "Now you don't have to worry about a ride, so just relax." Later, he took me down and showed me the laundry facilities. Needless to say, we are spending the night. All of this for a mere $25 for the both of us. We had a plush room with TV. We had the whole place to ourselves. These rooms usually rent for more than $100 per night. A small auditorium hosts plays four days a week that are free to thru hikers ($35 if you're not a hiker), but we are here on an off day.

We lounged in the big pool, took a hot tub. We were treated to dinner with Jerry and his family. We have been here only a few hours, but are overwhelmed by the kindness. We would never have experienced this goodness had we been successful in hitching a ride. Meeting Irv (maintenance guy) at 6:30 a.m. to catch our ride.

JUNE 30 | CLARK CREEK, 17.1 MILES, 1154.4 MILES TOTAL

Irv was right on time, and so were we. We had a good conversation as he drove us to Duncannon.

We ate breakfast at Goodies Breakfast Place in Duncannon, where we listened to loud, offensive racist talk amongst the locals. Things like, motherfucking niggers, goddamn Mexicans, we should ship all of them back where they came from, etc. I was about to stand up and say something when Cosmos intervened, "What would you accomplish?"

The whole restaurant had heard these guys and nobody said a word. Sickening.

I had a flashback. I was sitting on my bunker in the quiet of the night on radio watch/guard duty at a firebase in early June of 1968. I was "short," with a little over thirty days to go before home. I had borrowed a tiny transistor radio and was listening quietly to the one American station they had in Vietnam. I shouldn't have been listening to a radio in the middle of the night while on guard, but I felt confident we weren't going to get hit. I had the radio at its lowest volume in one ear, and my Prick 25 (war communication) headset in my other.

I listened to a couple songs. One was probably "Coming Home Soldier" by Bobby Vinton. The other? Probably "Soldier Boy" by the Shirelles. The station seemed to play these time and time again.

Then a special report came on. The moderator was talking about Bobby Kennedy, presidential hopeful. I was listening carefully, because I'd always liked Kennedy. He seemed a fair and honest man, one who I thought would try to fulfill promises I had an interest in. Like this damn war. Like the civil rights movement.

But the moderator was speaking in past tense about Bobby. At first I was confused, perhaps he was speaking about Bobby's brother, John. But no, he was in fact speaking about Bobby. I was stunned and full of anger, sadness, and rage when he said Bobby had been assassinated in Los Angeles at a political rally. I could not believe what I was hearing and immediately went to wake up the guys.

At first the guys were scared and panicky, and rightfully so, because they thought we were being hit. But I calmed them down and then delivered the news that Bobby Kennedy was dead. Assassinated. All were quiet, save one. My platoon sergeant looked at me and said, "You woke me up for that? So what if he's dead. They can afford it. He was nothing but a spoiled brat."

I wanted to put twenty rounds into his body.

We walked up to the grocery store to resupply. Cosmos and I got into a major spat over nothing. She went outside, said she was off the trail, and said this time she was serious. I got my groceries in a daze, alone, all the while wondering what life on the trail would be like without her. I was missing her even before she left. We were both in bad moods at the same time, a dreadful combination. She called her friend Brian Foster and gave him the news. Perhaps to cheer her up he told her she could have Lola (dog) when she returned. Cosmos loved Lola. She wept like I had never seen her. Sobbed. I don't believe for a moment her emotions were all about Lola. We have been through so many physical, mental and emotional struggles these past couple of months, weathered them all, and now we were looking at the end of our time together. This is why the tears and intense emotions surfaced. We sat and talked through our differences, apologizing. We then hugged, kissed, and moved on. My heart and spirit might break if Cosmos were to leave the trail.

Back to hitching a ride back to the trail. Got one from "Uncle Charlie" to the trailhead we'd left a couple days ago. The trail runs right through Duncannon and he gave us an historical tour of the town.

We then hiked 17.1 miles to Clarks Creek. Found a spot to tent next to a creek. As we ate dinner, we talked and talked, mostly about our relationship. We talked about the physical difficulty of the trail coupled with the added burden of being in a relationship and never getting a break from one another, 24/7. The conversation was both warm and open.

Cosmos is not sure about those new shoes of hers. Too early to tell.

JULY 1 | WOODS ROAD (NEAR WILLIAM PENN SHELTER), 24 MILES, 1,178.4 TOTAL

As I write this I realize my descriptions of the mornings are very repetitive. We tear down, have breakfast, pack up our shit, look for a possible destination for the evening, and move out. This is an everyday occurrence. Every single day we do the same thing. Tearing down is uneventful after being on the trail for more than three months.

We have grazed in the hills eating blackberries for seven days in a row. They are everywhere. Luscious. We found a flat area in the woods about a mile from the next shelter to spend the night.

Today, at various times, we saw Tall Grass and Coffee Bean (son and mom), Bill and Bill (father and son), and Robo, the guy from Grand Rapids, whom I haven't seen since breakfast at Fontana Dam, more than 1,000 miles ago. I was amazed to see his face. Hikers I know could be just ahead or just behind. I can figure out who is out ahead of me by looking at the trail registers in the shelter, but have no idea who is behind.

JULY 2 | BLACK SWATARA SPRING, 15.7 MILES, 1,194.1 TOTAL

Grazed once again. More blackberries. We still haven't hit the rocks in Pennsylvania everyone has been talking about. The first southbound thru-hiker, Trailer, crossed our path today. He left Katahdin (the beginning for him, the end for me) on May 3, 2009. Said he wanted to reach Springer Mountain by the end of August. Sixty more days, 1,200 miles. To me, hiking those kinds of miles so quickly doesn't allow time to enjoy the journey.

While hiking the five miles to Highway 501, Cosmos and I talked each other into hitching into Pine Grove (3.6 miles off the trail) to get breakfast and lunch. Isn't Pine Grove the town near "The Little House on the Prairie"? We got an immediate ride from a gentleman who dropped us off at an intersection in town. We asked where the nearest restaurant was and he just pointed to the right. We assumed he wanted us out of his car because we stunk. We said our thanks and started walking through town.

We soon strode by an old woman who was struggling, trying to carry her groceries from her car to her house. I smiled at her and offered to help (had my pack on). She reluctantly agreed, saying, "Just to the door," with conviction. So I dropped my pack and carried her bags of groceries to the door. She then opened the door to her apartment building, gave a little smile, and said, "Okay, you may bring them to my door inside." I did. She then introduced herself as Jeanette. I told her I was Naneek. She gave me a big smile and said thank you. I said goodbye and walked out. Cosmos was waiting for me, a slight smile on her face. She said, "You like to do things for people don't you?"

I hoisted my pack and we started walking, not knowing where we were going. We didn't walk twenty yards when a car pulled up with two women, maybe 60 and 90 years old. The 60-year-old says, "Where you headed?" "To get something to eat," we replied. She said, "Hop in. I will take you to the best place in Pine Grove." She didn't have to say that twice. And to a good place she took us, Buddy's. I feasted on broasted chicken, applesauce, beans and a salad. I ordered a Philly cheese to-go for dinner tonight on trail. And a chocolate malt to drink on the way to the trail-head. A splendid decision to come here off the trail. The food is one thing, but the bonus is meeting different people who are so generous and kind. Bunny (the 60-year-old driver) drove us all the way back to the trail. She even asked if we wanted to stop at her house and shower (we did stink). What an angel she was. And the older woman was a woman she hangs out with once a week to give her some company.

We said our goodbyes and got back on the trail, hiking eleven miles to the spring. We found a primo camping spot, set up, and feasted on our town food. We plan on a short hike of thirteen miles tomorrow, to Port Clinton. We want to hit the post office, then probably hike on or get some-one to drop us off at the trail eighteen miles or so ahead so we can hike back south. This, so we can be in Port Clinton for July 4. Cosmos wants to be in a city for Independence Day. That's the least I can do for my love, plus, rumor has it they are having a hiker feed.

My feet are numb, but the knees feel okay today, knock on wood. Or should I say, rocks. I was getting used to easy days, but now every step is rocks, rocks, and more rocks. Big, pointed boulders that are hard on the feet and knees, and are slippery when wet.

JULY 3 | PORT CLINTON, 13.1 MILES, 1,207.2 TOTAL

We arrived in town at around 3 p.m. and immediately went to the post office looking for a package of brownies from Charlee. Damn, nothing. My mouth was salivating all day today just thinking about them. Then we went to the outfitter looking for some different shoes for Cosmos to no avail. Her arches are hurting and having hurt feet when you have more than 1,000 miles to go is worse than driving a car with flat tires. Port Clinton is a cool little town. The barbershop has live fiddle music.

I befriended a little girl (Katrina) outside the outfitter while Cosmos shopped. She went to a neighbor, Mark, and asked him if he would give us a ride to Hamburg, where there was a Cabela's and he gave us a ride to the front door. More magic. Cosmos again looked for shoes without success. We bought some odds and ends and walked across the parking lot to a pizza place where we enjoyed chicken wings, pizza, and beer. As luck would have it, right next door was a Baskin Robbins. We consumed chocolate malts outside as we got in a long conversation with a blind man. We told him of our adventure and he was fascinated. There are now so many people I've met on and near the trail that I would love to have as a neighbor back home.

We walked across a highway to a hotel and got a room. I did the laundry while Cosmos napped. I talked with a trucker, who had myriad of questions about the trail. He was fascinated. He kept smiling and shaking his head. I also spoke on the phone with a high school friend, Lynn McCarroll, from Massachusetts, and good friend, Mac, back in Traverse City. Mac said he and some friends had chipped in and bought me a plane ticket from Boston to Cleveland at the end of the month. A party at Put-In-Bay, Ohio, looms. I said I would go on this annual trek with the boys, if I had less than six hundred miles to go. I am on track. Now that a ticket has been purchased, I have no choice. Plus, Lynn said she would pick me up, wherever I was on the trail, and take me to the airport in Boston.

After a long hot shower and a wonderful nap, Cosmos and I went to the bar in the hotel and played some pool. Saw Spicoli, the Scotsman, and Wolfpack.

We went to sleep early in a very comfy bed. As I lay there, I reflected on hiking more than 1,200 miles. I never dreamed it was going to be possible, but now I want to finish. I have come too far not to.

JULY 4 | PULPIT ROCK, 7.7 MILES, 1,214.9 TOTAL

I was able to make phone contact with my sisters this morning. I am extremely excited at the prospect of seeing my sister Eve in two weeks.

After indulging in the continental breakfast and watching Serena beat Venus at Wimbledon, we took a shuttle from the hotel to Port Clinton. Upon arriving, we simply had to stop at the barbershop. I got a haircut on my head, on and in my nose, on and in my ears, and topped off by a neck massage from the barber. Just like back in the day. Trail talking, world news talking, sports talking, local events talking. Cosmos got her hair cut by my barber's dad, Rocko. These guys seem wonderful, and we couldn't help but wonder about their life stories.

We walked down to the hiker feed with my little friend Katrina. Once again the event was sponsored by a local church. Great hamburgers, salad, potato salad, chips, cookies, brownies, and soda pop. Great people who put on a thru-hiker's gourmet dinner. On the way out of town, I bought Katrina a treat at a candy store. Then I gave her a big hug and Cosmos and I disappeared into the woods. While walking to the trailhead we saw Tag Team (husband and wife, 50-plus years old). Tag Along had fallen on the rocks and had a major shiner. Her eye was surrounded with painfully beautiful colors.

We hiked 7.7 miles to Pulpit Rock, on top of a little mountain (elevation 1,582 feet). We watched the Fourth of July fireworks from there with Woodsmoke (a section hiker) and two couples from the area. We had a great view and were treated to twenty-six separate firework displays from various venues all across the valley. The fireworks seemed small and distant because they exploded well below us.

My son Jake called. I love hearing his voice.

We pitched our tent at an observatory in a no-tent zone. I thought to myself, as I have many times on the trail, "How would anyone ever know if we tented here?" We pitched it late, just before dark, and were out early, even before sunrise. We could still hear fireworks as we dozed off.

JULY 5 | BLUE MOUNTAIN SUMMIT, 19 MILES, 1,233.9 MILES TOTAL

Cosmos is hobbling on her sore foot. At the Eckville Shelter, 7.5 miles out, we spoke with day and section hikers who were curious and full of questions about our hike and why we would attempt such a thing. I answered while Cosmos studied the map. She said there was a restaurant eleven miles ahead on the trail. I said, "It's a no-brainer. Let's go." We hiked another seven-plus miles to the Allentown Hiking Club Shelter where we stopped for a short break. Cosmos spotted a nest in the shelter with two, itty-bitty birds in it, and two unhatched eggs. I view this as another wonder of the trail. Momma is hanging out in a nearby tree waiting for us to leave so she can deliver lunch to the little ones. Again, I probably would have missed this beautiful sight were it not for Cosmos.

I set a strong pace after we exited the shelter. I was far ahead of Cosmos, breathing heavily, when I thought I heard an Eric Clapton tune. I stopped to listen. Yes. My ears did not deceive me. I continued my hike and the music got louder. I was closing in on it. The trail turned and I found myself hiking away from the sounds. I dropped my pack next to the trail and rumbled through the woods to seek out this music. I was knocking down branches and busting trail when I walked onto a lush, green, grassy clearing. I stared in astonishment as two guys played music under the bluest of skies. There were people sitting at tables, eating and drinking beer. I saw an outdoor bar! I was thinking, "Is this a mirage?"

I walked back to my pack and pointed my poles through the woods towards the music, hoping Cosmos would get the message, then I walked back and ordered a beer and listened to the music. Cosmos got the message and we ended up watching and listening to the music, drinking beer, and eating for three hours. At one point, the band even recognized us as thru-hikers, and the people in the audience gave us an ovation.

The owner of the restaurant approached us and said we could pitch our tent on the lawn if we so desired. We did. Then we filled up on water and turned in for the night, under clear skies. We are ready for tomorrow.

This was a grand day, indeed.

We found out Cruiser had contracted giardia. He was sick coming through Harpers Ferry from not treating his water and ended up getting off the trail. He went home to recover, but will be back on the trail in two weeks. Word has it he will skip Pennsylvania, then come back and finish after he summits Katahdin. MoFo stopped his hike in Boiling Springs, but may get back on trail in New Hampshire in August.

July 6 | Just Past Lehigh Gap, 17.5 miles, 1,251.4 miles total

We pulled out of our grassy paradise in the early morning.

Toward the end of our day we encountered a dangerous climb, some of it almost straight up. Dogs could not maneuver this part of the trail. We moved cautiously because one slip and you'd be history. I contemplated dropping my pack after I got through the roughest part of the climb and doubling back to help Cosmos. She would have none of that. When we got to the top, we were rewarded with a field full of blueberries. We stayed for an hour, filling up a baggie and grazing. Four young section hikers joined us. One refused to eat the berries because his parents had told him, "Don't eat any berries when you are hiking. They might be poison." These young guys were caddies when not in school and had taken a weekend to hike on the AT. Cool.

After gorging ourselves, we tried pitching our tent on a flat area in long grass on top, but the sight of several ticks changed our plan. We hiked on and came across wild blackberries. Then raspberries. We finally found a clear area way up on top, overlooking the Lehigh Gap. Coffee Bean and Tall Grass camped near us.

Cosmos' body is talking to her. Achilles. Foot. Shoulder. Her body just aches, as does mine. I haven't felt the last three toes on my right foot for 800 miles. Plantar warts on the bottom of the right foot cause me to limp. The knees are not great, but okay. "Why is quitting not even an option?" I thought to myself today. Determination, I suppose. And the people, adventure, and enjoyment all far outweigh the pain.

These rocks in Pennsylvania are killing us. Thirty-two miles to the end of this great state. This is day one hundred for me on the trail.

July 7 | Just past Wind Gap, 18.7 miles, 1,270.1 miles total

Fog hung over Lehigh Gap as the sun rose today. As we ate breakfast in pin-drop quiet and peace on the mountaintop, our thoughts turned to a zero day. Even speaking of an upcoming zero makes the trail's beauties intensify. We haven't enjoyed one in hundreds of miles. Pennsylvania, at least the eastern half on the AT, should be renamed Rockville. Huge Rockville. I get so frustrated being so cautious of my each and every move, afraid if I don't I am going to bust my ass and be off the trail.

We walked into town to the first eatery that was open. A sports bar. Great food. Well, not great, but good. Anything tastes great when you're constantly hungry. I packed out two desserts to eat before bed, then we turned around and hiked right back out of town, disappearing into the woods for another two miles to a flat camp spot. Always on top of the mountain.

We stopped for a break at the Leroy Smith Shelter earlier, and met two young guys, each with a wad of tobacco in his mouth. One of them is a firefighter, the other a future cop. One spoke of his dad being a Vietnam vet. He seemed sad when he said his dad never talked much about his war experiences.

I spent part of the day thinking about my mentor, Denny Leach, a soldier who made such an impact on my life. I thought about the orders to take hill after hill for reasons still unknown to me. We'd talked about it, Denny and I, many times, and we could never come up with an answer. I always felt a sense of security when he was near. We shared the same values. He knew this war was wrong. I sensed this in him from the very beginning. I have missed him all these years.

The rest of my day was swallowed up thinking about a sunny day in mid-September, 1967. I had been released from the hospital in Vietnam on my 21st birthday. I had always looked forward to my 21st, and yet here I was, back in the bush.

Less than a week later the "happy-go-lucky guy" of the class of 1964 was no longer. I had been in Vietnam more than sixty days and never seen the enemy. So far, this was a giant camping trip that was physically grueling for me, but nothing more. I had dropped 50-plus pounds, but had no fear. Why would I have fear? Twenty-one was an invincible age.

As we moved that day through a place called VC Valley, we came across some hooches (what GIs call the grass houses Vietnamese lived in) and we found a fresh fire nearby. That meant there were enemy in the area, an enemy none of us had ever seen. We set up a perimeter and sent sweeps (three GIs) out to all sides, maybe 75 meters or so. The perimeter was supposed to keep a keen eye for any activity, but this is usually the time guys start playing cards. Again, we had never seen combat so we didn't have that fear, and didn't pay attention like we should have.

I walked point on the sweep. We were out from our perimeter maybe fifty meters when we looked across a small valley (called a "draw") and saw three more hooches. One of the guys said, "Let's go check them out," and I happened to be in charge because, believe it or not, I had been in-country the longest. So I sent one of the guys back to our perimeter to get the rest of our squad; then we would go check out the hooches.

Maybe five minutes later, as we waited in the tall grass for our squad, Tom, the other GI crouched out there with me, whispered that he just saw three soldiers to his left (I was watching to the right) walking toward our perimeter. I assumed the soldiers in question were from one of our sweeps coming from another direction. I told Tom the same.

As I continued looking to my right and across the draw at the hooches, I heard giggling and whispering on my left, near Tom's location. Again, at first I thought it was another sweep, but in an instant I knew I was wrong. They were NVA. They had been walking back towards their hooches, now occupied by our company. They probably almost walked right in, but had seen our perimeter, went unnoticed by our guys, and scurried off. They were fast walking and smiling. I froze momentarily. I was stunned by what I was seeing. And then one of them, as if sensing someone was watching, looked directly my way. I looked straight into his eyes, and he mine. He was maybe ten meters away. We were in full view of each other. I could see fear. He could see fear. The entire ordeal took a split second, but it seemed like an eternity. The slight advantage I had was that I saw him first. I quickly raised my M-16 and fired on automatic before he could raise his AK-47. I think Tom fired as well. The NVA went down. My adrenaline was pumping as I ran around a tree and tried to get shots off at the other two as they ran down the valley and toward the other hooches. I fired a burst. One sprawled, hit in the back, but got up and continued to run, disappearing into the jungle as I tried to change the magazine on my weapon.

I slowly moved towards where the first NVA had been. I knew either I or Tom had hit him. I found him lying in the tall grass, covered in blood, his body jerking as if he were having a seizure. His eyes were wide open. He was KIA. I trembled inside. I tried to shake my emotions off, as if I were a macho-man GI and this was just another day at the office. I had heard stories about collecting souvenirs off dead NVA, so I began searching his body. Maybe I could find something to boast about to my friends back home.

First I found a map and then I found his wallet. Inside his wallet were photos. Photos of who appeared to be his sister and his mom. Just like I carried in my wallet. I found a picture of him posing with his friends. Just like I carried. My heart sank. My body ached. Plus, the adrenaline was still full throttle. Finally, our squad arrived. They seemed jealous they had not been the fortunate ones to face a person with an automatic weapon, with no choice but to kill or be killed. Someone said Tom and I were supposed to get an in-country R&R for this KIA. A prize for taking a life.

A SMILE ON A DREARY, SAD DAY.

I think about that soldier out here on the trail. I think about his family. For days after the encounter I was an emotional wreck. I covered my feelings well, but inside I began hating war. That young guy had a beautiful family like I did. He had friends like me. Maybe we could have been friends. I didn't feel guilt over his death. I felt sorrow and I felt anger.

When I think of him today, nothing has changed in all these years. He was one precious life gone from his mom and dad. Gone from his brothers and sisters. Taken away from his friends. I feel sorry for all who knew him.

JULY 8 | DELAWARE WATER GAP, 13.7 MILES, 1,283.8 MILES TOTAL

We were up and hiking at 6:15 a.m. We hiked like always, either Cosmos out front, or me, depending on the day and the mood. This day Cosmos was out front and we met up for a break at Kirkridge Shelter after about seven miles. With a zero on my mind, I feel strong today. The rabbit wants the carrot.

We made it to Delaware Water Gap just after noon. With the trail running right through town our first stop was the first place that served food. We were the only people in the Deer Head Inn for lunch, a fine dining establishment that was more than happy to serve a couple of stinky thru-hikers.

Then, per usual, over to the outfitter to look once again for shoes for Cosmos. Even though we just finished eating, I had a brownie and sundae while I waited for her. Unable to find shoes, off we hitched to Stroudsburg, Pennsylvania, and downtown to the Pocono Inn Town. Right on Main Street, a room for two nights, please, a nero (a short, fast morning hike) and a zero beckoned. It was relaxation time as our bodies needed a break. I did the laundry and we both took a long hot shower.

We taxied to the mall, with a movie on our minds. Before the movie, *Public Enemy*, was scheduled to start, we strolled around the mall. I got an incredible foot massage from a woman who was doing a promo for her massage business. Afterward, we walked to a grocery store for our resupply and then waited in the parking lot, approaching people as they left the store, asking for a ride. Cosmos is getting really good at this. Not long ago, she was a rookie when hitchhiking, but now she's a veteran at asking for rides. She simply walks up to whomever as they leave the store and asks if they are going that way (pointing), and nine out of ten times if the answer is yes they give us a ride. A young couple gave us a ride to the front door of the hotel.

A fun and talented duo played music in the hotel bar. We had some interesting conversations with people who bought us way too many drinks. We ended up in bed at 1:30 a.m., five hours past hiker midnight.

JULY 9 | DELAWARE WATER GAP, ZERO

As much as I wanted to sleep in, I was up at the usual time, but I was careful not to wake the Cosmos.

I ate breakfast alone and read the local paper's main story about a double murder by a skinhead in this town. He killed his wife and son. The bodies were found in the attic, where she had been storing food ever since Obama was elected, thinking the end was near.

Eventually Cosmos woke up. I had traveled around as she slept and located a place in town that trained massage therapists. As thru-hikers we could not pass up on this opportunity and while Cosmos said her massage was wonderful, mine was horrible. I would have been better off rubbing my back against the wall.

We got a ride to the library, and I updated friends and family and answered all my e-mails. I wrote to folks I hadn't communicated with in a long time and then, again, begged for a ride back to the hotel and succeeded.

After taking advantage of the pool and hot tub, we visited an Irish pub for an early dinner. This after Cosmos once again looked for shoes.

Another zero flies by.

8 NEW JERSEY AND NEW YORK

JULY 10
JUST PAST CAMP MOHICAN ROAD, 11.1 MILES,
1,294.9 MILES TOTAL

I could write this daily: I marvel at the miles I am putting on this body. Almost 1,300 now, walking over all types of terrain with a huge pack. Who would have thunk it?

After breakfast a taxi gave us a ride to the trail in Delaware Water Gap. We stopped back at the outfitter. I don't think we have ever gone through a town that had an outfitter without stopping. I order a wider brand of trail shoe (Vasquez) and they will send them up the trail to a mail drop. If I get a wider shoe, perhaps I won't have the numbness. Vasquez just started making a wider brand in my size last month. They are sending at no cost.

We visited a bakery in town, and then moved out. We hiked right out of Pennsylvania and into New Jersey, my eighth state.

I see Baltimore, Not Jack. Strange trail name, Baltimore, Not Jack. This is his fourth time thru-hiking. He said it takes him a year to recover and he always thinks he will never do it again. But then he thinks about all the wonderful parts of the trail, and he is off.

We are at a beautiful little spot overlooking New Jersey. I never would have thought New Jersey was this beautiful, always imagining malls and parking lots. After we set up for the night, we sat, ate, and talked near the edge of a cliff. We were surprised by the sight of a bear just below us, maybe twenty feet. It had no idea we were above as it wandered around in the bushes. I hung our bear bag very high in a tree before bed.

We saw gliders today from a mountaintop. We sat and watched them for almost an hour as they soared so quietly in the sky. We hiked a bit today with Mountain Man (the seventy-year-old), The Tag Team, and Bookworm, a self-proclaimed nerd who was very knowledgeable about all aspects of the trail.

JULY 11 | GREN ANDERSON SHELTER, 20.1 MILES, 1,315 MILES TOTAL

We made it to the shelter just before dark and found a spot to pitch our tent among eight others. The shelter is full. This is the most people I have seen at a shelter since Fontana Dam, three months ago. The rain poured down, but we managed to get the tent up without it getting wet inside.

Some of the people here I have not seen in a bit. Limbo, Momma Bear (dog, Husky) and Bird, to name a few. We hiked with some others and Mountain Man suggested we get off the trail after eighteen miles and walk up the road to Ken's Steakhouse. Our group included Mountain Man, The Tag Team, Matt from DC, and Bookworm. I over-ate some good chow including steak, salad, beer, wings, and two desserts.

While we waited outside we talked to a ridge runner (someone paid to walk and monitor the trail). He was walking with a cane. He showed us his leg, which was a deep yellow and black color from the knee down, wounded a week prior from a rattlesnake bite. He said that a half hour after he was bitten he was delirious. He'd radioed for help immediately and had to be assisted out of the woods to a vehicle and to the hospital by his co-workers. I feel paranoia setting in. Most people on the trail have seen a rattlesnake, but not us.

We hiked on and every time I saw a twig on or just off the trail I would jump, thinking rattlesnake. Damn, how long is this going to last?

We had rain and lightning all night. Not a good night's sleep. I did pass 1,300 miles today.

JULY 12 | UNIONVILLE, NEW YORK (THE MAYOR'S HOUSE) 20.1 MILES, 1,335.1 MILES TOTAL

My son Jake is 20 years old today. Where has the time gone? What was I...42 when he was born? Oh, to be 42 again.

We were up early and the first ones out of the shelter area. I am fascinated watching other hikers milling about trying to get their shit wired tight before they depart. In the rain.

I hiked ahead of Cosmos to the Sunrise Mountain pavilion, a couple miles up the trail. This is a beautiful, flat spot on a mountain top. We tried to get here last night, but darkness and rain stopped us. While waiting for Cosmos, I stretched my aching body for a bit. When she arrived we enjoyed the view for a while and then moved on, the next stop, High Point State Park.

Upon arrival, we dropped our packs in the park office and walked the mile to the beach and concession stand. Gatorade, hot dogs, cheese fries, and more. We sat and talked, wanting to go swimming, but the water was too full of people and the beach overly crowded on this beautiful July day. We walked back, packed up, and began the nine-mile trek to Unionville, New York, and the Mayor's House, which we had heard so much about.

Cosmos hiked ahead, out of sight, while I called Jake to wish him happy birthday. He said he would love to hike the last part of the trail with me.

I met Tiger (a seventy-ish man) as I came around a bend on the trail. He had blood streaming down his cheek. He had slipped on some rocks and fallen into a tree. I tended to him and put a Band-Aid on his cheek. The cut was nothing too serious, but he will be bruised. Tiger said he was a retired psychotherapist.

I hiked hard to catch up with Cosmos and left Tiger behind me some-where. The trail improved, with few rocks and beautiful meadows. The legs feel weary. Cosmos waited for me at a road and we talked for a bit, waiting for Tiger to catch us, and then power hiked the four miles to the Mayor's, wanting to make it in time for dinner. I called the Mayor's House when we were on a mountaintop, and a man who fielded calls told us, "We will hold dinner for you. Call when you reach Lott Road, and we'll send someone to pick you up." More trail magic. More trail angels.

We arrived at Lott Road, where a guy named Dick picked us up and took us to the Mayor's. There are seven other hikers here. Dick put an ice-cold Bud in my hand and said, "This one is free, the rest are a quarter apiece, and four is the maximum allowed." Fair enough. Then he said, "When you are done eating, get your laundry together and give it to me. Then you two get a shower."

We had an ultra spaghetti dinner with corn on the cob, coleslaw, beans, and watermelon. What a treat. Not just the food, beer, and hospitality of the staff of this house, but the camaraderie of the hikers, including fellow thru-hikers Schooner, Ferdy, and Union Break (so named because he takes breaks daily at 10 a.m. and 3 p.m.).

The house was full so we pitched our tent in the backyard on soft grass. As part of the deal to stay here, we are supposed to watch a motiva-tional video. I am thinking to myself, "A thru-hiker needs a motivational speech?" The Mayor wasn't there so we didn't have to watch.

After dinner, the Mayor's friend took us to town to resupply. We went inside the grocery store, and the guy just sat in the parking lot waiting for us. Goodness abounds. I have asked myself many times, "What's in this for them?" Feeling good about giving, I guess. They do have a donation cup, but most hikers have little money. I left forty dollars.

We had a peaceful sleep on the lawn. As I drifted off, I was hoping that tomorrow would be as easy a hike as the last nine miles today were.

JULY 13 | BEARFORT MOUNTAIN, 20.7 MILES, 1,355.8 MILES TOTAL

An older man made breakfast this morning and would accept no help preparing the food or doing the dishes.

We met the Mayor just prior to departure. He had been visiting in another city. The Mayor used to be just that: the Mayor of Unionville, New York. What a kind and generous man. Dick gave us a ride to the post office, then to the trailhead.

We did have an easy hike today--flat, and we felt like we were in cruise control. Cosmos passed 1,000 miles today. To think at one time she was going to hike 100, maybe 200 miles, and now she has done over a thousand.

We hiked for a bit with Union Break, a tall, lanky, gentle man. What a good guy, very mellow. He started his hike over a month later than me. He spends little money and hikes quickly, doing big miles. Probably won't see him again.

I was out front this day. Cosmos was somewhere behind hiking with Matt from DC. Eventually, darkness loomed. I was trampling around in the woods looking for a flat spot; I am always baffled why flat spots in this huge forest are so hard to find. All I want is a simple little flat area to pitch a little tent and spend the night.

Eventually, Matt from DC found us a spot on a big flat rock. We got the tent up and had a wonderful dinner. Before dinner I gave Cosmos a 24-ounce beer I had packed to surprise her, commemorating her 1,000 miles. We slept under the stars, sans rain fly.

JULY 14 | JUST PAST ARDEN MOUNTAIN, 17.3 MILES, 1,373.1 MILES TOTAL

We were up early with ice cream on our minds. I had read in my trail bible about an ice cream place being down Highway 17A, which we were to cross. I reached the highway first, ahead of Cosmos, so I left a note on the trail telling her of my whereabouts. She missed the note, but did, however, have an innate sense of the whereabouts of ice cream, arriving an hour or so later.

For the hiker, extreme disappointment. The ice cream place doesn't open until noon. This according to Coffee Bean and Tall Grass, who are waiting and reading. It's 10 a.m. Do we wait or move on? We could do another five miles before they open, but we decide to wait. This is supposed to be the best homemade ice cream this side of Moomers, in my hometown.

Matt from DC joins us. We have five thru-hikers who have hiked off trail and are willing to wait two hours to indulge in sugar. Oh, the luxuries of life. We will nap, read, talk, or whatever until someone opens this place. Tall Grass informed me of all the places along the rest of the trail to avoid, and to not miss. Info given him by a hiker legend and I write it all down in my bible, *The Thru Hiker Handbook*. Where would I be without this great resource? Written by Bob "501" McCaw, my 2009 edition has directed me continuously, without fail. Thank you 501.

The number-one place is the Long Trail Inn, in Vermont, home of the best Guinness beer on the trail, Cosmos' favorite.

When the ice cream place finally opens we learn quickly the reason it is so highly touted. Great homemade ice cream. The bonus was all the fun we had waiting, which led to laughing and talking about our lives back in the world.

We left with a belly full of ice cream and were greeted with a tough, tough climb. I had to take my pack off once and toss it up, because I couldn't scale the rocks with it on my back.

I waited on top of the mountain for about an hour for Cosmos. We ended up traveling 17.3 miles to just past Arden Mountain, where we pitched our tent and ate dinner to the sound of the New York Thruway. We could see the thruway from the mountaintop. Doesn't quite feel right, but such is diversity.

We are only 62 miles from seeing my daughter, Morganne, my sister Eve, and her Woodstock family. Seems like just the other day that this meeting was more than 1,000 miles away. I reflect on the many ups and downs I have experienced on this trail. One day I feel great, and think I have this down. The next day I feel like I am just beginning my hike, feeling fatigue from beginning to end. The only philosophy to have is to just keep walking; all the body parts and mind will eventually "kick in," just like in life. The first 20 minutes are always the hardest. Keep smiling.

Speaking of smiling, in April of 1968 we were set up at a firebase. Actually, the firebase was Hill 1338, the hill on which we suffered so many casualties four months earlier, and at that time my worst day on earth. Now the hill is totally stripped of any vegetation and is a huge firebase. The hill was now quite secure. We were set up here for a few days to guard the base. The bunkers are now enormous. One could stand up inside them and walk around. They were equipped with an area specially dug for sleeping, card playing, eating, and reading. In our bunker were the RTOs (radio telephone operators), our platoon leader, Lieutenant Terry, and a platoon sergeant.

This day we were supposed to get a couple of replacements, new guys. Also, rumor had it we were to get hot chow from base camp. These were two good reasons to celebrate, because neither one of these happened often.

A chopper landed and Lieutenant Terry went to greet it, knowing our platoon's replacement was on board. He brought the guy down to meet us. Inside the bunker we all introduced ourselves. Dushing was small in stature and seemed quite shy. He was from Tennessee. His fatigues were clean, as was his steel pot. Everything on him was brand new. We talked for a few minutes about this and that. No, never once did we mention how many days we had left. I vowed I would never do that to a new guy.

Suddenly the sound of another chopper filled the air. Hot chow had arrived. Rejoice!

Dushing simply watched us with curiosity. In the bunker with Dushing and me was a good friend, Phillips, a tall man (boy) with an average build. He had lots of baby fat, but likened himself to the actor Robert Mitchum. In fact, he liked to be called Rob, even though his name was Jim. Phillips was a prankster.

I seized the moment. When Phillips asked me if I wanted to go get in the chow line, I thought for a moment, then said, "No, I don't think so. I think I'm going to have flies for dinner tonight." Phillips looked at me, nodded his head up and down with a mischievous look on his face, and said, "Damn good idea, Keenan. We haven't had flies in a long time, and there are lots here to choose from."

And so, with the shy Dushing looking on in bewilderment, we swatted and killed flies in our bunker and ate them for dinner. With each tasting we would say, "Mmmmmmmm." Dushing silently left our bunker. It took great effort not to laugh outloud. Of course we stopped eating flies and made some C-rations in our bunker. We did not eat hot chow that night, as good as it sounded, because we wanted to keep Dushing thinking this is the way it is out here in the bush.

Fast forward a few weeks. We had moved and moved with little contact with the enemy, but intelligence informed Grizzly there was a force of NVA in an area and we were to combat assault in.

Morale drops when we get orders such as these because we all know if the reports are true, casualties are in the near future.

We choppered first to the Dak To airstrip to resupply. Then we waited, as a misty rain fell on a silent group of GIs, sitting stretched out on the wet clay, minds swirling as to what might lie ahead. Not a word was spoken.

As we sat, Dushing arose and stood among us. He looked like he was about to give a speech. He no longer had clean fatigues, boots, and steel pot. He looked grubby and dingy like the rest of us. A trace of jungle rot could be seen on his neck. He had our attention. He looked intensely at me as he opened his rucksack and dug around inside. He looked proud as he produced a C-ration white bread can 2 ½ inches high and 3 inches in diameter.

Dushing opened the lid, which had previously been opened, but was now full of something other than the white bread. Then he proudly went from person to person to show off what he had: a can full of dead insects--flies, roaches, mosquitoes, bees, moths. A wide range of creepy crawlers. He reached inside and squeezed out its contents.

He then smiled gingerly, eyeballed all of us, opened wide, and jammed as much as he could into his mouth. His cheeks puffed like a squirrel with nuts. He chewed and chewed as we all watched astonished. Eventually, after gagging a few times and swallowing and swallowing, he had a clear mouth. He smiled once again, opening his mouth to show it clear and clean. Everyone in the platoon clapped with enjoyment. Dushing was the man.

As he performed his act, the thought of choppering into a hot LZ and the casualties that go with such a mission was furthest from our mind, even though our departure was moments away. Although these moments of joy seem grotesque to a "normal" human, our choices of entertainment were limited. This one was a highlight, remembered by many to this day, I am sure.

I cannot bring myself to set up at the bottom of a hill or mountain while hiking the AT. I need to be on top. I can't quite shake the feeling of not wanting anybody to sneak up on me, or have a clean shot at me from on top of a mountain. I still get that ambush feeling, but they are much less intense since the day I started this journey. As different as night is to day.

Atop a battered hill.

JULY 15 | FORT MONTGOMERY, NEW YORK, 19.4 MILES, 1,392.5 MILES TOTAL

We climbed and descended Bear Mountain this day. Funny thought: "Wouldn't it be nice if there were bridges from mountain top to mountain top, so we don't have to continually go up and down?"

Saw a first today. I was far behind Cosmos, moving slowly, when she yelled at me from atop a small mountain, "Where are you?" "I'm coming, struggling today," I shouted back. "When you get up here you are going to shit yourself." I climbed on, wondering what she was talking about. When I reached the top I saw blueberries everywhere, a welcome sight, but nothing earth-shattering. Cosmos pointed to the east, and there in the distance was the New York City skyline. Masses of tall buildings. So far away, yet so near. The Big Apple from the AT.

At the West Mountain Shelter we stopped for lunch. We had seen a lot of section hikers in New York, but this particular shelter graced us with a man setting up his tripod to take a photo of the shelter. He is friendly and very funny. We talk for a bit, then Cosmos and I eat lunch on a rock near the shelter. The guy takes a photo of himself standing in front of the shelter, then gets out some weed and asks me if I want to partake. I decline, but tell him I don't mind if he does. So he lights up and gets on his phone. Tells whomever is on the line, "Okay, I have a photo of the place where all the craziness began." I yelled at him, jokingly, "You talking to your therapist?" He nodded yes, and smiled. Forty years ago his teacher brought his class here on a weekend outing and this is his first time he's been back. One of the things he had to do in therapy was go back to "where all the craziness began." He invited us down to his car for some beer and further discussion. We declined, but a part of me wanted to hear his entire story.

Saw Union Break today. He was just sitting in the woods a bit off the trail, thinking. I love that guy.

We have had mostly glorious weather the last two weeks. Today, 70s, 80s. We summited to the enjoyment of a wonderful southerly breeze. While we rested atop Bear Mountain, we met a man who was incredibly encouraging regarding our hike. He inspired both of us. I should have written down some of his words of wisdom, for my own personal reflections and to share with others.

I had heard about a bar in Ft. Montgomery that served chicken wings unsurpassed by any in New York. That was the mission, although Cosmos didn't quite agree with me. I had the craving, thinking about my hometown Brady's Bar and their luscious wings. We saw an antique car show in a field below as we came down the mountain, but hiked on. I was salivating for those wings. After walking on a highway for a mile or so, we found the bar, almost like another mirage. We walked in, dropped our packs, found a booth, and got ready to chow down, only to hear the waiter say, "Sorry, folks, the kitchen is closed." Ugh. I got the look from Cosmos. We'd hiked nineteen-plus miles to be told this? I was demoralized.

We had one beer while contemplating our next move. I asked a guy if he knew where the nearest restaurant was and he said there was one down the road. I asked him if he could drive us there and he said he had no car. I was tired and hungry and called a little motel and made reservations for the night. Five minutes later, a woman who had been sitting at the bar with a friend, walked up to us and said, "If you want, we will drive you to the restaurant." Trail magic once again. We finished our beers, threw our packs in their trunk, and away we went. We had dinner together and wonderful conversation. They may meet us up the trail next month if all goes well. Trish, a social worker, and her friend Linda, a pharmaceutical rep.

While we dined, Spicoli came in. We talked for a minute while he stared at our food, like a begging dog. We gave him some ribs, wings, and shrimp to share with Wolfpack and the Scotsman. He left to find a room and showed up about twenty minutes later begging Trish and Linda for a ride somewhere. While we were eating dinner! He bothers me ever since he lied to me about the pot that was in the Slim Jims. I looked at Spicoli with furrowed eyebrows and he moved on.

After about a two-hour dinner, we said our goodbyes to Trish and Linda and walked to our room. Meeting people on the trail is a highlight for me.

JULY 16 | NEAR DENNYTOWN ROAD, 14.5 MILES, 1,407 MILES TOTAL

Up at 8 a.m. I slept in. We had breakfast at a bagel place across the street from the motel. The woman who owns this motel gave us a ride back to where we had left the trail, the Trailside Museum in Ft. Montgomery. The AT runs right through it.

After spending a few minutes at the museum, we hiked across the Hudson River, the lowest point on the AT. I felt very strong today. I got way ahead of Cosmos. The trail crossed a road next to a market and by the time Cosmos arrived I'd consumed a sandwich and a beer, water, and Gatorade. Scotsman, Spicoli, and the Wolfpack followed her in. Unbeknownst to Cosmos, I packed a couple of sandwiches and Cheetos out of this place for dinner tonight. I want to surprise her.

Blue blazing? The Flying Scotsman, Spicoli, and Wolfpack hiked down the road instead of the trail today. I was way out in front of them, busting my ass, and when I came to a road and a clearing where we were to camp, there they were. My eyebrows furrowed once again. That would be classic blue blazing, skipping parts of the trail. If you are going to hike the trail, hike the trail.

Cosmos arrived. I had pitched our tent in an open area near the road. A light rain fell after we ate our sandwiches. We got in the tent early, because of the influx of mosquitoes. I hiked hard today. Tomorrow I get to see my sister and daughter and the entire Woodstock clan.

July 17 | Highway 52, 15.8 miles, 1,422.8 miles total

I woke up excitedly, only to be engulfed by Mike Mosquito and his family as I emerged from the tent. We tore down and were out of the area in a hurry. Today is a big day. We will meet my nephew, Geoff, and my daughter, Morganne, at Highway 52. A nero, to be followed by a zero.

As we approached Highway 52, after hiking fifteen-plus miles, Geoff drove up. Timing is everything. We were out of the woods and into his car, which felt surreal. We stopped at the first store we passed to buy sandwiches, chips, pop, and beer, then continued on to my sister Eve's house.

Radiant was my sister as she emerged from the Rainbow Lodge. She looks like a queen. Cosmos told Eve she smelled wonderful.

Cosmos and I took long showers and she napped for a couple hours while Eve and I played "Screw Thine," a family card game. Eve took my money while boasting to the nth degree; I walk all this way to get to her house and, just like a sister, she takes my money.

Morganne arrived from New York City. How wonderful to hug her, to look at her. I am so proud of her and I felt myself beaming, like my mom would have. What a joy to see my family after all those miles. Cheyenne, Molly, Eric, Ian, Marshall. I wish all my kids could be here, plus my other two sisters. Nephew Ian gave me many wonderful smiles and laughs. Love is in the air.

We played cards late, all money going to my charities: Women's Resource Center and Veterans for Peace scholarship fund. The family plays cards all the time and whoever wins puts their money in a pot, to be given to me when I finish this trek.

It poured rain from about 3 p.m. until late in the evening. Poured! We picked good days to visit, to nero and to zero.

JULY 18 | WOODSTOCK, ZERO

Up early as usual. We did our laundry. My sister made quiche for breakfast, and Cosmos gave me an unbelievable foot massage. We went shopping to Woodstock for a few hours, then back for dinner. We had ourselves a true zero day, pure relaxation.

JULY 19 | NEAR NEW YORK HIGHWAY 55, 7.2 MILES, 1,430 MILES TOTAL

Packing up and ready to go. The stay was too short. Time flew.

I have a hard time separating myself from watching the British Open Golf tournament. Tom Watson, at 59 years old, was leading until the end of the last day. But he bogeyed the last hole when he needed a par to win, then lost in a playoff. Bummer. But Mr. Watson is very inspiring. I think of myself hiking all this way at 62 years old and compare myself, humbly, to him.

Geoff and Molly drove us back to Highway 52 after we took a photo of the family and said our goodbyes. Saying goodbye to my sister was especially hard today. I so love that woman.

Off we go into the woods. As we depart Molly says, "We dropping you off, and you disappearing into the woods seems so bizarre." Geoff adds, "Yeah, a bit more bizarre is that they are walking to Maine."

I am comforted knowing Cosmos had a good time these past couple days. She seemed to feel at home.

9 | CONNECTICUT AND MASSACHUSETTS

JULY 20
KENT, CONNECTICUT, 25.9 MILES, 1,455.9
MILES TOTAL

I thought the new shoes I had ordered were coming here. Not. They are coming to Cornwall Bridge.

We hustled the miles today. My body said today's hike was a bit much as I traveled, but always when I get to where I am for the evening, I feel fine, saying to myself or to Cosmos, "That wasn't that bad." But this time the map had said downhill the last five miles, it wasn't, and I was pissed off. For motivation, I just tried to keep Cosmos in my sights. I did a lot of swearing today. My legs were weary and my knees ached.

I called a motel from a mountaintop and reserved a room. Whoever took my reservation said they would pick us up on the highway when we came out of the woods. We waited and waited. Finally, we started walking. By the time we get there, the restaurant in the motel will be closed, I thought. And it was. We did get a room in Kent after eating pizza at a local pub. Saw fellow hikers Schooner and Ferdy. We have been seeing them on and off since the very beginning, as they started the same day as me, almost four months ago.

As I was putting the key in the door to our room, I was bowled over by the sight of Tall Grass. He and Coffee Bean were in the room next door. Small world, as we hadn't seen him in weeks. We were sad to hear Coffee Bean had badly sprained her ankle. They were going to the doctor tomorrow to get a prognosis and I pray it is a short healing process. They are inspirational, this son and mom combo.

JULY 21 | CORNWELL BRIDGE, CONNECTICUT, 11.1 MILES, 1,467 MILES TOTAL

We had breakfast at a cool little restaurant on the way out of Kent this morning. Cosmos talked me into going to the doctor for my feet. I tried to get in, but no luck. The next opening was in the afternoon. We will be long gone by then. Cosmos didn't like my decision, but I had been hurting for months and I knew what the doc would say: "You need to let your feet rest." Resting for any length of time is not an option. I don't think there is anyone on the trail at this point who isn't hurting. This is the tenth state I have walked through. Boggles my mind.

We walked in the rain all day. We had a nice walk next to a river for about four miles. We were high stepping on the flat surface and exceeding three miles an hour.

We spent the night in Cornwall because I had to visit the outfitter in the morning to pick up my shoes. We got a room at a little motel and attempted to dry out our gear. In the next room were a couple, trail names Simple Man and Ice Fingers. They had left Springer Mountain in Georgia three weeks before I did and we have never seen each other before. Also at the motel were Limbo, Bird, and Momma Bear.

We hung our stuff all over the room to dry and then walked down the street and visited the "Spirit Store" having heard they give two free beers to thru-hikers. The rumor was true.

Cosmos was upset with me because instead of paying attention to her, I watched TV and read the paper. I am in one of those moods. I just felt like being alone. We ironed things out. Our "moments" are few and far between now.

JULY 22 | JUST PAST FALLS VILLAGE, CONNECTICUT, 15.2 MILES, 1,482.2 MILES TOTAL

Our plan of leaving town early was thwarted because our gear failed to dry in the room. We waited until the sun rose above the trees to hang it out to dry. After a siesta, we packed up and headed to the outfitter. I was excited to pick up my new shoes and they fit perfectly. Size 12 wide; my feet are growing but I'm shrinking. Age!

We ran into Storyteller. We had not seen him in months, thinking he was off the trail. He informed us Coffee Bean was off the trail. The prognosis from the doc was torn cartilage. Tall Grass may go home with her. When we saw him in Kent, he had been phoning home to tell his dad of his mom's condition. In a way I hope he continues on his own to completion. But knowing him, I would bet he is homeward bound with his mom. He is a grand hiker, but an even greater son and person. Coffee Bean is a very frail-looking woman, but strong. She must only weigh a bit over one hundred pounds. She plays violin in a symphony. Tall Grass has been so very patient with her, always hiking with her, always catering to her, always encouraging her. They made a great team. The bonding they did on the trail will be life-long. Dad was supposed to come, but because of medical reasons he couldn't so Coffee Bean took his place. She did her level best not to hold up Tall Grass and they hiked strong.

We had bigger hills today. The mountains are coming. The hiking has been relatively easy since Virginia. I have been thinking about the White Mountains of New Hampshire since the end of March. They are looming. Southbound and section hikers that have passed through there all say the same thing: "Wait till you get to the Whites. They will kick your ass." Very few people are positive about the Whites.

We set up camp next to a fast-moving, very wide river complete with huge, thunderous falls. We started today's hike fording that river. We found ourselves in thigh-deep, flowing, rushing rapids. We had spent a good half hour walking up river looking for a place to "rock hop" across, to no avail.

We ran into Schooner and Ferdy on the trail, all of their gear hanging from trees and foliage, drying out. We decided to hike with them for a bit. I was bringing up the rear when I noticed everyone had stopped and were looking left down a slight valley in the woods. I looked down and there was the biggest bear I've ever seen. Huge, maybe six hundred pounds. This monster bear was muddling its way through the brush, looking for whatever. It started walking up the hill toward us, just banging down shrubbery as it went. We were frozen. I had my camera at the ready, but was feeling leery. Cosmos stepped back slightly, and when she did, a twig broke. The bear didn't even glance our way, but instead did a one-eighty and lumbered down the hill away from us. The forest seemed to shake as it ran. It stopped at the bottom and stood up, this monster bear, looking our way. Schooner made a funny mouth noise and the bear responded by cocking its head this way and that, like a puppy. Schooner made another noise with the bear continuing to cock its head back and forth, appearing baffled. We walked on. Yet another unforgettable moment.

We had some tough downs today. Scary. I fell so hard one time my ring flew off my finger.

We tented by a spring close to Prospect Mountain.

We are trying to get to Vermont by July 29, but to accomplish this we must average seventeen miles a day. I should say I am trying to get to Vermont by July 29. Cosmos does not like my hiking agenda. She disagrees with pushing, simply because I want to have fewer than six hundred miles to go before I get off trail for my four-day trip to Put-In-Bay to meet my friends. She does have a point. But she is going to meet and hike with her mom and brother when I get off the trail for those four days, so she will be able to slow down then and relax.

JULY 23 | PLATFORM AT LAUREL RIDGE CAMPSITE, 15.8 MILES, 1,498 MILES TOTAL

I hiked briskly the 6.6 miles to Salisbury, Connecticut, and waited by a road for Cosmos to catch up. We had planned a lunch in this charming little town. There was a speed limit sign near downtown that had 30 mph limit, and a digital read-out for "your speed." The device measured Cosmos at three mph.

We invaded the local grocery store and prowled around. To a hiker, everything looks good. I ended up buying some fried chicken from the deli and four bottles of various liquids to drink. We dined in an outside table area that was surrounded by a quaint variety of little shops. Spicoli, Scotsman, and Wolfpack joined us.

After stuffing ourselves we slowly walked back to the trail. As soon as we got there I told Cosmos to go ahead of me, I would catch up. I actually asked her to move on because I could tell I was about to have a major and thunderous diarrhea attack.

I fell once again on the trail, this time on a treacherous rock downhill. If it weren't for a tree I grabbed on the way down I shudder to think what could have happened to this old man.

We are tenting on a platform, a flat area made of wood just wide enough to pitch a small tent. On different sections of the trail, depending on how active the volunteerism is from local hiking clubs, these platforms are built because there are no flat spots. They are a welcome sight for a weary hiker. To me, this is trail magic. Here there are two platforms. One is the home of Ice Fingers and Simple Man, thru-hikers we had never met prior to a couple days ago. We had a nice chat over dinner. Then the heavens opened up once again and the rain poured.

We are now in Massachusetts, state number eleven.

JULY 24 | TOM LEONARD LEAN-TO, 19.1 MILES, 1,517.1 MILES TOTAL

After tearing down in the rain and packing our wet gear, we were off. I love being in a tent when it rains, the pitter-pattering is soothing to me. Cosmos commented about being under pressure regarding the hike. I do understand. We are pushing a bit.

The walk was tough for me today, but it seemed not to be for her. She seemed spry. I struggled early and throughout the day. My legs are sore. I know I need to average sixteen miles a day to get to Bennington, Vermont, by Wednesday. That will be where Lynn (my high school friend) will pick me up. If Cosmos and I start early every day, we shouldn't have a problem.

We stink beyond normal. Sometimes the smell wakes us up in the middle of the night.

I fell twice again today. Fatigue is a factor. The terrain is rocky. That, coupled with what feels like straight-down hills is a recipe for falling down. The rain makes the rocks slippery, almost ice-like. I try to be careful, but easier said than done.

The mosquitoes were horrendous today. Even with DEET (ultra-bug repellent that makes my skin crawl) they were all over me.

Kbar, Soundtrack and Penny Whistler the Dueler are here or tenting near this lean-to, as are Ice Fingers, Simple Man, Spicoli, Scotsman, and Wolfpack.

Both of my legs (hamstrings) severely cramped late in the night. I woke up from a dead sleep and had knots like golf balls. I straightened my legs and was quivering, trying to knead the knots, to no avail. I was all the while trying not to disturb Cosmos, just gritting my teeth. The rain was pouring down, so I couldn't roll myself outside and "walk it off." Finally, Cosmos woke up to me moaning and quivering. I scared the shit out of her. She thought I was having a seizure. She deeply massaged my hamstrings until the cramps subsided. My first cramps on the trail.

I passed 1,500 miles today.

JULY 25 | UPPER GOOSE LAKE CABIN, 21.1 MILES, 1,538 MILES TOTAL

We hiked hard today to this beautiful spot on the trail. The place reminds me of the scenery in the movie, *On Golden Pond.* We are at a large cabin/hostel on a beautiful lake. After claiming our bunks, Cosmos went swimming near a dock while a fellow hiker played the violin. Cosmos and I borrowed a canoe and glided around the lake in the still waters.

We are meeting more and more southbound hikers. Most think they have got it made because they have completed the White Mountains. Nothing could be further from the truth. I met four south-bounders, three young guys and a younger woman. I talked to them for a bit, sharing info about what lies ahead and giving them tips on various places to stay. Before departing I asked them for their trail names. They called themselves The Sibs. Three brothers and their young sister, aged 18-24. As I hiked off I thought how proud their parents must be. And perhaps worried.

We are up and out early. We have been hiking these last couple weeks with or near Spicoli, Scotsman, and Wolfpack. They pass us, we pass them. The Scotsman is manic, and always funny. The last couple days we have also hiked with a guy named Tank. Tank is a big guy, with a whopping black beard, who wears a kilt and knee socks. He always has a lit cigarette hanging from his mouth, whether he is going downhill or up. A character indeed.

As we neared the end of the day, planning on stopping for the night at the next shelter, we came across a cooler in the middle of the woods, full of cold soda and treats. Next to the cooler was a journal to write your thanks. The magic was from Birch, a woman who'd hiked more than nine hundred miles earlier to complete her hike (she had been hiking various portions of the trail for a few years). I sat down with Cosmos and was drinking a wonderful, cold beverage on a hot day, reading the journal. Lo and behold, I found an entry from Rugged Shark. He'd signed the journal just the day before on July 25. His entry said he was going to zero at the Birdcage tomorrow. I looked at Cosmos wide-eyed and said, "That would be today." I asked the Cosmos if we could push to Dalton, a few more miles. She agreed.

The AT cut right through the city of Dalton. The instructions on the map said to find the local Sunoco station and have an attendant call a guy named Rob at the Birdcage. We did. Moments later Rob picked us up in his van. Rob opens his home to hikers at no cost. In fact, he will not take your money. He lets you do laundry, opens up his shower with dry towels for you, and gives you "hiker clothes" to wear after you shower while your laundry is drying.

When Rob pulled up to his house with us, I saw a clean-shaven dude sitting on the porch reading. It was Rugged Shark. I had been following/chasing him for 1,300 miles, and I finally caught him. I got out of the van and yelled at him, "Hey, what's your name?" He looked up and said, "Rugged Shark." He stared at me for a moment, stood up, and said, "Naneek? Is that you?" And down the stairs he came. We embraced excitedly, so happy to see each other. The first thing out of his mouth was, "God, you stink." I introduced him to Cosmos. What a bonus to once again see this special man. I really connected with him long ago and knew he would be the type of person I would know forever.

We have been hiking in some serious mud the last four days. The weather? Rain at night, sunny days. Terrain has not been too bad, but my feet are all fucked up. I have lost toenails, have at least four numb toes, plantar warts, and cracked heel skin. But I just keep walking. My morale is high.

> One of the reasons I keep pushing on, and the very reason I make my way through life, is the war experience. When problems and concerns enter my life I often think of war. I longed for regular life problems and concerns when I was on guard duty in the middle of the night, after an all-day firefight. I longed for the problems and concerns in "the world" as I lay on the cold ground after walking point all day, fearing for my life every step of the way. Oh, how I missed home. Oh, how I missed those easy problems and concerns.

Eight hikers stayed at Rob's. On couches, on the floor, or in the basement on mattresses. Rob took photos of everyone and placed them in his 2009 album. Underneath your photo is your trail name and hometown.

July 27 | Cheshire, Massachusetts, 9.3 miles, 1,568.1 miles total

I woke up early and walked to the store, had a little breakfast by myself, and read the local paper.

We did the relatively short hike to this small town, where we searched frantically for ice cream. I was surprised to see Gail (refuses to have a trail name) with the little umbrella she still carries. I must admit I did not think I would see her at this point in the journey, though she may have felt the same about me.

We bussed to Pittsfield, Massachusetts, looking for civilization. Out of habit we exited the bus when we saw an outfitter sign at a local mall. And what's this, a movie theatre? We bought some tickets, the largest popcorn available, and brought our stinky bodies into the theatre. We sat alone on one side of the theatre so as not to offend anyone. The movie? *The Ugly Truth.* Horrible! But the popcorn was good and the movie, no matter how horrible, was a nice diversion from the trail. I've learned to expect the unexpected out here.

Cosmos and I treated ourselves to a good dinner at a pub and a wonderful stay at a little motel.

A continuing trend: The majority of the south-bounders are not friendly on the trail. They tend to keep to themselves. They don't seem to want to stop and chat. If I were in their shoes I would seek out any and all information I could on what lies ahead.

July 28 | Sherman Brook Campsite, 15.6 miles, 1,583.7 miles total

I had breakfast by myself at Friendly's, a little diner across from the motel, and let Cosmos sleep.

We bussed back to Cheshire and found the trail and hiked back into AT reality. Today was a tough day for me, with lots of big ups and lots of big downs.

We have been running into Gail consistently. Today we were on a mountaintop clearing, eating a snack while taking a break. I had chaffing on my ass and was about to put cream on the affected area when Cosmos came up with another memorable quote: "Go behind a tree to do that, will you? As soon as you stick your finger up your ass, Gail is going to come out of those woods and see you."

She said this with a perfectly straight face and we both laughed uncontrollably. I did go behind a tree. And Gail did not come out of the woods.

We got off trail a couple miles from the site we were seeking and walked down Highway 2 to a grocery store/deli in North Adams, Massachusetts, famished.

We asked a woman who was sitting on her front porch if we could leave our packs in her yard for about an hour and she approved.

After finding what we needed in the grocery store, we sat out front on a bench and attacked the food. Lots of fruit. We had our boots and socks off, letting them dry, and were the subject of more than one double take. Satisfied and quite plump, we walked back, picked up our packs, and disappeared into the woods.

We found a platform two miles into the woods and pitched our tent.

I will miss Cosmos terribly when I am in Put-In-Bay. I love that we are getting along. We have our moments of stubbornness and assholerishness, but 90% of the time, we relish each other. I so wish our relationship could work. Age is such a huge factor; a 35-year difference can be hard to navigate. She is at having-a-family age, and I am at grandpa-to-a-family age. But we love each other. Damn. I will always feel close to her in that she helped me love again, just when I thought I had too many emotional walls, the result of the hurt I experienced as my marriage ended.

My heart will ache when we are no longer this close. I have unconditional love for her. I want her to be happy. We will forever have a huge bond that nobody can possibly tamper with. She will always be mi carina. We have so many remarkable memories especially for having known each other for less than a year. Hiking this trail will bond us forever. We often wonder what other hikers think of our relationship. I have heard some rumors: That we are a father and a daughter; that she is a lesbian; that we are just friends; that we met on the trail and hiked at the same pace, but never did I hear, "they are lovers."

10   Vermont

We had a tough hike today, complete with mud, rain, and slippery, dangerous rocks, especially on the downhills. I was particularly careful today, and now I have fewer than six hundred miles to go as I head to Put-in-Bay to see my bros.

We hitched the five miles into town and Cosmos got a room for the evening. After showering, we walked downtown in the rain to meet Lynn at the Madison Brewing Company for dinner. Lynn is awed we have hiked this far. After dinner, she drove us to the room so I could pick up my pack. And then it was goodbye to Cosmos. Long hug. It rattles me how much I will miss her. She is special. She will go to a hiker celebration here, and then meet her mom and brother in a couple of days. I will catch up to her somehow, somewhere, down the trail.

1,600 miles, twelfth state, 577.8 miles to Katahdin.

July 30 – August 1 | Zeroes, 1,600.5 miles and holding

I lay in bed last night unable to sleep, thinking about the similarities between R&R in Vietnam and getting off the trail to join my friends for a little R&R. On this journey I made the decision that I would do this R&R thing if I had fewer than six hundred miles to go. Done. In Vietnam, I told myself I would not go on R&R until I had fewer than ninety days to go. Done. In both instances, most of my journey needed to be behind me. I always wanted to think of that "carrot" in front of me when I was in the war. I think the reason I wanted to do the same thing on the AT is PTSD- related. In Vietnam, some took their break early, with many months to go before DEROS (going-home date). Their philosophy was: "I may never get the opportunity. I could die any day." So when the opportunity arose, some jumped. And many died later. Maybe they were right.

Lynn dropped me at the airport in Boston. The ticket was waiting for me at the courtesy counter thanks to the goodness of one of my all-time favorite friends, Mac. I feel out of my element in the airport. Yesterday I was in the middle of a sixteen-mile hike in the middle of the woods, and now am surrounded not by trees, but by people bustling around, all in a hurry. I carried my pack onto the plane. People looked at me strangely as I walked the aisle of the plane. I realized then my pack stunk of me, even though I was showered and clean.

I arrived in Cleveland, grabbed my pack from the overhead, and put it on, just like yesterday in the woods, feeling extremely excited about reuniting with the boys.

As I approached the exits of the airport, there they were, standing off to the side. Mick, Mac, Ellis, and Kevin, all holding signs that read, NANEEK, LUCIFER, OHHS, 64. They had big grins on their faces and so did I. Paul and Egg, two other friends, are at our site on the island of Put-In-Bay. Other friends, Thom and Sid, cannot be here, so that will be a big void. Thom's wife Sandy is being tested for breast cancer and Sid had Traverse City Film Festival commitments. I crossed my fingers and said many prayers for Sandy.

We left the airport and headed out to Put-in-Bay. I think to myself, "Now this is really trail magic." We boarded the ferry like it was just another end-of-July vacation with the boys, but I can't help but think about the fact that I have hiked more than 1,600 miles to get to this point.

Paul and Egg greeted me with open arms and warm smiles when we arrived at our tent site. Egg offered to carry my pack and I agreed. He carried it to the spot I was to pitch my tent, dropped it, and looked at me with the Egg scowl and said, "Whew, that thing's got some stench to it."

I proceeded to drink a bunch of beer with the fellas, telling stories of the trail all the while. We went into town and I ate chicken at my favorite outdoor eatery on the island. My feet were bothering me. They are so swollen it scares me. When I wake in the morning the swelling is down. But when I stand and move around, they get huge, all the way up to my ankles. With the swelling comes a constant, dull pain. The sandals I had purchased in Bennington will no longer fit my swollen feet.

We played in the Tenth Annual PNB Golf Open. My game sucks. My feet are so sore, and I'm having a hard time walking. But I do have Ellis as a partner, and what could be better than that.

After the tourney it was into town to a pool party. Tons of drunk folks in the pool drinking beer and hanging out. I am in the pool only minutes when a young guy taps me on the shoulder and says, "No sweaters allowed in the pool area," referring to my hairy chest and back. We both laughed.

This behavior went on for three days. The highlight for me was just seeing the boys. I spent time staring at each of them, just appreciating my friends.

I had a wonderful time, but I miss Cosmos, and, though I can hardly believe it, because of the physicality, I miss the trail.

AUGUST 2 | ZERO

I am off the island. We had a breakfast on the mainland per usual. Mick gave me a Smartwool t-shirt, thinking I might be able to use it on the trail. My biggest worry now is how I am going to get my boots on, with my feet swollen like they are. They look like if I stuck a pin in them they would explode.

The boys dropped me off in Cleveland at the airport, driving way out of their way. I got very emotional hugging them goodbye, and I had to get myself in the airport before I started sobbing. What an incredible gesture of love, bringing me to PNB. All these guys, including Paulie and Egg, praised and encouraged me continuously. I needed their support.

My friend Lynn picked me up at the airport and assured me she would get me to the trailhead whenever I wanted to get there tomorrow. The drive to the airport from her house is over an hour. She took me to a grocery store where I resupplied, then to dinner and a pleasant chat. Back at her house, she helped me pack. She was quite amazed at the things I needed and didn't need. The whole process was foreign to her and would have been foreign to me four months ago.

We have a two-hour drive tomorrow to get me back on the trail, so rising early is a must. I need and want to get back on that trail, so I can catch Cosmos. I feel a driving need to hug her, and I want to be back in the woods.

AUGUST 3 | STORY SPRING SHELTER, 19 MILES, 1,619.5 MILES TOTAL

Lynn dropped me at the trail at 9 a.m., in Bennington, Vermont. After saying my thank-yous and my goodbyes, I immediately got back in a groove. I had been so concerned with my feet, but once I got my shoes on and started hiking, all was well.

I kept thinking, "Yesterday I'm having breakfast with the boys near Cleveland and here I am in the middle of the woods doing a nineteen-mile day in Vermont." I finished at 7 p.m. I had some big climbs today, but felt surprisingly strong considering the swollen feet, the food consumed, the 100 beers drank, and lack of exercise the last few days.

As I came around a turn on the trail this morning, there sitting on rocks was The Tag Team, husband and wife thru-hikers, both in their late 50s. They had stopped for breakfast. When I came up on them, I startled them, and both said in unison, "Naneek!" I hadn't seen them in weeks; I may never see them again, as I will be putting in some big miles these next few days. I also saw Witness, a young, energetic thru-hiker, and Mountain Man, a 70-year-old thru-hiker. I was days ahead of them at one point. The trail is like a walking city – you never know who you will run into. And when you do run into someone you haven't seen in a while, well, it's quite the treat.

One other person is here at this shelter where I call it quits for the day. Miles (for hiking miles and miles) is very quiet, and a thru-hiker. There were no flat spots to be found around the shelter, so I pitched my tent inside the shelter to avoid being eaten by bugs. I crashed hard after a quick dinner.

The terrain today was quite muddy, but I am focused on doing the miles to catch Cosmos.

AUGUST 4 | TOP OF BROMLEY MOUNTAIN, 24.1 MILES, 1,643.6 MILES TOTAL

The last part of today's hike was straight up a black diamond downhill ski run, to the top of Bromley Mountain (3,260 feet elevation). I am tired. I reckon that forty-three-plus miles in two days after three days of partying will do that to you.

I did some swearing today.

I found Soundtrack and Kbar in the warming hut, here for the night. I quickly pitched my tent outside, as this area is infested with mosquitoes, and ate dinner in the hut with them.

Highlights (and lowlights) of the day:

Great sunrise.

Climbed a fire tower at the 7.5-mile mark.

Mud, mud, mud.

A young guy smoking a joint as we looked out over Prospect Rock. I declined his invitation to partake.

Got sidetracked when my mind drifted and I ended up on a blue blaze, then in knee-deep water. Had to backtrack.

Stratton Pond. In a word, magnificent.

No problems with swelling feet.

Soundtrack playing the flute at sunset.

Full moon.

AUGUST 5 | BULLY BROOK, 22.2 MILES, 1,665.8 MILES TOTAL

I am out before sunrise once again.

I met a thru-hiker named Slapshot at a shelter. He is so named because he wears his hair in a mullet, inspiring his friends to say he looks like Barry Melrose, the hockey commentator and coach. Then I caught a guy named Everready, a long-time section hiker in his tenth year of hiking the trail. He will complete next year if he stays healthy. He asked if I was a thru-hiker, and then asked me how far I had hiked today, and I told him seventeen miles, with a little more than five to go. He just looked at me, shook his head, and said, "Damn, you must have legs of steel."

I have great respect for section hikers. They do this once a year for a couple weeks. They just get their "trail legs" under them, and then have to get off trail. Then do the same thing next year. Section hiking may be more difficult than hiking through.

I hiked by gorgeous and pristine Little Rock Pond, where Boy Scouts from a local troop took turns jumping off a big rock on the other side of the pond, their voices echoing.

> As I watched the boys I had the little flashback of our company hiking down a river in Vietnam, knee deep. We had our five meters apart going for us, when I noticed the guy in front of me had a couple strange black marks on his neck. I asked him to hold up so I could remove them, but when I neared, I was sickened by what I saw. Leeches. The black marks were leeches on his neck. I got on my radio and let the rest of the company know. We were holding up for a moment when I noticed I had one on my hand. And my arm was covered. And my legs. Ditto for everyone else in the company. We pulled out of the river and spent a good hour burning those suckers off our bodies. We used cigarettes. Light one and put the hot ash end near the blood-sucking leech and it simply drops off. So gross.

I keep looking in the shelters for a note from Cosmos, but have found nothing to this point. I become disappointed at not finding anything.

I have a big day ahead of me tomorrow, up Mt. Killington, 19.2 miles. I want to get there by 4 p.m., before the snack bar on top of the mountain closes. I have a burger and ice cream on my mind.

I found a picturesque area overlooking the valleys below, complete with a flat spot to pitch the tent. Heavenish. I cooked a great meal of chicken and pasta, then ate a big fat candy bar for dessert.

No fly on the tent tonight. I will look at the stars.
A restful night with a bright moon.

AUGUST 6 | KILLINGTON MOUNTAIN, 19.2 MILES, 1,684.1 MILES TOTAL

I hopped out of the tent early, ate a little breakfast, packed up my shit, and moved out. The time was 6 a.m. After walking three miles or so at a rapid pace down the mountain, thinking about a myriad of things, I realized I was seeing blue blazes on the trees, not white. Damn, I had missed a turn. I had to climb back up the mountain I had just come down. Eventually, I found my mistake, and figured I had added at least three miles to my day's journey. I got up in the dark to make this mistake?

After I found my way back on the trail, I saw a big plump porcupine waddling down the trail in front of me. I quickly forgot about the blue blaze screw-up and realized I never would have seen this cute little critter if I had gone the right way in the beginning. He heard me coming and hustled off the trail, if you can call a snail's pace hustling.

Today's hike was hellacious. The sixty-five miles in three days to get to this point after partying with the boys has taken its toll. The ups were big, the downs were steep, and they were coupled with enormous jagged rocks. I feel tired and weak, but determined to summit. I rested two miles from the top, knowing I would make it by 4, snack bar closing time. I drank mass quantities of water today, and feel like I sweated out the same amount.

I arrived at the summit of Killington Peak and felt major relief. I searched and found the shelter. There were three packs in it and I recognized one: Cosmos'. I have hiked 84.6 miles in four days, in the big mountains of Vermont. I pushed myself to do something I had not done before, and I probably won't ever do again.

After dropping my pack, I took a short hike up to the top of the peak, looking for the snack bar at the ski resort. Slapshot joined me. We found it, and there, sitting by the window, were three people: Cosmos' family. She spotted me. I stunned her. The elation I felt when I saw her was indescribable. I could tell she felt the same way. I met her brother, Reese, and her mom, Leah. I ate some snack bar food and we chatted. Cosmos just stared at me, saying she couldn't believe I hiked that far, that fast.

We all walked back down to the shelter and sat around and talked for a while, then took a different trail to the top to watch the sunset. A beautiful one it was. I met a young guy there named Doug, a tall, bespectacled cross-country runner and pianist. He is hiking with his mom, his best friend, and his best friend's mom, to the Long Trail Inn.

Cold tonight, but cuddling up to Cosmos was warm and wonderful.

AUGUST 7 | LONG TRAIL INN, BETWEEN RUTLAND AND KILLINGTON, VERMONT, 9.7 MILES, 1,694.6 MILES TOTAL

I got up early and watched Reese and Leah pack up their stuff. They have been hiking for a few days and seem to be in great spirits. We hiked swiftly, and then blue-blazed off the trail to the Long Trail Inn. I remembered the Tall Grass quote from way back at the ice cream place: "The world's best Guinness." And my Cosmos loves Guinness.

We arrived at 3 p.m. Hiking with Leah and Reese was a treat. For not being on the trail long, they seem to be strong hikers, yet are already starting to have those little aches and pains familiar to all thru-hikers. They have been with Cosmos for six days, which was a wonderful thing for their family. Leah now must have a good idea of what her daughter is accomplishing.

The Long Trail Inn is one of my favorite spots on the trail, equipped with great food (shepherd's pie), great desserts, great beer, and quaint little rooms. Cosmos is sleeping in her mom and brother's room, but sneaking down here from time to time.

Later in the evening we were treated to some great live Irish music courtesy of the Blarney Band. I met an older man (my age) who was hiking the long trail, a 272-miler. He was elated he had come this far and was determined to finish. He asked me if I was a hiker, at which time I informed him I was hiking a hundred miles or so of the Long Trail, but was actually hiking the Appalachian Trail. He asked if I was a section hiker. I said no. He then asked, with a puzzled look on his face, if I was a thru-hiker, I said yes I was. Then he asked how far I had come to get to this point. When I said, "almost seventeen hundred miles," he about shit his pants. I will always remember that look on his face.

Doug, the pianist and cross-country runner from the trail, played the piano for us later in the evening. He played two songs, making them both up as he went. His music was so beautiful, I almost cried. Cosmos met me in my room for a goodnight kiss.

We will go to a hiker feed in Rutland tomorrow.

AUGUST 8, ZERO

We were up early and treated to a breakfast (part of the deal when you stay here) that rivaled Deb's in Damascus, Virginia. Eggs, French toast, fruit, etc. Doug played a couple more songs after breakfast. I notice he has eyes for Cosmos.

Cosmos and her family bussed to Rutland, and I walked to the post office. After picking up a package from my sister Charlee, I hitched to Rutland. All the years since I last hitched and now, on the trail, the action feels so comfortable.

Cosmos's family and I secured a room at the Comfort Inn in town. After a relaxing swim and hot tub, we went to the hiker fest, a celebration honoring thru-hikers. It was a nice event, although somewhat boring. I think this was the first year they had it. There was decent live music and a few vendors, but the highlight for me was playing croquet with Cosmos and her family. Cosmos bought a dress at a thrift store and looked gorgeous in it. I feel a connection with her mom and Reese.

I am in bed fairly early after a trip to Ben and Jerry's. There are masses of thru-hikers here.

AUGUST 9

Zero, though didn't mean it to be.

We had breakfast, continental style, which in no way compared to the Long Trail Inn.

Cosmos's family left at 9 or so for Michigan. They loved hiking and both Reese and Leah committed to hiking the entire trail someday.

We gathered up all our stuff and together took the bus back to the Long Trail Inn to head out where we left off. Our plan was to blue blaze up the trail to the white blazes, but by the time we got back to the inn from Rutland, we were hungry again. So we ate another fantastic Long Trail Inn meal, then we ran into Tall Grass at the bar, who was there with his fiancé. We had no idea he even had a girlfriend. After we were done eating and shooting the shit with Tall Grass, we had killed a lot of daylight hiking time. By the time we would get back on trail, it would be 2 p.m. We looked at each other mischievously and said, "Let's do another zero." And we did. This place is like a magnet. We can't get away. We relaxed, napped, watched some TV, ate another good meal, and played some games. We took some photos of Tall Grass's feet, which were unbelievably filthy. He will be off the trail soon, as his mom is home and he wants to finish the trail with her someday.

AUGUST 10 | WINTTURI SHELTER, 16.6 MILES, 1,712 MILES TOTAL

We had to treat ourselves to one more awesome Long Trail Inn breakfast before we embarked to the trail. We immediately got back in the groove. It was so good to be back with Cosmos. I can't say I breezed through this day, because after zeroes I usually struggle a bit. I gave much thought today regarding what lies ahead in New Hampshire. The White Mountains. I keep telling myself to remember what I'm Fine told me twenty miles into this hike: "When you get to the Whites, you will be in such great physical condition you will blow right on through them." But still, I feel intimidated thinking about those mountains.

We had hummus and peanut butter sandwiches for dinner, Butterfingers and Snickers for dessert. Interesting that this shelter, which could hold up to ten people in a pinch, is vacant. There are seven other thru-hikers here, and all are tenting. There was lots of storytelling and laughter during and after dinner. I love the goodness of this trail.

We were all in bed early. I passed 1,700 miles today.

AUGUST 11 | PODUNK BROOK, 17.8 MILES, 1,729.8 MILES TOTAL

We were schooled by the heavens again last night. The rain flowed. The tent started leaking just enough to be irritating, but we were up in the early a.m., treated to beautiful sunshine. We ate breakfast and planned a sixteen miler today, but then we saw an option of getting off the trail after 3.4 miles and walking down a road .02 miles to the On the Edge Farm, an eatery. We took the option. I wolfed down a whole blueberry pie and some ice cream. Then I chugged a Gatorade, packed out some ham, chicken, chips, Fritos, and Cheetos for dinner tonight, and headed for the white blazes.

I wonder how long it will take me to recover from this trek. I fell many times today, which is incredibly rough on a body, but I was strong and I made it to West Hartford before the store closed, running into Jellyfish and Slapshot.

I waited at the store for Cosmos. When she arrived we hiked right on through town and into the woods, finding a nice flat spot to tent just off the trail. We no sooner got the tent up when the rains came.

We are closing in on New Hampshire, my thirteenth state, where we will resupply and possibly do a zero. Or maybe a nero.

New Hampshire

AUGUST 12
HANOVER, NEW HAMPSHIRE, 8.4 MILES, 1,738.2
MILES TOTAL

Only one more state ahead of me. Hanover is the home of Dartmouth University, and New Hampshire is the home of the White Mountains. This state will be a challenge.

When we walked across the Connecticut River Bridge, separating Vermont from New Hampshire, a guy was sitting and waiting, just inside New Hampshire, with a couple coolers and chairs. He waved us over with a huge grin on his face, saying, "Are you thru-hikers? I have trail magic for you," and proceeded to dole out cold beer, soda, and cookies.

Don't Panic, Winging It, and Tarzan (other thru-hikers) joined us. They had recently hiked the Pacific Crest Trail. I asked them about the differences in the two, and Don't Panic quickly responded, "I liked the Pacific Crest." I took that to mean the AT does not suit her as well.

We walked into town (the trail goes right through Hanover) after the trail magic, and plopped down at a bus stop, waiting for a ride to a motel on the outskirts of town. We sat and watched all the students hustling and bustling around town, taking it all in.

We found a little motel out of town. I did our laundry and we took a hot shower and hitched a ride from two students back to town. The first thing we did was go to a pizza place where thru-hikers get free pizza and beer.

I walked across the street to the local bank to use the ATM, and the name of the bank happened to be Lake Sunapee Bank. I was pleasantly stunned, remembering staying near Lake Sunapee in New London for a couple weeks one summer way back in 1963. My friend and I hitched there more than forty years ago. My sister Eve worked at Lake Sunapee Country Club. I caddied there. Great memories flooded my mind.

I went to the library, the outfitter, and the post office, then to a little restaurant for pizza and beer with Slapshot, Otter, Jellyfish and Windbreaker, the banjo player, whom I hadn't seen since Woodshole, back in Virginia. It was fantastic fun hanging with the fellow hikers off the trail, even though most of our conversations were "trail talk." A major part of the AT experience is hearing others' experiences on the trail.

Cosmos and I went to Ben and Jerry's for dessert. I had a very relaxing evening, although Cosmos was a bit stressed, having been on a bus all day, looking for gear.

I received my WRC (Women's Resource Center) Patagonia shirt in the mail. Women and children who are victims of domestic violence is one of the charities for which I hike.

I also received my winter sleeping bag from Thom, and sent my lighter one home. It's going to get cold up above treeline.

AUGUST 13

Zero, but it wasn't supposed to be.

I shaved yesterday with a dull razor left in the motel room. My face looks like someone hacked it with an ice pick.

Today is my sister Eve's birthday, and I started my day by giving her a call.

We bussed to town and found a little eatery named Lou's, where I devoured an omelet. Cosmos is searching for a winter sleeping bag and wants to go online to buy one, so to the library we went. She saw Storyteller and he informed her he was getting off the trail. After 1,700 miles! He didn't want Cosmos to say anything to anyone as he wanted to quietly move on.

While she searched, I got caught up on all my e-mails, but my thoughts kept drifting to the Whites. We are only forty-five miles away. I find myself intimidated, and trying to stay motivated because we have such big hikes ahead.

I had another brilliant idea. "Hey, Cosmos, why don't we just hang out here for a bit, go to a 4 p.m. movie, pig out on some popcorn, and then hike into the woods just a bit and tent?" She agreed. Cosmos got a good sleeping bag. Then we went to dinner at a local eatery.

I feel no motivation to hike. We headed to any movie that was playing after dinner. The movie turned out to be an Iraq war movie, "The Hurt Locker." It was very intense. I wish I hadn't seen it because it conjured up war thoughts when I thought I was getting a handle on those powerful feelings. I became quiet, saying I was tired.

We went back to the motel to bed. After watching that war movie, I lay in bed and said to myself, "I need to get back on the trail."

AUGUST 14 | TRAPPER JOHN SHELTER, 16.7 MILES, 1,754.9 MILES TOTAL

We bussed into town early and had breakfast at Lou's. We were packed up and ready to go and I knew I was in for a long day of thinking after the movie last night, but the hiking turned out to be easy today because my mind was elsewhere.

There are seven other hikers here, and again, none staying in the shelter. All are tenting. Otter. Jellyfish. Others.

Slapshot had a friend pick him up in Hanover and drive him to the nearest airport, where he flew to Jamaica for a friend's wedding. From the AT to Jamaica, now that's a first. He said he will catch up with everyone when he gets back on the trail. A tough task given the fact he will be eighty miles behind the way everyone is hiking these days.

We ate our meal with all the folks, all thru-hikers. More storytelling and laughter. These people all seem so genuine with no hidden agendas.

Rested gratefully this evening, thankful that Cosmos was by my side.

AUGUST 15 | MOUNT CUBE, 13.4 MILES, 1,768.3 MILES TOTAL

We had huge uphill climbs today. And, as always, rocky and dangerous downhills.

We went up and over Smart Mountain, taking a break at the firewatch station, and then hiked on to Mount Cube. We are back in the deep woods, like down south. No cell service. We thought we were at our destination, arriving early. I was excited for some relax time, but we had misread the map, and could see Cube in the distance. Damn. We hiked on.

The top of Cube is a series of huge boulders, some flat. We are spending the night, cowboy/cowgirl style. No tent will be pitched. We will simply sleep on our thermarests on top of the boulders, under the stars and the moon.

We ate dinner and quietly watched a beautiful sunset over the mountains.

It seems like every time I look up I see beautiful mountains, lakes, streams, and trees. I am overwhelmed. I feel blessed to still be a part of this. I feel fortunate I can walk. As sore as I am, I am trying to savor these moments of bliss, because we are getting close to our destination. And then what?

AUGUST 16 | GLENCLIFF, NEW HAMPSHIRE, HIKERS WELCOME HOSTEL, 13.2
MILES, 1,781.5 MILES TOTAL

We were up before dawn, but ate breakfast together watching a beautiful sunrise. I long for my friends and children to experience just a fraction of what I see daily.

I am packed and ready to go. Had a bit of dew on the bag, but packed it up as I am anxious to get moving. I had a great night here on the Cube. Every once in a while I woke, rolled onto my back, opened my eyes, and gazed at the stars for a bit before I fell back asleep.

Cosmos chose to stay and let her bag dry. I have happy feet and move out. I hiked all day by myself, feeling good. I took two breaks. The first was at Ore Hill Shelter. As I sat at the shelter, listening to the quiet and ate a Snickers, I heard a loud noise and movement to my front, maybe ten meters. I didn't move. I felt fidgety to put it mildly.

> Eventually, the noise moved the other way through the forest. I breathed a sigh of relief and once again was left to my thoughts: Someone saying "I hear movement," and my friend, the late Sergeant Andretti.

I took my second break overlooking Mt. Moose and a beautiful, picturesque pond. I saw my first fox. I waited for Cosmos to catch me and we walked to Glencliff, New Hampshire, and the Hikers Welcome Hostel. Uncle Walt is caretaking the place and they offer tons of movies. I did the laundry while Cosmos showered, then it was my turn (Uncle Walt had a great outdoor shower). He gave us a ride to town to resupply, waited for us, and then dropped us at a small pub/restaurant so we could eat dinner. We ate with Hammock, a nice guy, thin, with long dreads. I told him the story about I'm Fine and his dreads. He was so inspired by the story he later cut off his dreads at the hostel.

We hitched back to the hostel and got a ride from a young woman. Others offered, but they were too drunk. We ended up pitching our tent on the lawn rather than staying in the hostel because of the bugs and heat. Plus the tent is home, a place we always feel safe. This night, hiker midnight was 9:30 p.m.

We probably would have stayed up and watched a movie, but the guys were watching regular TV, a Rocky marathon. "No way," we said. Here we have a hostel with all these great movies, and these guys are watching a Rocky marathon on regular TV, complete with commercials.

Tomorrow, after months of anticipation and hoopla, we will enter the White Mountains. The time is here. Up Mt. Moosilauke, elevation 4,802 feet, from our location of at 1,000 feet. We will summit in six miles. Here we go.

AUGUST 17 | LINCOLN, NEW HAMPSHIRE 9.5 MILES, 1,791 MILES TOTAL

We are up early, feeling anxious and antsy at what lies ahead. We had a slight delay because Cosmos had a package coming to the post office across the street. We ended up pulling out at 8:15. I am nervous, feeling similar to how I felt when I first started hiking back in March.

The trail was flat for just a bit, then we began ascending. We were into the Whites. They are upon us. Or, we are upon them. After all those months and months of anticipation and wondering if I'm capable. After all the talk from the south-bounders about how treacherous and difficult this section is, I am here. All those discouraging words and now we are about to find out for ourselves.

I gave Cosmos a kiss just before we started climbing Moosilauke at 8:30. A big climb it was.

We summited at 10:30, and I was elated. *That wasn't bad,* I thought. I'm Fine was right. I pretty much bounded up this mountain, my adrenalin driving me, never even stopping to catch my wind. *I can do this,* I thought. This is the first time on the AT I have been above tree line. Clingmans Dome was higher, but not above tree line. Cosmos was right behind me and we treated each other to a snack on top, chatting with other hikers. I called my son Jonathon to tell him of my accomplishment, knowing he would be excited for me.

I wandered around the top of the mountain and struck up a conversation with a couple guys who had day hiked here, an all-day event. These guys, Woody and Ned, were simply awed that I had hiked more than 1,700 miles. This is something they have always dreamed of. Woody sported a beard, was 55 or so, and soft-spoken. Ned was about the same age, was clean-shaven and inquisitive. Both seemed quite educated. Woody gifted me a loaf of his homemade banana bread before they began their descent. I brought it over to my fellow thru-hikers and shared.

Some thirty minutes later, we began our descent. We are trying to get to Eliza Brook Shelter, seventeen miles from the beginning. On the way down I passed Woody and Ned.

The descent was frightening, extremely rocky throughout. We were heading almost straight down, 3,500 feet in three miles. I remember MoFo saying the descent was like an elevator shaft. Today was not the day to fall, because one slip and I would be history. But it was tremendously beautiful, with waterfalls cascading down on one side of me and deep woods on the other. We passed many day hikers who were on their way up, seemingly all asking, "How much further to the top?"

Halfway down I got off trail a bit and found the Beaver Brook Shelter just to check the register to see how far out front other friends might be. Cosmos waited on the trail. The banana bread guys, Woody and Ned, hiked by Cosmos and offered up their condo for the evening if we so desired. Cosmos didn't seem interested.

After checking the register, I hiked on (I am faster on downhills than Cosmos is, she is faster on the uphills). I made it to the bottom and passed a parking lot, about to sit and wait for Cosmos and there in the parking lot were the banana bread guys. I talked to them for a bit, and they once again extended the offer of a condo for the evening. They said they would buy some cold beer, take us to dinner, and get us back on the trail tomorrow at whatever time we desired. These were extremely nice guys. I felt connected.

Cosmos arrived and I met her on the trail and delivered my best sales pitch about staying with Ned and Woody. I talked her into it. She wasn't pleased at first, "You change your mind so much," but she relented. We threw our packs into the back of their car, and we rode with them to Lincoln, New Hampshire. We had hiked a total of 9.5 miles. Not a big day miles-wise, but for us a big day psychologically. I know I can climb these mountains, this being one of the biggest, according to the map.

Ned and Woody were exemplary hosts. Ned stopped to get some beer, we went back to their condo, chatted, drank beer, and ate some snacks for about an hour. Then they took us to the pool and hot tub area. We swam, soaked, and talked. Then we were treated to a luxurious shower, if a shower can be luxurious. It sure felt like such. We were expecting to open our thermarests and sleep on the floor of this one-bedroom condo, but Ned had spoken with the condo boss, who allowed us to stay in a private bedroom adjacent to theirs, equipped with a huge king bed, a big bathroom, and cable TV. As I describe the room, it sounds like an ordinary room. For a thru-hiker, after almost 1,800 miles of being in the woods, it was pure extravagance.

We had dinner in town and lovely it was. I feel like I have known these guys my whole life. They are easy company. After dinner, we hit an ice cream place (of course), then back to the condo, and bed. Sweet dreams.

AUGUST 18 | LONESOME LAKE HUT, 13 MILES, 1,804 MILES TOTAL

Ned knocked on our door at about 6 a.m. We were packed and ready to go. He and Woody took us to the post office, deli, and breakfast.

At the post office was a package containing a Patagonia Yesterdog t-shirt complete with my name, Naneek, on the back, sent to me by Yesterdog owner Bill Lewis, a friend I have known since high school. Yesterdog is a well-known hot dog spot in Grand Rapids, Michigan. I love this shirt.

Bill Lewis has always been a special person in my life. A quipster is he. Bill, Steve Bourgoin, and I lived together at 122 Mayfield in Grand Rapids. This was our first venture from our parents' wings. It was November of 1966, I was 20 years old, and all of us were out of school (a dangerous move with the war raging in Vietnam), but prepared to enroll at Grand Rapids Junior College in January of 1967.

We moved into this house for one reason: to party. And party we did. We rented a furnished house from an elderly couple who had moved to Florida and only charged us a hundred bucks a month. None of us were working so we charged our friends $10 a month to come and party any day, anytime. We came out ahead on that deal. A typical day for us? Get up at 1 p.m. or so. Bill would cook dinner, Steve would go to the store and pick up a case of quarts, and I would set up the Monopoly board. We rotated our daily chore. We had a party every night of the week. We only allowed our friends to drink quarts, as we could turn them in for a deposit now and then and get a free case.

All went well for a couple months until we got the dreadful correspondence from Uncle Sam ordering us to get our physicals. And, what seemed like only a couple weeks later, came that fateful letter: "Greetings, you are hereby ordered to report to the bus station in downtown Grand Rapids, MI, on February 7, 1967. From there you will be transported to Detroit, for induction into the United States Army." Failure to show was a $5,000 fine and five years in prison.

The party was over.

Bill, Steve, and I got on the same bus for Detroit. We went through basic training together. When we got our orders for advanced individual training, Bill and I got infantry, Steve got air reconnaissance, all of us went to Vietnam and all of us somehow survived. After a while there, Bill, the quipster, sent Secretary of Defense Robert McNamara his "two-week notice." He thanked McNamara for giving him a job when he was unemployed, but he had decided to pursue other opportunities. Neither the food nor the living conditions suited him.

He got no response, but those he shared the letter with got a good laugh.

Even though Cosmos and I hadn't spent all that much time with Ned and Woody, we still found it hard saying goodbye, their generosity of a night in the condo being the ultimate trail magic.

After getting back on the trail and hiking a few miles, we stopped for lunch near a stream. Zipper, a tall, thin, attractive woman and a former teacher walked up looking haggard and disheveled. She said she was struggling big time today. We all know that feeling.

We hiked off after lunch and found more waterfalls, one complete with a swimming hole. I went skinny dipping. Cosmos was uncomfortable with me doing this, but I said, "We are out in the middle of the White Mountains. The only people we could possibly see are thru-hikers, and they certainly don't give a shit." Cosmos hiked on alone, but the swim rejuvenated me. I caught up to her and we hiked hard up Mt. Kinsman, elevation 4,358 feet. The scene was sheer beauty.

The hike down was ugly! The beauty turned to misery and my knees took a beating. The danger of the downhill had me proceeding with extreme caution.

We hiked the tough miles to the Lonesome Lake Hut. We had heard about the huts in the Whites before, but had no idea they were so large. We are used to the shelter lean-tos that sleep six to eight people, but Lonesome Lake Hut is huge, equipped with a giant kitchen and several bunkhouses. It was surreal to step out of the woods and see this massive structure. They have a "Cru" (students from various colleges) that works the place for the season. Section hikers pay around $90 per night to stay here, and they are usually filled to capacity. Reservations are required for the section- and day-hikers, whereas thru-hikers can work for lodging and food at no cost. We call it "work for stay."

We arrived near dark and were treated to delicious leftover chicken soup and bread, and for a bonus, ice-cold lemonade. I washed windows and sills and Cosmos did the dishes. The work-for-stay includes leftovers after breakfast tomorrow morning, but we will be long gone by that time.

Jellyfish, Otter, Miles, and others are here. We are all in bed at hiker midnight.

I have now walked more than 1,800 miles.

AUGUST 19 | AMC-GALEHEAD HUT, 15.9 MILES, 1,819.9 MILES TOTAL

How can I ever explain to my friends, my family, and others the astonishing beauty of this experience? There are writers and others who have hiked the AT who have described what I am seeing daily far better than I. I simply know that you have to experience this trip to believe it.

I drank the best water of my life today at a spring, a bit past the summit of Mt. Lafayette.

We stopped for a break atop Mt. Lafayette, gawking at the beauty surrounding us. We couldn't help but notice two section-hiking couples carrying huge, huge packs. One of the guys had a .357 magnum strapped to his waist, and the magazines for it secured around his ankles. This is the first weapon I have seen on the trail. We hiked quickly past them.

We summited Mt. Lafayette (elevation 5,249 feet) and Mt. Garfield (elevation 4,488 feet). These were tough climbs, but also exceptionally rewarding. Hiking the AT is a spiritual experience. I feel like a grain of sand on a beach in these mountains. Every difficult climb is rewarded by magic at the summit. The hiking over the past months has been beautiful in its own right, but this beauty is in another league.

Cosmos and I had some differences over the mileage we are doing, but we ironed them out. The only time we have differences these days is over mileage. She struggled today. There were no flat spots out here to pitch a tent so we had to keep moving to reach the hut, as darkness was descending.

This hut was teeming with thru-hikers when we arrived. The Cru usually allows a max of four thru-hikers work for stay; then, if more want to stay, it is $15. If there is leftover food, we can eat. We paid. We ate. There are no beds available, all being full with day and section hikers, but the thru-hikers are allowed to sleep on the floor or on the dining-room tables. Lights out at 9 p.m., which is perfect for us.

Some older section hikers, who had reservations, came in late, well past 10 p.m., as they struggled to get here. Everyone was in bed, but they had reservations. It was dark in the dining room when they arrived, but the Cru fixed them a meal and they quietly ate dinner at the far end of the room. One section hiker saw all the bodies sleeping on the tables, but didn't know what they were because of the darkness. He said to his friend, "What is that stuff on all the tables?" The Cru guy said, "Thru-hikers." Those of us who were still awake laughed aloud, as did the guy who asked the question.

AUGUST 20 | CABIN AT THE CRAWFORD NOTCH GENERAL STORE, 14.7 MILES, 1,834.6 MILES TOTAL

We were on the trail before sunrise. Our initial climb was a steep one up South Twin Mountain (elevation 4,902). We summited and watched a stunning sunrise. Fog and clouds were hovering, making the rise of the sun incredibly beautiful. These times make me feel so free.

We hiked on to the Zeeland Hut and stopped for some soup. We met and talked with the Cru. Jellyfish and Otter were there, taking a break for lunch.

As we were hiking down South Twin, we met a southbound woman section-hiker who spewed negativity about what lay ahead for us. She said not one positive thing and then, as if to prove her point, she fell into a bush along the trail. It was quite funny, although I didn't laugh at the time.

We hiked past Ethan Pond and onward to Crawford Notch, where we were met with trail magic as we hiked through a parking lot. A man talking to a section hiker treated us to cold soda pop and chips. We talked with him for a few minutes when another man pulled up in a car and offered to drive us to some cabins at Crawford Notch. Done deal. Can't pass that up. We are in. The guy dropped us off at the Crawford Notch General Store and we got a cabin for the night. Another hiker is also here, Hitch.

I did our laundry. I found out where Hitch was staying and invited him over for some hot dogs, chips, and beer. Cosmos is a splendid host. She starts a fire, I get some hot dogs and fixings from the store, and she makes us a meal like only she can, out of hot dogs. We sit around until 11 p.m. or so, just shooting the shit. It turns out Hitch had been off the trail, injured, and was just back on it. After tomorrow, I probably will never see him again, even though he heads north, same as us.

AUGUST 21 | LAKES OF THE CLOUDS HUT, 11.2 MILES, 1,845.8 MILES TOTAL

After packing up, we had a quick breakfast at the store. Then we tried hitching by the road, and for a change, had no luck. Minutes later, Hitch, who was sitting in the front of the store, yelled and waved at us. He had a guy who would give us a ride to the trailhead.

The driver was going to drop us off at the trailhead, but not where we left off. We would actually miss some 200 meters of the trail. I asked if he would drive down this two-track and drop us where we left off. He agreed. No problem. At this stage I will take no shortcuts. I will do every inch of this trail.

We were up in the mountains all day. The twenty-five-mile section between Crawford and Pinkham Notch is called the Presidential Range, the peaks all being named after former Presidents.

We met three women thru-hiking south. We talked with them for a bit and told them they were close to the Nauman tent site, where they were stopping for the day. They seemed like fun people to hike with for a few days, but they are going the wrong way. We see few women on the trail. The ratio is probably 20:1, men to women. I don't know why, other than fear. Women hike as strongly as the men.

We had what seemed like a straight-up climb to the peak of Mt. Webster. Then down. Then up to Mt. Jackson. Then down. Then up Mt. Clinton. Then down. Then up Mt. Pierce. Then down. Then up Mt. Eisenhower. Then down. Then up Mt. Franklin. Then down. Whew!

On one of the summits, gray jays ate cashews out of Cosmos' hand. They landed on her hand and ate from it.

Met up and began hiking with the Wiz Kid at Mizpah Spring Hut. We contemplated whether to push on, because of a possible storm moving in. It was early so the decision was made, the goal being the hut before Mr. Washington, the highest point in the Whites. Wiz Kid is with us.

The storm moved in on us quickly. First the rains came. We are above treeline, so we had no cover. The rocks were slippery, the hike treacherous. The rain kept coming, and we kept walking. Then we got the high winds. Then thunder. Then lightning, cracking all around. Bizarre, as we were actually in the storm. It wasn't above us, we were right in the middle of it!

At first I wanted to keep pushing, as we were but a couple miles from our destination, but the storm was too intense. I had never been in this situation before, and became concerned for our safety. Lightning was cracking and the thunder was penetrating my brain. There was no joking around at this point. We were all scared. We got off the trail, hid behind some boulders, and put Wiz Kid's poncho over us. We crouched and waited, soaking wet, praying we wouldn't get hit by the lightning. I was shivering and started thinking about hypothermia. We stayed about a half hour, not moving and just when we'd decided we should hike on as the storm was beginning to subside, a crack of lightning hit dangerously close. We tried to laugh to keep from crying. We stayed for a few more minutes, letting the storm lessen and then made our move. I was miserable. I was shivering and cold, but said nothing to Wiz Kid or Cosmos about my condition. They led out. I followed, shivering and scared. We hiked quickly and the walking warmed me. We could see the storm moving southeast. The terrain and sky once again turned beautiful, with the clouds hovering.

We could see Mt. Washington when we were hiking. I have dreamed of this for months. I felt elated as we neared the Lakes of the Clouds hut. We hiked 11.2 life-changing miles today. I am so glad to be here.

When we entered the hut we found it packed with section hikers and about ten thru-hikers. The thru-hikers sat at a table away from the day and section hikers, who were somewhat awed by the thru-hikers' presence. They were very inquisitive.

We were treated to a great meal and dessert after the paying customers had finished their dinner. Thru-hikers love leftovers. If someone doesn't eat the food, the Cru has to hike it off the mountain. They hike all the food up here, and they don't want to hike it back down.

Once again it was work for stay, and I was directed to straighten the bookshelf, which took me all of ten minutes. Cosmos was in the kitchen, scrubbing down the cupboards. She quit after she saw me doing nothing. Wiz Kid did a workshop, which was a question and answer for all the patrons. The folks had lots of questions regarding the thru-hike.

Lights out at 9 p.m. I blew up my thermarest and put it on a dining table, crawled into my warm sleeping bag and, with a full stomach, put on my headlamp, and wrote this. What an eventful day it was. I am happy for my life. Mother Nature sure got my attention.

AUGUST 22 | OSGOOD'S TENT SITE, 10 MILES, 1,855.8 MILES TOTAL

As was planned, we were up and gone before the section hikers were out of bed. We summited Mt. Washington (6,288 feet) at sunrise, accomplishing another milestone. We stayed up here for a bit, trying to get phone service to call my sisters, my son Jonathon, and the rest of my children, hoping to tell them of my whereabouts. Nope.

Once on the trail, an older woman section hiker (my age) approached, hiking towards us with her husband. Neither of them were carrying packs, so they probably had driven a car to a side trail. She was heading up towards Mt. Washington while we were descending. She did not budge on the trail, offering no room for us to stay on trail with our large packs, so Cosmos walked just off the trail to let her by. The woman said snootily, "No, honey, don't walk on the tundra. You don't want to ruin the growth up here." I am behind Cosmos and the woman looked at me and said, "Can't teach 'em anything, can we?" I responded, "She has hiked fifteen hundred miles. She knows what she is doing." The woman's husband responded, "If she's hiked fifteen hundred miles, you would think she would know better."

Ugh. End of conversation.

We stopped at Madison Spring Hut for lunch. The Cru served us bottomless vegetable soup, bread, and lemonade. We probably should have stayed there, as nightfall was approaching, but we pushed on.

Climbing down Mt. Madison took more than three hours. The mountain was a mass of huge, jagged boulders. There was no dirt to be seen. We had to be cautious, trying hard not to slip, knowing we would bust our asses if we did. Rain and slippery boulders are a bad combination for Naneek.

We fell short of our goal today, the terrain, fog, and rain slowing our progress. We pitched our tent on a platform in the rain. We settled in after eating our dinner. I am keenly aware of my senses and offer up a startling observation to Cosmos. "We both reek."

My eyes close to the sound of pouring rain.

August 23 | Carter Notch Hut, 10.7 miles, 1,866.5 miles total

We left the site at 8 a.m. and hiked quickly the 4.7 miles to the Pinkham Notch Lodge in 2.5 hours. A remarkably easy hike it was. We are going to have some kind of brunch before we complete our day's journey. I saw a guy with a Tybee Island (Georgia) shirt on and got so excited to talk to him. I approached him and started talking about Tybee. He looked at me and politely walked away. *Do I look that bad?* I thought. *Do I stink that bad?* I guess I do.

We are going to try to conquer the Wildcat Peaks today. All rocks, of course. As I put my pack on, I looked to where we are headed. I just shook my head.

The hike ended up being almost straight up. It sure felt that way. We summited Peak E and looked down 2,500 feet to the lodge below. It looked miniscule. Again, as I have so many times in the past, I pinched myself. Cosmos was out in front of me somewhere when I came upon what I thought were three section hikers. They were reluctant to let this old man pass, but I was a moving machine and blew right on by.

We had phone service on top. I called my children, Morganne, Jake, Jonathon, Colin (no answer, haven't had any correspondence since May), and my sisters. I wore a huge smile the rest of the day.

We hiked on until 5:30 p.m. We did, in fact, conquer all the Wildcats, five peaks. Up and down. Elevations of 4,041; 4,063; 4,270; 4,270; and 4,380 feet. I kept thinking, if only there were a bridge from peak to peak!

I passed a guy along the trail who was trying to fix a trekking pole, swearing. He was trying to restore it with duct tape and a branch. Good luck. He said it was his hiking partner's, and he had stepped on it and broken it because he was tailgating her. Prairie Dog is his name. A tall, strapping man, with a quick wit, he had long hair and a scraggily beard. He wore a kilt and a woman's headband.

Cosmos is out in front of me once again and soon the Prairie Dog passes me. I am heading up a steep section, one where you don't want to lose your footing and fall, because you will be dead. I thought I saw Cosmos up front of me, then realized it was another woman. She was slow-moving, deliberate with her steps, and very talkative. Her name is Angry Beaver, the Prairie Dog's hiking partner. She would not let me pass, so I talked to her and listened to her talk. We had a long conversation, and she was very likable. She is dark-skinned, short, and strong looking. Solid. She doesn't look like your typical thru-hiker.

After hiking a few miles with the Beaver, I heard a flute playing ahead, and the Beaver said that we must be getting near the hut, because the flute I hear is Prairie Dog. He always plays the flute when he is finished for the day.

Down we go to the hut. We worked for stay. Prairie Dog, Beaver, Cosmos, and I cleaned a storage room and had fun doing it. Then we had a great meal. Beaver and Cosmos partnered up against the Dog and me in a game of euchre. Miles is here, along with two young southbound flip-floppers. And of course there is an abundance of day and section hikers occupying all the bunks.

Miles is a bespectacled, dark-haired, twenty-something small in stature. He weighs in at probably 130 lbs. or so. He tells us the story of hiking into Hanover, New Hampshire, from Vermont. The trail runs right through town, and he is walking along, feeling very thirsty and hungry when he sees a cooler. His heart races. *Trail magic,* he thinks, as he approaches the cooler on a hot summer day. He opens it and finds two Gatorades, a sandwich, and a fruit salad. *This is wonderful,* thinks Miles, and he sits down on the grass, eats half the sandwich, drinks one of the Gatorades, and begins eating the fruit salad, just kicking back. All of a sudden he hears a scream and sees a guy running from across the street yelling, veins popping out of his neck, "What the fuck are you doing eating my lunch, Goddammit!" The guy was a construction worker. Miles was taken aback. He tried to explain trail magic and trail angels. He tried to pay for what he had eaten. He apologized over and over. The construction worker finally let Miles be on his way, but not before he told him he had prepared that lunch special for this hot, Friday afternoon. A funny tale, especially the way that Miles told it.

Some thru-hikers were turned away from the hut because there was no room. They had to move on. It pays to get up early and get to a hut before other thru-hikers arrive.

All the Crus have been wonderful, but this one was my favorite. They are truly thoughtful. A hiker came in late. There was no room here, but this guy was hurting from cold and aching badly. He could barely talk. The Cru got him some hot soup and bread and covered him with blankets in a bed in their room.

I slept on a table once again. Believe it or not, they are comfy.

With some luck, we hope to get to Gorham, New Hampshire, tomorrow. A zero could be beckoning. We haven't zeroed in more than 250 miles.

AUGUST 24 | GORHAM, NEW HAMPSHIRE, 15.2 MILES, 1,881.7 MILES TOTAL

I know I have said it before, but today could have been my worst hiking day ever. My knees ached. My feet ached. My back ached. It felt like my hair ached. I fell at least six times. I broke a trekking pole. Some dogs, owned by day hikers, barked and ran at me violently as I approached a shelter. I didn't care. All the beauty I saw today? I didn't care.

We went over Carter Dome, Middle Carter, and Mt. Moriah, then straight down 3,000 feet to Gorham. Cosmos had a jump in her step today. Not I, as I trudged along, head down. Even visions of a zero couldn't bring joy.

I found myself looking around today, feeling anxious. I should say my eyes darted back and forth. This is the first day in a long time I have seriously gazed about, looking for enemy. I tried to make myself relax, but could not. The stress sapped my energy.

Cosmos was standing in a parking lot as the trail winded down, talking to a couple of people. One guy had the trail name Hammer. He is a former thru-hiker out doing trail magic. He drove us right to town and dropped us at the Top Notch Inn. Ah, a hot tub just outside our door, next to the pool. I was almost completely exhausted. Some days you have it, some you don't. Physical stress is one thing, but today I had mental, emotional, and physical stress.

Cosmos and I had a great dinner at J's, next to the motel. I don't know if I would be where I am on this trail were it not for her. Just having her there when I suffer is reassuring.

In the morning we were lying in bed talking, planning our zero-day activity, when the owner opened our door with his key. He said, "Oops, I mistook the room, thought you had gone." Really, with our boots drying outside the door?

We are now actually out of the White Mountains. Unbelievable. In eight days we hiked more than one hundred, truly incredible, miles. Some days are extremely difficult, but never did I not feel proud of myself at day's end. All the months I had spent thinking about the Whites, and now they are a lifelong memory.

AUGUST 25 | ZERO

When the owner of the motel opened the door on us as we lay in bed, we immediately decided to move on. We moved to the Royalty Inn. This place also had a pool and hot tub, but we would never use them.

While Cosmos went to the store for food, I made my way to the library to update my correspondence to the folks back home. Afterward, I went to the local outfitter, per usual. I phoned the manufacturer of my shoes and pack at the outfitter's. The webbing of my shoes is ripping. We have been in mud and wet constantly, but these shoes are but a few hundred miles old. Then there is my pack. It is coming apart, but I do have lots of miles on it. The owner of the outfitter verified to the manufacturers my story. Both manufacturers (Osprey for the pack, Vasquez for the shoes) are extremely understanding and generous. After talking with the outfitter, Vasquez said they will send new shoes and Osprey said they would send a new pack to the Rangeley, Maine, post office. Right on. All I need to say to these manufacturers is, "I am thru-hiking."

Cosmos and I went to Mr. Pizza's for dinner. I arrived there a little earlier than her and bought her a martini. When she arrived, she had a card for me. We were thinking strongly about one another at precisely the same time.

I iced my knees for two-plus hours today. We had a nice zero, but it was way too busy.

I slept soundly in a soft, soft bed, resting my aching body.

AUGUST 26 | GENTIAN POND CAMPSITE SHELTER, 11.8 MILES, 1,893.5 MILES TOTAL

I ate breakfast alone. How quickly things can change for two people in a relationship. Cosmos and I were at odds over something stupid. I wanted to be alone. She wanted to be alone.

I had fruit and eggs while reading the paper. The first thing I look for when I read the news is how the Detroit Tigers are doing.

When I arrived back at the room, Cosmos and I looked at each other and smiled, aware that what we were at odds over was so very trivial. We talked it through, packed up, and hiked to the post office. We were a bit sad, as we had no packages waiting. Cosmos asked a guy coming out of the post office if he would give us a ride to the trail. He obliged. She is way better than me at the art of ride getting. It may help that she is a beautiful and fit woman. Who wants to pick up a scraggly old man?

When we arrived at the shelter after a short hike, we were treated to reunion time. The Rugged Shark is here, as is Prairie Dog, Angry Beaver, and Gritty. We pitched our tent on a platform away from the shelter and came down to eat with all these folks. It was a wonderful meal, with people sharing food and stories. There was lots of laughter, and lots of trail talk. I love to trail talk. I wanted to talk deep into the night, but hiker midnight came early, and the air became chilly.

How do you tell day, section, and thru-hikers apart? If a day hiker drops food on the ground s/he throws it away. If a section hiker drops food, s/he blows it off and pops it in their mouth. If a thru-hiker drops food? Pick it up and eat it without question.

As I hiked today I came upon a magnificent, mirror-like pond. I stopped and stared a bit. The pond was so quiet and peaceful. I thought to myself how nice it would be to camp here and that if I were a moose I would hang out around this pond. A spontaneous materialization occurred—a moose appeared. She slowly walked in the water in front of me, looked over my way, and began to eat dinner, dunking her head to the bottom of the pond and bringing up vegetation. How beautiful. Cosmos caught up and we watched together.

We have had rain the last three hiking days, making the rocks slippery. Although I broke one of my poles (the same pole I had fixed at the outfitter) today, I did not fall. I find myself walking very carefully these days.

I am looking and feeling very grimy. When I am in a town, some folks treat me indifferently, much like back in my post-Vietnam hippy days when a lot of people looked at me with my long hair and judged me as a pot-smoking, draft-dodging, non-working lazy hippy. They were only right on some counts.

I wonder if these people look at me indifferently simply because I look straggly and unkempt. They couldn't know how much I reek merely by looking.

12   MAINE

It is very cold today, with the temperature in the 30s.

We went up Mt. Success (elevation 3,565 feet), then down, then up and over Mt. Carlo (elevation 3,565 feet). These are tough climbs and extremely dangerous downhills. I reflected back to Vietnam, when my days in-country were numbered. My tour on the AT is nearing an end, and I feel extremely cautious. I do not want to get hurt at this point in my journey.

We took a break with Gritty, Prairie Dog, and The Captain next to a sign in the woods saying, "You are entering Maine, the way life should be." This is state number fourteen. I have walked my way through thirteen states, and 1,900 miles, which in itself is incredible to think about. 277.5 miles to go.

We arrived at the shelter and tented on a platform. Gritty, Prairie Dog, Angry Beaver, Cowboy, Captain, Mudslide, and Pudgie Pie are camping here, along with a south-bounder who has been hiking for two months and has only progressed to here, 277.5 miles. He is averaging fewer than five miles a day. He won't get finished until next year at his pace, but he seems to be having a great time and is equipped with a fantastic attitude.

Angry Beaver is a young strong woman. Prairie Dog is a big strapping man. They complement each other well. He occasionally hikes with her (breathes down the back of her neck he is so close), and other times he is way out ahead of her. She just plods along, always making her destination. If anyone has any questions, like, "I wonder how far to the next shelter," or "I wonder how far to the next water source," one need go no further than to ask the Beaver. She will know.

The Captain is a former military man who is attempting to complete a long section of the trail. He talks like a military man, i.e. niner, niner, I copy, roger that, etc.

Mudslide and Pudgie Pie are two very nice folks and very religious. Cosmos asks me not to say "fuck" in front of them. She does not trust my mouth in front of strangers.

Our shelter group just sat around eating dinner and shooting the shit until eventually, one by one, people disappeared into their tents, exhausted after the long day. I was in bed before 7 p.m. Mahoosuc Notch, a treacherous one-mile, boulder-infested part of the trail looms tomorrow. The day will be difficult. As I drift off, I think, "I am eating too much candy. Will I quit eating all this sugar when I get off the trail?"

AUGUST 28 | BALDPATE LEAN-TO, 13 MILES, 1,915.8 MILES TOTAL

We are up before the sun rises and off to the infamous "Notch." I am astonished to see a series of huge, small house-sized and jagged boulders, as far as my eye can see through the forest. As I hike, I move cautiously. I shifted to the side many times as young thru-hikers rock hop, almost running and jumping to the next rock, at a rapid pace. One slip would result in great damage to their bodies. I rock hop too, but not so quickly. In fact, I was having a difficult time of it, trying to maneuver my way through this mass of rock. It took Cosmos and me two hours to go one mile.

After a short breather, we went up Mahoosuc Arm (elevation 3,770 feet), down, then up further to Speck Mountain (elevation 3,985 feet). We stopped for a snack at the beautiful Speck "pond," adjacent to the Speck Mountain Shelter.

In Maine, what would be called lakes in Michigan, are called ponds. They are gorgeous. They are untouched. There are no cottages or boats on them. The water is calm, almost glass-like.

It is now official. We are out of the White Mountains. I thought it was official in Gorham. I have memories that will forever leave me in awe of those mountains.

I hiked a bit today with Rugged Shark. We talked of memories of the Smokies. Both of us, from time to time, would say to each other, "So nice to be hiking with you again." I love that man. He said he plans to sail the Great Lakes upon completion of his hike.

We had trail magic today. Chips, Gatorade, and candy at Grafton Notch parking area. The Captain, Jellyfish, and Slapshot are here, enjoying the generosity of trail angels.

What a beautiful day it was, in so many ways. We tented on a flat spot near the shelter. Cosmos urged me to hang my pack in a tree, but I declined as I was worn out, opting to place it under my rain fly. The rain began at 1 a.m. or so. At 2, Cosmos woke me up and said she thought mice were getting in my pack. I rolled over and listened. Fuck! Those little critters were trying to get my candy, which I had left in the side of my pack by accident. I had to put my head lamp on, get up and out of the tent, in the dark, in the rain, nude, and hang my pack with the bear bag. Before I hung my pack I had to shake it out, making sure all the mice were out. What a bummer. Talk about disrupting slumber. I spouted some select language. The mice had eaten a hole in my side pack. I should have listened to Cosmos. Maybe two hours later, I was able to fall back asleep.

AUGUST 29 | ANDOVER, THE CARETAKERS, 8 MILES, 1,923.8 MILES TOTAL

The rain fell hard throughout the night. We tore down in the cold rain, shivering all the while. When we walked past the shelter on the way out, everyone was sleeping, including Rugged Shark. Evidently, they were going to stay here instead of walking in the rain. The thought of doing a zero in a shelter never appealed to me. We filled up our water bladders and bottles from a nearby stream and hiked on. We made our way up the peak of both West (elevation 3,662 feet) and East (elevation 3,810 feet) Baldpate Mountains.

The short eight miles we hiked today could have been the scariest yet for me, rivaling my hike outside Hiawassee in the blizzard, some 1,800-plus miles ago. East peak was the culprit with its rocky, smooth surface. The weather? Rain, sleet, and high winds. Cosmos started crying, but regained her composure. I needed her to be strong because I was scared shitless. We were freezing cold and getting driven all over the mountain by the high winds, unable to keep our footing. Thoughts of getting blown off the mountain were constant. We slanted our bodies into the wind, but were still getting pushed sideways. There was nowhere to take cover. Eventually, we made our way to the north side of the mountain, safe. Cosmos hiked strong and was a great leader.

After the initial scare, we passed by some beautiful sights, including swift rapids in the river and tall waterfalls. We rock-hopped across this river, being careful not to stumble, as we would be swept over the falls. It was difficult to appreciate the beauty as I was chilled to the bone.

We crisscrossed the river, seeing many waterfalls. More beauty. Eventually, we made it to a road. I was freezing, shivering, so we decided to try and hitch into Andover, after hiking only eight miles, but a brutal eight miles it was. Made me think we should have stayed at the shelter and zeroed with the other thru-hikers.

We were having a problem getting a ride when a pickup pulled over. A young dude bounded out and of course told Cosmos he had room for only one in the cab. Me? The old man? No. The beautiful woman hiker, Cosmos? Yes. I rode in the back of the pickup, which already had a four-wheeler in it. I had to lie down on the open tailgate and hang onto the axle of the four-wheeler. I could not see where we were going. I simply closed my eyes and held on. I sang the song "Hurricane" in my head. I prayed. When the truck hit a bump, I would be lifted into the air. It was a harrowing ride.

It turned out the guy was a bear hunter, and the pickup truck in front of him was full of bear bait: donuts! We eventually were dropped at a restaurant in town, and I was never happier to put my feet on the ground.

We ate a big meal in a very uncomfortable state, as both of us were soaking wet. I needed a shower and warmth in a big way. We walked to a hostel in town. They were booked up inside, but we could stay in a bunkhouse in the back. We went back there, but the place was damp and cold and the entire place was filled with religion-themed material. We called the only other hostel in the area, and were delighted when Caretaker drove over and picked us up.

A hot shower awaited us followed by a hot dinner. I, and other thru-hikers, smoked pot out of the Caretaker's vaporizer. Much laughter and eating of munchies ensued. I feel a special connection and bond with Prairie Dog and Beaver, as our paths continue to cross.

Hiker midnight this night was 9:30 p.m. The sun will shine tomorrow. This was a tough day for me, both physically and mentally, but all days seem to end on a good note.

AUGUST 30 | CARETAKER'S, 10.1 MILES, 1,933.9 MILES TOTAL

Caretaker dropped us off at the trailhead in the early morning. He stopped in town to pick up other thru-hikers, and almost lost Jellyfish out the rear of his truck, driving off before he was securely in the bed of the truck. Caretaker is always stoned. He was wounded while serving in the military and shared some of his stories with us last night. His wife, Laura, is very nice and a great cook. Both of them aim to please the hikers.

We hiked 10.1 miles today to a stream near a road, stopping for a break. Our plan was to go further, but as we sat eating a snack, a truck pulled up by the side of the road. Guess who? The Caretaker! He said, "Are you sure you don't want to come back for another night? Your room is still open." We looked at each other and smiled. Back we went.

We did in fact sleep in the same bed and once again we had a great meal and drank a bunch of beer. And, we again smoked a bunch of pot through Caretaker's vaporizer. We talked endlessly. Our night turned into a full-scale party, finishing with a soak in their huge hot tub, sans clothes.

AUGUST 31 | SABBATH DAY POND LEAN-TO, 17 MILES, 1,950.9 MILES TOTAL

We are up early and chow down on cornflakes and fruit. Laura and Caretaker are smoking dope immediately. I passed. We are hiking out. The Dog and Beaver decide to zero here.

We take a couple pictures before Caretaker offers us a ride to the trailhead. Prairie Dog, the Beaver, Laura, and the Caretaker piled into the van. I wondered at the time why everyone was going. We headed toward the AT, but detoured to an old cemetery, because Laura wanted to take some pictures. This diversion was unexpected to me, but the others knew what was happening. She lined us up, each in front of a specific gravestone, including herself. Then, she took one shot of us clothed, lying down in front of our assigned tombstone. The next shot, she asked us to be nude. It's cold outside, and I am thinking about the bizarreness of what is happening. I looked at the others and they were quickly disrobing, so I followed suit, getting naked and lying down in front of my tombstone. Laura placed her camera on a stump, setting the camera on automatic, and raced for her place. We repeated this twice to get the ideal shot. I am thinking to myself, how would we explain this to the folks back home? I won't soon forget this morning: six people lying naked on graves in the cold.

We were finally dropped off at the same spot where Caretaker had picked us up yesterday. We said our farewells to all, knowing we would never see them again. I was disappointed Prairie Dog and the Angry Beaver decided to zero.

We hiked a hard seventeen miles to Sabbath Day Pond Lean-to. The last hour was in the dark because we thought we were closer than we actually were. The terrain was not conducive to night hiking, with jagged rocks and large roots everywhere.

We were both happy to have had a big day, because we now have but 9.4 miles to Rangeley, Maine. We pitched our tent quietly near the shelter and ate via headlamp, whispering when we spoke, cautious of not waking other hikers sleeping in the shelter. I am in bed quickly after bear bag and cleanup duty. My sleeping bag feels glorious. It is cold here tonight.

As I snuggled in my bag, I reflected on the Caretaker and his incredible war stories. When he got stoned he went on and on. I stayed quiet throughout. He was an airborne ranger, infantry, and evidently saw a great deal of action. He knew I was a Vietnam vet, and I left it at that.

Hearing the Caretaker, or anyone for that matter, speak of war and talk of experiences in war always makes me wonder: Was he telling the truth?

September 1 | Rangeley, 9.4 miles, 1,960.3 miles total

A trail magic guy gave us a ride into town. His wife is out for a day hike, and he was waiting in a parking lot with a cooler full of goodies. She went by me southbound about forty-five minutes before I arrived here. She was a large, big-boned woman and as she passed, exchanging hellos, she was breathing heavily. Her stature led me to believe she would not hike a great distance. Come to find out, she had thru-hiked this trail. And she has thru-hiked the Pacific Crest Trail, some 2,400 miles, from Mexico to Canada. Judgmental was I.

On the way into town, we picked up a hiker walking with his dog along the road. After we dropped him off, we found out he had hiked the AT, the Pacific Crest, and the Continental Divide trails. A "triple crowner" they call these folks. There are few people who have done this. He has done it three times. Incredible. He is a hiker's version of Babe Ruth or Hank Aaron. What an honor to meet Let It Be.

We got a room in town and realized as we settled in that just maybe we are getting off trail a bit too much. I rationalized we don't usually do zeroes, but neros.

I went immediately to the post office, excited to receive a new pack and shoes. I did get the new pack from Osprey. A shiny new red pack. I sent the old one back. Didn't get the shoes from the Vasquez folks, so I called them and they informed me they should be there. I also got a package from my sister Charlee, full of caramel corn and brownies. Her fudge package never got to me, and she sent it over two months ago. Oh, the little things. Thank you, my sister.

I also received my Veterans for Peace shirt. I finally get this shirt with only 220 miles to go. I will wear it with pride and answer any and all questions regarding my affiliation with the wonderful group.

We went out to dinner and later stopped at a bar for a beer and met Let It Be, the Triple Crowner himself. A humble, gentle man he is. He has been hiking on and off, mostly on, since 2001. This is his third dog. He has been in the woods for more than eight years!

September 2 | Zero

We are up at an early hour, prepared to move on after the post office. Yes, I got my new shoes from Vasquez, and they fit my feet comfortably.

I then went to the local library, got on a computer, and reserved a plane ticket from Boston to Traverse City. It is now setting in that I am almost done. I cannot fathom this journey is nearing completion. Unlike Vietnam,

I am not sure I want this to end. Perhaps this is the reason we are slowing down.

> In the last month or so in Vietnam I was unusually nervous. After being over there for eleven months, I was on high alert always. I had problems sleeping at night. We were moving around on various missions as always, but had had little contact with the enemy, and that's what scared me. We were overdue.

We hitched a ride out of town and toward the trail. Near the trail was a grocery store, a perfect place to resupply. There, standing alongside the road, near the grocery store, feeding his face like a little kid, was Rugged Shark. We thanked the driver for the ride, grabbed our packs, and hopped out of the car, happy to see the Shark. He was waiting for a ride from a hostel owner in the area.

We talked for five minutes or so and were about to say our goodbyes and head into the store when along comes hostel Bob to pick up the Shark. Two others are passengers in the back of the car, the Angry Beaver and Prairie Dog!

We had full intentions of hiking out today, but we are weak mentally and were easily talked into zeroing at the hostel. How could we resist hanging out with four of my favorite people on the trail, Rugged Shark, Prairie Dog, Angry Beaver, and of course, the Cosmos. How many chances am I going to get to do this? We went to the hostel and dropped our packs, and Bob brought us back to town so we could hang out, eat dinner, and drink some cold beer. Hostel Bob is about eighty years old and lives in a cottage on a gorgeous pond. He has two bedrooms upstairs with bunk beds. He loves to share his digs with thru-hikers.

In town we had great fun. Rugged Shark caught a buzz and started talking politics, a no-no with a buzz on. He was trying to push my liberal buttons, he being very conservative. His strategy didn't work. I was having too much fun with these people. The Prairie Dog drank one of the ever-famous Prairie Fires. So did I. A Prairie Fire is comprised of a shot of cheap tequila mixed with a shot of Tabasco sauce.

We ended up at the ice cream place in town and I consumed two hot fudge sundaes before Bob picked us up at the grocery store, where we had gone to resupply. Rugged Shark bought a fifth of something to drink back at the hostel. We all watched a movie at the hostel before bed, "Shawshank Redemption."

Woodsmoke is here at the hostel. He is the sixty-five-year-old section-hiker who does big-mile sections. We had not seen him since sharing a boulder with him and watching fireworks on July 4. Remarkable how these amazing things continue to happen on the trail.

SEPTEMBER 3 | ORBETON STREAM, 13.4 MILES, 1,971.7 MILES TOTAL

I got up around 3 a.m. or so to pee. The Rugged Shark and another hiker were still talking downstairs, trying to kill that bottle. They had a major buzz on.

Bob cooked us breakfast in the early morning, then offered us a ride to the trail. Prior to departure, Rugged Shark made an appearance looking like a truck had run over him. He slowly said, with glassy eyes and a foggy brain, "I am zeroing." I am thinking I will never see this dude again on the trail, but that our paths will cross again.

Bob dropped Prairie Dog, Angry Beaver, Cosmos, and me at the trail. We thanked him for all his kindness and generosity. Cosmos and I set a quick pace as we hiked the 13.4 miles to Orbeton Stream. We both felt exhausted, so we set up the tent and settled in. We had some big climbs today, over Saddleback Mountain (elevation 4,120 feet), and past Poplar Ridge Lean-to. We had awesome views today, again, too beautiful for words.

When we were getting ready to eat, the Dog and Beaver happened down the trail and set up with us. Who would have guessed that this woman, the Beaver, who would not let me pass her a couple hundred miles ago, would become one of my closest buddies on the trail?

After dinner, we had a couple candy bars for dessert, then bed. We have another big day tomorrow. I have said that so many times these past five months, "Big day tomorrow." Yep, they all are.

September 4 | Stratton, 18.8 miles, 1,990.5 miles total

I struggled big time today. I could barely pick my feet off the ground the last few miles.

We had two big summits today. Over Sugarloaf Mountain (elevation 3,650 feet), down, then up and over Crocker Mountain, both south and north peaks (elevation 4,040 and 4,228 feet) and then, of course, the downhills. Treacherous at times. But there was great beauty above treeline.

I was worn out upon arrival. It was just one of those days for me. I didn't have "it." We were supposed to meet the Beaver and Dog at Horn's Pond Lean-To, but didn't make it that far. We left a note on a fence that we were going into Stratton to get something to eat. I was thinking maybe that would rejuvenate me.

We got some trail magic from two folks, a man and woman, who gave us a ride to town. They also gave us a cold beer from their cooler. I couldn't even talk to them I was so tired, letting Cosmos do all the talking.

We ate dinner at a small restaurant in town. Mudslide and Pudgie Pie were here for dinner as well. We ended up getting a bed for the night above the restaurant because I was hurting. After taking a shower, I plopped down in bed and was out. I feel like I have been walking for five months.

SEPTEMBER 5 | WEST CARRY POND LEAN-TO, 22.6 MILES, 2,013.1 MILES TOTAL

We are up early to a new day. I feel so much better. We ate a hearty breakfast at a restaurant across the street. I saw a south-bounder here and tried to make conversation with him. Nope. He was too cool for us. He probably thought we were day or section hikers. He had no idea we had only 187 miles of the entire AT to go. We knew he had over 2,000. He had better change his ways if he plans on going on. His attire was jeans and a cotton hunting shirt. When he gets wet, he will suffer.

We hitched a ride to the trail and were picked up by an older gentleman in a pickup. When he stopped we jumped out of the back and when I leaned in the passenger window to say thanks, he asked gently, "You're not a thru-hiker are you?" When I said yes, he said, "If you don't mind my asking, how old are you?" I said, "Sixty-three in a week." He shook his head and gave me a calm smile and said, "Congratulations, you are an inspiration to many. Very impressive." That man breathed new life in me.

We hiked two-thousand-plus feet over Avery Peak (elevation 4,090 feet). The views were glorious, as if we were walking in the heavens. I spoke with many section and day hikers today. It is Labor Day weekend, so the folks are out enjoying the beauty.

We could see Mt. Katahdin from Avery Peak. I stared in awe for a few seconds.

After lunch I hiked out, and the downhill was treacherous. After reaching the bottom and hiking for a few minutes, I stopped and waited for Cosmos, thinking she was right behind me. I waited for almost an hour. The reason I waited? I wanted her to take my photo. I am standing next to a tree. On the tree is a sign that says, "If you are northbound, you just passed 2,000 miles." Two thousand fucking miles! Cosmos arrived, took my photo, and off we went.

I was feeling good today. The comments from the old guy who dropped us off this morning were in my brain all day. I got out ahead of Cosmos again and waited at the Little Bigelow Lean-to for her. When she arrived, she seemed to be doing okay, so we decided to try to get to the next shelter, another 7.3 miles, or find a flat spot and camp along the way.

The terrain was very rocky. Never was there a flat spot. We ended up hiking hard into the night, over two hours in the dark, until we made it to the lean-to. What had been a nice hiking day turned extremely strenuous.

I had no appetite and neither did Cosmos. We pitched the tent. Immediate sleep followed.

September 6 | Cabin in Caratunk, Maine, 14.1 miles, 2,027.1 miles total

We are up early and feeling good. Today is glorious. What a great day to hike. Cosmos was out in front of me and I heard rumbling and scraping in the pines just off the trail. *My first thoughts were to hide. Get down, Tim! I took another deep breath and waited.* I waited for several minutes to see something, my heart racing. *Was I going to see a moose exit these pines? Perhaps a bear? Certainly not an NVA. Certainly nothing that was going to harm me. My shoulders dropped to relaxation mode.* The movement shifted and I moved on without incident.

I was hiking alongside a large pond and saw a lone canoe far out in the glistening water. It was just past sunrise. I stood by the shore and waved at him or her, got a return wave, and walked on. As I walked the trail beside the pond, the canoe came slowly towards me. Finally, I stopped and waited for it. Cosmos had taken a seat and was waiting as well. It was a man out for an early morning paddle who became curious as to who waved at him. We talked to him for about twenty minutes, then he pushed on. Nice morning.

We are now hiking alongside a beautiful river (the Kennebec), with wonderful, flowing rapids. The trail winds in and out of the forest, and the earth is covered with rich green moss. The forest was enchanting. I got goose bumps many times today.

At one spot in the river, the water appeared deep. And with the sun beating down on a beautiful morning, what better time to go for a swim. Off came the clothes, and into the cool, gently flowing rapids I went. Cosmos was reluctant to take her clothes off. I said, "Cosmos, you aren't going to see another person out in these woods. We are in the middle of nowhere, in Maine. What's more, when are we going to get another opportunity like this?" No sooner had Cosmos shed her clothes and joined me in floating around this beautiful river than a southbound hiker walked by and started a conversation. I thought his presence was quite funny. He was in no way offended. Why should he be? And we had a beautiful swim. I said to Cosmos when he left, "We will never see that dude again, no big deal." Eventually, we pulled ourselves out of there and got back on the trail.

We hiked on and got to a point on the trail where we needed to cross the river via anything but our own feet. The rapids were intense and we would surely be washed downriver. This is where we had to wait for the "ferry," as described in my handbook. I had thought about the ferry coming for the last couple hundred miles, and had jokingly fantasized that it would be like a riverboat, adorned with all the amenities of the old west, i.e., bartender with a handlebar mustache, dancing girls, people playing blackjack, beer with a huge head on the frosted mugs, dinner. But I was jolted back to reality. The ferry was a canoe operated by Hillbilly.

Hillbilly is a knowledgeable man who has lived here all his life. He tells stories as we paddle up river, staying close to shore. Cosmos is in front, paddling, I am in the middle, and Hillbilly is in back. We have to paddle way upriver, then when Hillbilly gives the word, paddle frantically to get across to our destination, the trail. We ended up exactly where we wanted to be. After we exited, Hillbilly pointed to a white blaze painted on the floor of his canoe, telling us it is illegal to try and "ford" the river. He said many have tried, few have succeeded. Most that try need to be rescued as they are swept downriver by the powerful rapids.

Once we were on dry land, we looked across the river and could see the Dog and the Beaver. Hillbilly got right back in the canoe and headed across so we decided to wait for them. Hillbilly's position is paid for by the county. Five months of the year he does this, paddling section- and thru-hikers across the river. We were his tenth customers today. And he refuses to take tips.

The Dog and the Beaver make it over. As we put on our packs, Hillbilly informs us that if we are hitching, we should be walking, not just standing there with our thumbs out, because the locals don't like to pick up hikers that are lazy. I think to myself, lazy? We have walked more than two thousand miles, and they think lazy? We got a ride from a woman in a big shiny SUV to a place called Northern Outdoors. I almost felt guilty getting in the vehicle because we smelled so ripe, and the vehicle was immaculate inside.

Instead of hiking on, we ended up chipping in with the Beaver and the Dog and got a cabin by the river. This is an outdoor place that offers whitewater rafting, and there are lots of people around. There is a pool and a hot tub that was only lukewarm, so we don't utilize either. I just came from a nice swim in the river. The pool didn't appeal to me.

We had dinner here, then retired to our cabin for a game of euchre, men versus women. After a while Cosmos felt sick and had to lie down, so the women had to forfeit.

We then called it a day. I had a bed available upstairs, but wanted to be by Cosmos, because she was sick. I have been trying to change her view of me as "the most non-nurturing man I have ever known."

I slept on a comfy sofa, but got little sleep because it turns out this is party central to all these folks who have been whitewater rafting all day.

September 7 | Moxie Bald Lean-to, 18.8 miles, 2,045.9 miles total

What a beautiful, yet chilly day today. We almost zeroed. We had planned to go whitewater rafting, but the temperature isn't where we want it to be. Too cold for rafting, but perfect for hiking. We took a shuttle to the trail after stuffing ourselves at a fine breakfast buffet.

We traveled up, then down Pleasant Mountain (elevation 2,470 feet), then up and down Moxie Bald (elevation 2,629 feet). We ascended 1,130 feet in .9 miles coming up Pleasant Mountain, which is almost straight up.

I have a mere 133 miles to go. This is getting scary. I am feeling strange. Here I am almost done. Then what? What will I do with myself? I so wish Cosmos would have started with me from Springer. Her anticipation and excitement of being on the summit of Katahdin will be different than mine.

Maine has been so beautiful. Seeing and feeling magnificence is so much easier when the weather is good. Today has been cool and sunny. We have seen no rain yet in Maine, even though locals have said they have seen more rainfall this year than in half a century. We hit it right.

We ate dinner and camped next to a wonderful, still pond. And we even had a picnic table, a first.

September 8 | Monson, Maine, 17.9 miles, 2,063.8 miles total

Yet another memorable Cosmos quote this morning. First thing out of her mouth: "I have asked you time and time again, when you wake up, please refrain from thrashing about like a madman. And while I'm at it, your language is atrocious in the morning, too." That was a good one, coming from the "homecoming queen," who can spew words rarely heard from a woman.

We forded two rivers today. We took a break and had a snack overlooking another mirror of a pond. I say mirror because I could shave while looking into it. I could put on makeup, if I wore any.

We made our way into Monson and hit up the local store for some treats, then secured a bed at the Lake Shore House, a hostel. The first thing that amused me here was the selling of t-shirts that read, "Washer up front, liquor in the rear, sleep on top."

The little pub and restaurant borders the water and has great beer and food. Wonderful, kind people run the show. They cater to thru-hikers.

I did our laundry and visions of a zero once again danced in our heads. We will wait for the Dog and Beaver before we make our decision.

SEPTEMBER 9 | ZERO

The Prairie Dog and Beaver finally showed last night, and the first thing out of the Dog's mouth was, "We zeroing tomorrow?" Okay! We had breakfast down the street at Shaw's, another hostel. All-you-can-eat pancakes and eggs were served up. This place is teeming with thru-hikers. Wolfpack, Pudgie Pie, Mudslide, Gail, Schooner, Ferdy, and Soundtrack to name a few. There are some section hikers here as well. Shaw's is a nice hostel indeed.

The woman who runs our hostel gave Cosmos and Beaver a ride to the next town to resupply. Monson is a small town; population can't be more than a few hundred. There are no grocery stores.

I went to the library across the street after Cosmos left to use the computer and it dawned on me that this is my last entry before summit. Oh, my god. Seven days to go. I can't grasp this. I am feeling euphoric, but a part of me doesn't want it to end. Life is so simple out here. Eat, drink, hike. Stay warm. Embrace the people on and off the trail.

Later, I relaxed by the water on this beautiful, sunny day and watched Mudslide and Prairie Dog fish. I lay in the hammock, ate some snacks, drank a couple beers, and chatted with folks.

Mij, another thru-hiker, from Japan, is here. All these miles we have both hiked, and we had never crossed paths. Mij, stands for "Made in Japan."

We ate dinner with Prairie Dog and Beaver, played some euchre, and crashed.

SEPTEMBER 10 | LONG POND STREAM LEAN-TO, 15.1 MILES, 2,078.9 MILES TOTAL

We were up early and headed for breakfast at Dottie's, and her all-you-can-eat pancakes. We then hitched a ride to the trail and off we went, hiking on extremely rough terrain that was nothing but roots and rocks. We arrived at this shelter a bit before dark, and actually slept in a shelter for the first time in months. We had it to ourselves. Prairie Dog and Beaver are here. And we met the Sawman, who had a nice fire going.

We saw lots of southbound thru-hikers today. They are southbound to Springer? I'm thinking they have begun their journey too late. Those White Mountains will be cold by the time they come through. Odds are against their completion.

We saw many mice in and around the shelter as we were eating dinner. Hope they don't crawl in bed with me as I sleep. The fire was comforting to doze to. Thank you, Mr. Sawman.

We entered what's called "The Hundred-Mile Wilderness" when we left Monson. That means no resupply for one hundred miles. They say we are supposed to have provisions for ten days through here. That would be for section hikers, and those not in trail shape. We have provisions for five days. We plan on hiking right on through this wilderness. As we look at the map it doesn't look that difficult. But the signs warn us not to take this section lightly.

SEPTEMBER 11 | WEST BRANCH OF PLEASANT RIVER, 15.3 MILES, 2,094.2 MILES TOTAL

The anniversary of the New York City tragedy. War. War on NYC. For all of us who watched on TV, the scene was like a sci-fi movie. Unreal.

For anyone who has seen combat, the sight was all too familiar. People displaced, terror stricken, not knowing where to go or how to get there. Bodies strewn about. Chaos. First responders giving their lives to save others. Heroes all. Reminded me of early November of 1967. I remember November as most Americans remember 9/11.

This is when we, A Company, 3rd of the 12th Infantry, were relocated via convoy from VC valley to near Dak To, close to a beautiful river. We were to stay there for months, so we were told, our mission being to guard a bridge. We built super bunkers with literally thousands of sandbags. I sent a letter home asking for a tape player so I could send tapes home and my family and friends could reciprocate. Maybe my little sister, Cindy, could put some of the Top 40 music on a cassette for me. I missed my music. Normally, I would never ask for a tape player because it would add weight to my rucksack, but in this circumstance, perfect. We were going to have it made. Hot chow every day. Maybe some beer. Swimming and washing in the river. All good. If I was going to be in a combat zone, this would be the place to be.

All of that changed when one of our squads, on a routine patrol through a village on the other side of the river, found a young Vietnamese man. There are never young men in villages; they are usually in either the NVA/VC or the South Vietnamese Army. We might find old men or young, young boys in a village, but that's it. We brought the man in for interrogation and he spilled the beans. He informed us there were two regiments of North Vietnamese soldiers in the hills around Dak To. Bad news. A regiment could comprise up to 5,000 men.

The next day another unit came in and took over our just-completed super bunkers, as we were ordered to combat assault (chopper in) to the foothills outside Dak To. The young man, actually a member of the NVA, gave us a location where his comrades in arms were located.

Our unit was composed of two companies, A&B. I would guesstimate we had 250 guys total in both companies. That number would dwindle considerably in the following months. One company ideally has 250 soldiers, but I don't think we were ever at full strength. We were hoping and praying the guy in the village had given us wrong information. Most of us had never seen combat before. The majority of us viewed our tour to this point as a giant camping trip with weapons.

I don't remember why, but B Company was on the first birds in. A Company (ours) followed. When we were all on the ground, and in this open field as I remember, we regrouped and received our final orders on where to go and when. B Company led out once again. Tomorrow it would be our turn. We moved slowly, everyone staying five meters apart. We were to go up what turned out to be the first of many hills in the "Battle for Dak To." The hill was approximately 2,000 meters from our departing point. As we moved slowly, cautiously forward, one could almost hear a pin drop. Although most of us had never had contact with the enemy, we believed the intelligence, but hoped it was wrong. But somewhere in our guts we thought something was going to come down.

And then it happened. AK-47, M-16, and machine gun fire rattled the jungle. Everyone hit the ground and sought cover. I could hear screaming. I could hear chaos. I felt panic. B Company had walked into an ambush. And when you have never been involved in such horror, your natural reaction is to hide, take cover, perhaps even run. One never knows how he will react until faced with the moment. You don't charge on like in the movies. B Company was in disarray and decimated. They had to leave wounded and dead fellow soldiers up on that hill, the site of the ambush. We were to find them the next day. The troops that survived said they thought all people that were left were dead, but there was no way of knowing.

We spent a long, harrowing night about 300 meters from the summit of the hill. We quickly dug half-ass bunkers and settled in them as best we could, not giving a thought to building one of our hooches. We were scared. We exited the holes from time to time to keep from cramping, but when we did we risked getting killed by incoming mortar fire, which the NVA leveled on us when they thought we might be out of our holes. All night we worried about the next morning, when one of our squads, not the entire company, was to head up that hill. The reason we sent a squad? Better seven guys perish than the whole company.

When morning came, our company commander called in air strikes on the hill. God, was it harrowing with five-hundred-pound bombs exploding only two or three hundred meters from our location. This, plus we knew the enemy was waiting for us. I was not a member of the squad that went up that hill, but I was sick with worry for them. It seemed to be suicide.

The squad moved out and maintained radio contact in whispers as they moved. Then they reported seeing a dead GI, then another. Then a dead NVA, then a dead GI. And on and on. They made it to the top unopposed. Thank you. Upon receiving this word, we saddled up and headed to the top. As we moved up that hill I will never forget the feeling I had seeing a dead GI. Only a couple days earlier he had been playing cards on his bunker by the river. And now his spirit is gone. He had family. He had friends. He was a man I knew. I tried not to cry. Some of our dead appeared to have

been attempting to crawl back to our perimeter, but bled to death
en route. The experience was sobering to me. I had just turned 21,
a boy really. I don't remember how many we lost that day, but it
was too many. The experience was gut-wrenching. And there was
no time to grieve, to mourn. This could be happening again tonight,
or tomorrow, or the next day. I was petrified beyond my wildest
imagination. This turned out to be the beginning of me becoming a
hard-core grunt, with little regard for the life of the enemy.

This is what took over my mind this day on the AT. All day I thought about
it. But I had relief. I was okay. I was with friends. There was no danger.
My hiking friends had no idea how I fed off them this day. Although the
hike was difficult, I moved forward with two polar emotions. I was both
sullen and joyful.

The day also rekindled my frustrations of America's involvement
in war. If our involvement in war could bring lasting peace, maybe
the price of life would be worth it. But how many times is there a
winner in war? Does war bring peace? Innocent people die. Innocent people are maimed. Innocent people are going to lose their
minds. And this includes the troops involved, because they are
innocent. A soldier that is involved in combat will have those memories forever. The visions will always remain. Families watch as
their sons come home different people. Shame on politicians that
continue supporting war, but have no idea the meaning of the word.
What price glory...

The fifteen-plus miles today were so difficult. I don't know how many
times I have said to myself, "You should be in shape now. This shouldn't
be that hard." 84.1 miles to go.

We found a little flat spot near the river to pitch our tent. Prairie Dog
and Beaver camped nearby, and we shared dinner together in the darkness using our headlamps as candles. How romantic. We shot the shit and
laughed. This is one of those simple happenings on the trail that mean so
much. Especially today. The others had no idea how much their presence
and joy meant to me.

Hiker midnight comes tonight at 8 p.m. We have rivers to ford and big
climbs tomorrow.

SEPTEMBER 12 | MOUNTAIN VIEW POND, 18.2 MILES, 2,112.4 MILES TOTAL

We had easy traveling for a couple miles, and then it was a big up, followed by a treacherous down on Whitecap Mountain (elevation almost 4,000 feet).

We tented tonight at a beautiful pond. There seem to be thousands of water bugs. We see enormous fish jumping in the pond. This is serenity at its finest. Quiet and peaceful. Blessed has his tent set up a couple hundred meters from us. Blessed is a laid-back, kind, and spiritual man, who wants to be a preacher someday. I would go to his church, as he seems saintly. He wandered down by us for a chat and said he got up this morning and watched moose eat from the floor of the pond. Then he did a zero here, by himself.

Whitecap is the last big climb before Mt. Katahdin. It's now 65.9 miles to terminus. I passed the 2,100-mile mark today.

I know I have written this so many times before, but am freaking out thinking I am actually going to complete a thru-hike of the Appalachian Trail. I have put the stops on being on edge out here. I give thanks, I am grateful, and I am so blessed.

As we talked earlier today to a couple from Germany on top of Whitecap, another hiker reached the peak and greeted us. Moments later he looked at us with a puzzled expression and said, "Aren't you the two that were swimming in the Kennebec River near Caratunk?" I gazed at Cosmos, remembering what I had said to her when this guy came upon us swimming in the river minus clothes: "We will never see that guy again as long as we live, so don't worry about it." Oops. Cosmos slipped me a mild smirk.

We hit the bed early, feeling comfy, warm, and relaxed. We will try to pull a twenty-miler tomorrow, my birthday.

SEPTEMBER 13 | WHITE HOUSE LANDING WILDERNESS CAMP, 20 MILES, 2,132 MILES TOTAL

I am 63-years-old today. I wondered, as I lay in bed before I arose, "How many people my age have completed a thru-hike?"

We got up early (6 a.m.) and ate breakfast overlooking the pond. We hoped to see a moose, but no luck. I thanked Cosmos for hanging in there with me. She is an extraordinary woman, putting up with me all this time in the woods. We had a great day together although my feet ached more than normal. They have been hurting for months and I pray I am not doing irreparable damage to them.

We hiked on and off with Blessed, Mij, Prairie Dog, and the Beaver.

We saw many ponds and lakes today. Maine is ranked right up there as my favorite state. The weather may have something to do with my attitude about Maine, as it has been perfect for hiking. Cool and sunny.

We knew from looking at my hiking bible that if, after hiking twenty miles, we walked .09 off trail and followed the signs, we would come to a big lake, not a pond. At the dock there should be an air horn for us to blow. This would summon a boat from the White House Landing Wilderness Camp, now a hostel. This all sounded right up our alley. We found the air horn, blew it once, and waited. From a distance we could see a guy getting in his boat. He started the engine and roared across the lake to pick us up. A beautiful boat ride to the camp.

I showered and went to the main cabin where dinner was to be served. Great company greeted me with fellow hikers Gail, Blessed, Prairie Dog, Beaver, two section-hikers, and Cosmos. There were two choices on the menu, burgers or pizza and a huge salad. What a way to spend a birthday. I was beaming.

After dinner, we went back to our bunkhouse and played euchre by candlelight with Dog and Beaver. The boys won both games.

I spoke with my sister Eve. She is so proud of me. Everyone is proud of me. I am proud of me. I also spoke with Jake, Morganne, Dawn, and Mac on this birthday.

As I reflect late this evening, I drift again to the importance of having Cosmos as my hiking partner. The fun we have had on this trail is priceless. Hopefully, that fun will continue. She was my constant trail angel. A special birthday, indeed, and one I will never forget.

Four days to summit Katahdin.

SEPTEMBER 14 | RAINBOW SPRINGS CAMPSITE, 19.6 MILES, 2,152 MILES TOTAL

Up early once again, packed and ready to go. We had breakfast at the main cabin, blueberry pancakes and eggs. All we could eat. It was great to have breakfast with all the hikers. It does seem like a little family. We took some group photos and said our goodbyes to the owners of this fabulous place, then boated across the lake and back to the trail.

I am enjoying hanging out with Beaver and Dog, two 23-year-olds with great energy and spirit. I have a special bond with them.

We went 19.6 miles today, or, as Bullet would say, "nineteen and change." Bullet impressed me as a hiker with an extreme ego. On one occasion, he was way out ahead of his brother and showed up at a shelter where we were tenting. His brother showed up later in the evening, extremely fatigued, and asked Bullet, "How far did we go today?" as he was huffing and puffing. Bullet responded casually with, "twenty-one and change."

We pitched our tent and ate dinner near the shoreline of Rainbow Lake. Today we hiked alongside a beach, along a river, and alongside creeks. I counted twelve stream crossings today. All day was just glorious with radiant sunshine continually peeking through the trees.

I am getting a rash or something. I hope I don't have the bed bug thing going. Last night at the hostel, I slept on the mattress and simply pulled my bag over me without getting into it. Time will tell. I am restless and anxious thinking I only have twenty-six miles to go.

SEPTEMBER 15 | THE BIRCHES CAMPGROUND, 20.9 MILES, 2,173.1 MILES TOTAL

We finished the Hundred-Mile Wilderness in five days and change, averaging almost twenty miles per day.

We initially hiked to Abol Bridge Camp store. On the bridge before the store, we had a breathtaking view of Katahdin. Her peak is in the clouds. She looks so massive and imposing. I am not intimidated at all looking at her, knowing I have come this far, summited so many mountains. I look forward to standing on her peak. I look forward to seeing the sign that says Mt. Katahdin, northern terminus, accompanied by the mileage back to Springer Mountain, 2,178.3 miles.

The Dog, Beaver, Sawman, and Mij are all here at the store, in great spirits, eating whatever they have to offer and drinking beer.

As much as I wanted to sit and celebrate with the others, I had to hitch to the nearby town of Millinocket and hit the post office, which had packages from my friend Mick and my son Jonathon. I also was to pick up a package we had sent ourselves when we were way back in Hanover, New Hampshire.

I got a ride from some folks in a camper, who took me out of their way and dropped me in Millinocket. At the post office I received the three packages. The one from Mick contained some brownies and sweet stuff. Wrapped in some paper at the bottom of the package was a small bottle of tequila. This is perfect for tomorrow's summit. A celebration drink. Thank you, Mick and Deb. Jonathon and Jennifer sent me brownies and other sweets. Thank you. I needed to send something home because with all these goodies, my pack was too heavy, so I sent my raincoat to make room for brownies and tequila. Bad move. Dumb move.

As I was opening my packages at the post office, in walked Cruiser, who I had not seen since he left the trail in Harpers Ferry, West Virginia, with giardia, some one thousand miles ago. He had summited Katahdin yesterday. Now he is trying to hitch a ride back to Pennsylvania and complete the entire state, which he missed because of his giardia. When water isn't treated, we all risk the chance of getting it.

After the post office, I tried to hitch a ride back to the Abol Bridge. I was having no luck. From a corner traffic light I saw an old man get out of his pickup and sit on a bench. I walked down to his location and asked him for a ride, telling him I would give him gas money. He said, "You a thru-hiker?" I said, yes. He said, "You going up Katahdin?" I said, yes. He said, "Anyone that wants to climb that mountain is a fool. I won't give you a ride. Do you know what's up there?" I laughed, thinking he was joking with me, and said, "No, what's up there?" He said, "A pile of goddamn rocks, that's what. Go down there and keep hitching. Someone will give you a ride, but it won't be me."

I ended up doing a first for me, going door to door and asking for rides. Time was of the essence and I needed to get back to the trail. I had another nine miles to hike today, and Cosmos was waiting for me. The first three doors I knocked on turned me down, although all were friendly, they just didn't have the time. Finally I saw a couple on an enclosed porch. I went up and knocked on the door. The woman came to the door and said, "Can I help you?" I told her my plight, and she looked at her boyfriend (a Billy Bob Thornton look-alike), and gave him the order, "You go and give him a ride. You can use my car." And away we went. I had a great conversation with Billy Bob, as he told me all about the history of this quaint little town in Maine.

I eventually arrived back at the store to find Dog and Sawman with a major beer buzz going. I said, "Boys, we have over nine miles to hike before Baxter State Park." They said, "Come on Naneek, we are going to do a beera-mile challenge." I said, no way.

The Dog and Sawman left the store before Cosmos and I did. When we hiked out the mosquitoes were horrendous. I could not slow down without them lighting on me. I hiked hard and got ahead of Cosmos. I waited a few times for her, but had to keep hiking because of the bugs. I eventually passed the Dog and Sawman. They were doing the beer-a-mile thing, and of course again asked me to join in. Nope. I hiked on. The trail paralleled the Penobscot River and was very flat, so I made good time.

The beer-a-mile boys ended up stripping down and going over "Little Niagara Falls." They with their buzzes in full form, just eased into the water, and then let the rapids take them over the falls. The river, like most rivers, is full of major rocks and is very treacherous. Cosmos happened by them before they went over the falls, and they begged her to video their adventure and she reluctantly agreed. Miraculously, no one got hurt the day before Katahdin. Those boys were crazy.

I sat overlooking a pond waiting for Cosmos for about forty-five minutes before entering Baxter State Park. I did some major reflecting on my trail journey. What am I going to do now? I will be seeing my family, or at least some of them, very soon. What will come of Cosmos and me? What is my son Colin up to, and why hasn't he spoken to me in months? What will life be like off the trail? Will I go through withdrawal?

I gave thanks once again for having the strength and perseverance to walk this distance and actually enjoy the journey. And oh, the beauty I have seen. And the people I have met along the way. And the thoughts and emotions of Vietnam I have weathered. And the love I have for my hiking partner, a bond that will never be broken. And I think about life back in society, the importance put on material things. Out here the philosophy is eat, drink, sleep, keep your sleeping bag dry, and keep hiking. That's it. No frills.

I felt so very proud of all my fellow thru-hikers who were able to complete. And do it while white blazing with a full pack.

Those strong emotions made me think how proud I was to have known Leo Hadley, first lieutenant, in Vietnam. It was July 4 in Vietnam. If I was to do my entire twelve-month tour, I had but eight days to go. But few did a full tour, because they got what was called a "drop," getting out a few days early. Lieutenant Hadley was the 4th platoon leader, but had been promoted to company commander when Captain Foye left. I knew him very well and had a great deal of respect for him.

We got orders the day prior that our company was to perform a helicopter combat assault the next morning. We were heading for the same hill that was a "hot LZ" in late February, the hill that took the life of Sergeant Andretti and Top. The NVA were back. I was to be on the first bird out. Do you think I was scared? I had been here 11 months, 23 days. I felt I had seen more combat than anyone in this company, having never missed a firefight. I did not want to die now. Don't put me through eleven-plus months of misery and then take me out.

The night before we departed I approached Lieutenant Hadley. "Lieutenant Hadley," I said, "I have only eight days to go to my actual outdate. I should not have to go on this mission. I have paid my damn dues. Please." His response? "I asked Grizzly (battalion commander) yesterday if we could send you back to base camp, because you had so few days to go." Grizzly said, "It's a twelve-month tour. He goes on the assault." Asshole. I think I speak for my entire platoon in saying we had a deep-seated dislike for Grizzly. I hesitate to use the word hate. Our opinion was he knew little about what was happening on the ground, and seemed aloof regarding the casualties we suffered. When it came down to it, the number of casualties when he was our leader was 660, nearly an entire battalion wounded or killed. Seemed like when we had a person killed and a couple wounded, a week or so later we would get one replacement.

I went that day. First bird. I had a bad feeling, but as we descended I could see no sign of the enemy. And my eyes were fixed and intense. We landed with no resistance. Four days later I went home.

I thanked Lieutenant Hadley for going to bat for me with Grizzly.

Less than six weeks later, Lt. Leo Hadley was killed in action as the result of an ambush. He and thirteen others died on August 14. Grizzly had sent two platoons near the Laotian border. News of this came via letter to my home from a fellow soldier. The war followed me home. And it never left.

Eventually, I left the serenity of the pond and hiked on to the state park and the Birches Campground. Baxter State Park reserves a spot on one end of the campground for thru-hikers for no charge. It was nightfall when I walked in. A campfire roared. Other thru-hikers, soon to end their journey, were trail talking, rehashing over 2,000 miles' worth of stories. Some are hikers I had never met. They have been on the trail for as long as me, and I am just meeting them for the first time at the base of Katahdin.

The Angry Beaver is here, and she is more than a little angry. First thing she says is, "Have you seen Prairie Dog?" I told her I saw him at the store, but made no mention of the beer-a-mile challenge or the Little Niagara plunge.

Cosmos arrived a few minutes after me. Later, Prairie Dog and Sawman appeared. Prairie Dog is so excited about his naked plunge over Little Niagara that he wanted to share this excitement and the accompanying video with the Beaver. She would have none of it. Peace was eventually restored and we all ate dinner together. I shared my brownies and other goodies with them.

The Dog, Beaver, Cosmos, and I slept in the shelter. I know the night will be a restless one, like the day before Christmas when I was a little boy waiting for Santa. I have but 5.2 miles to summit Katahdin. The weather is supposed to cooperate.

SEPTEMBER 16 | APPALACHIAN TRAIL LODGE, 5.2 MILES, 2,178.3 MILES TOTAL

I rise and immediately think of my cousins, Doug and Denny Baker. Today is their birthday. I will always remember this day.

We are up at 7 a.m. Others have already torn down and are gone. We had breakfast, chit chatted with some fellow hikers, packed our things, filled our water, checked the weather on top, and began the summit of Katahdin. On this final day, we were the last ones out of camp, Cosmos and I. Unusual.

We started the day hiking alongside a creek, and it was beautiful, but my adrenaline was pumping. I felt so strong I couldn't contain myself. Cosmos was out ahead, but it didn't take long before I passed her. And I continued to pass other hikers, nine in all. They could hear me coming and cleared out of my way. I was running up that mountain. I waited for Cosmos every couple hundred meters or so, and didn't mind the wait. I wanted to be with her when I summited. She is my teammate. She has been my inspiration.

Big boulders and dangerous climbs slowed us down. I took a really bad fall at one point. I slipped off the side of a rock and had to tuck my head into my chest to avoid a head injury. Luckily, I only hurt my arm and knee. When I looked up at Cosmos after the fall, she was holding her breath. We eventually made it past the big rocks and were above tree line. The last climb turned out to be tough, like all the others on this long hike in the woods.

As we hiked on, I knew we were getting close to the top. I could just feel it. We were in and out of the fog, and I had to pay particular attention to every rock, for they were all slippery, so I was looking down most of the time.

As I trudged forward I looked up and saw figures of people moving around ahead, in the fog. Sort of like "night of the living dead." I couldn't make them out. Then I saw the sign I had read so much about prior to leaving on this journey. The sign I had seen so many pictures of over these last five-plus months: The Katahdin sign. The Northern Terminus. I HAD MADE IT!

I looked back at Cosmos. She looked so proud. When I saw her smiling I was overcome with emotion. I had to stop and gather myself. I had to weep. I had to hug her.

I had hiked 2,178.3 miles. In 172 days. I cry as I write this.

We hiked the remaining few yards to the top and touched the sign. There was the arrow that pointed south: Springer Mountain, 2,178.3 miles. I remembered vividly Colin dropping me off at Amicalola Falls State Park, and the sign pointing north that said "Katahdin, 2,183 miles." I just stared at this sign for a while, dreamlike. I kept staring at Cosmos with a grin on my face.

Blacklist, Bullet, and his brother were there. It was noon. September 16, 2009. I sat there for a bit by the sign. We took some pictures. Although I was feeling extremely proud, I also didn't know now what to do with myself.

Cosmos found a porn picture stuck in a rock next to the sign. Evidently, someone carried that picture the entire length of the trail, and left it at the summit. We both drank a shot of tequila, and hid both the tequila and the porn pic under a rock for the Prairie Dog and Beaver.

A camera crew arrived before we descended the mountain. They were filming a documentary of a guy who had thru-hiked in 1955.

After an hour or so at the top of Katahdin, we hiked back down, somewhat reluctantly. I wanted to savor this accomplishment. To bottle it. To bask in it.

It took more than five hours to descend, very carefully. I said to myself more than once, "Here I am, having just completed this long journey, but I could still fall to my death." Eventually, we hit flat land by the stream and made our way back to the park, signed in saying we had completed, and waited for the shuttle to Millinocket. We saw Gail, Schooner, and Ferdy in the park, as they were to summit the next day. I felt a huge sense of accomplishment, but didn't want to be too joyful, as Cosmos still had four hundred miles waiting for her from Tennessee back to Springer Mountain in Georgia.

The end of my tour in Vietnam? Four days from my actual coming-home date of July 12, I sat on my bunker in the dark on radio watch, deep in the jungle. As I monitored our listening posts and ambush patrols outside our perimeter, I was surprised by a voice on the airwaves I did not recognize. The voice shackled (shackling is code, i.e., Kilo is for K, Delta is for D, Zulu is for Z, Alpha is for A, etc.) out the letters I was longing for. He said, "Please be aware that at 0800 hours a chopper will be out to pick up the element Kilo, Echo, Echo, November, Alpha, November. (KEENAN) He will be coming back to base camp to DEROS." In other words, I was going home. I WAS GOING HOME! And this was July 8, four days earlier than expected. I immediately thought of surprising my family.

I was unable to sleep the rest of the night. At dawn I rose, as did everyone else. I was nervous about leaving. I had mixed feelings. Yes, I was more than elated to be going home, but I felt a sense of loss at the thought of leaving these soldiers and friends I had come to know so well. We had survived life and death situations. I knew that many of them would die or be wounded in the coming weeks and months. I just knew it. I was going home, but could not be happy. I could not feel the joy.

I divided up all my gear. I gave away my canteens to those who were short of them. I gave away my poncho liner. I gave away most of my ammo, my grenades, my claymore, my entrenching tool, my C-rations, my heating elements, and my sandbags. I had a nearly empty rucksack after I turned my Prick-25 radio and extra battery over to the next RTO.

And then in the distance I could hear the whirling of chopper blades. I knew it was time to say my goodbyes. I struggled, holding back tears just thinking about it. I made my way to our first bunker and shook a hand before I grabbed and hugged. It was Palmer, a guy from Georgia who had been in country almost as long as me. I bit my lip, trying not to cry. Then I went to John Phlugh, he who sang a great rendition of Kenny Rogers' "What condition My Condition Was In." And I was done. The tears flowed. I couldn't talk. Some of the guys laughed at my emotions, perhaps wanting to cry themselves. Others cried with me. I had embraced all in my platoon by the time the chopper was to land. Talk about bittersweet. I was leaving this horror, going home, but also leaving my friends. As I ducked my way on board with help from the door gunner, I realized I was the only passenger. My eyes foggy, I looked out at the jungle as the bird lifted off. There, waving goodbye, all with sadness in their eyes, was my platoon. Some had tears. Some had soft smiles. I would miss them. I would always remember.

The chopper brought me to Dak To. Then I took a Chinook to base camp. I was there two days checking out. When I turned in my rucksack the sergeant in charge confronted and quizzed me on the whereabouts of all my equipment I had checked out a year ago, i.e., entrenching tool, machete, canteens, ammo, etc. I told him that I got new gear throughout my tour and that stuff changes hands on a day-to-day basis. I could not believe he was asking me these questions. Finally he pounded his fist on his table and said, "What you fuckers don't realize is that there are two wars going on here, soldier, one out there with the enemy, and one right here at my fucking desk." And he was serious. I almost puked.

I hooked up with Mike, a friend who I went through AIT with and who was a mortar man like I was supposed to be. We found the location of my former platoon leader, Lieutenant Lawton, and roused him out of a deep sleep. We drank beer and laughed like there was no end, celebrating our survival. After day two in base camp we flew to Cam Ranh Bay to catch the flight home. Our "freedom bird" ended up being delayed so Mike and I walked around the base smoking pot given to us by an Air Force guy.

Finally our plane arrived and when we lifted off the ground, a roaring cheer echoed through the cabin. We were officially homeward bound. After 11 months, 26 days, and 13 hours, mostly spent in the bush, I was going back to the world. We ended up arriving in Seattle "before" we left Vietnam (time change). Mike and I decided to enter the bathroom together and smoke what was left of a joint we had saved for just before touch down of our flight. When we attempted to squeeze our bodies into the bathroom the pot smoke was so thick we could barely see ourselves in the mirror. We had only to breathe the air to catch the buzz, as others had the same idea.

We were whisked away by bus after clearing customs, the destination being Fort Lewis in Washington. Once there, we were treated to a steak dinner (oh, how nice of Uncle Sam), told where our next unit would be in the states, and were given our "dress greens." My destination for my final six months was Fort Carson, Colorado. I would have to report in 35 days. I scoffed at that news. From the beginning of my army tour, I was always told if I survived Vietnam I would get 45 days leave. I thought to myself, "I am taking 45 and I don't care who knows it."

Once dressed, it was off to the airport and the flight home. Mike and I talked about the possibility of protesters at the airport, as we had heard from replacements and read in papers sent from home of the many protests going on back home. We had heard about people spitting on us in the airports, heard of people calling us "baby kill-ers," heard of grandmothers yelling obscenities, heard of violence towards us. But the airport in Seattle was incident free, although there was no "thank you for your service" from folks in the airport as there is now. We both breathed a sigh of relief and Mike and I said farewell, as he was off to home in Wisconsin.

My plane was to land in Chicago, and then I was to connect to Grand Rapids. The flight to Chicago was eventless. I deplaned and headed for my connecting flight. I was dismayed when I arrived at my gate to find the connecting flight had been canceled. What to do? After checking with the ticket counter, I found the next flight to Grand Rapids was leaving in three hours. Three hours? No way could I wait three hours when I was 150 miles from home. I had been over 10,000 miles away in a combat zone for a fucking year. I was so excited to see my parents, sisters, and friends I couldn't sit still. Back to the ticket counter I went and canceled out. The airlines gave me my money back. I decided to hitchhike home.

I exited O'Hare and got the first cab I saw. Money was not a factor. The cabby asked where I was going and I said, "Get me on a road to Michigan, if you will." He nodded his head and away we went. He asked me where I was stationed and I told him I just came home from Vietnam. We exchanged pleasantries along the way as he drove for miles until he dropped me off, telling me that if I stayed on this road it would take me into Michigan. I thanked him, got out of the cab, and reached into my pocket for my wallet. He said something like, "Hold it soldier, this one's on me. Thank you for what you have done." I was flabbergasted, what with all the stories I had heard regarding protests and such.

I waved goodbye to him after a big thank you and stuck out my thumb. I hadn't waited five minutes when a car pulled over occu-pied by a young family: husband, wife, maybe 21, 22, and a little girl, perhaps two-years-old. I got in the backseat with the little one and the parents asked the same series of questions as the cabby. What is your name? Where are you going? Where are you coming from? I told them and they asked some more questions. We drove a few miles and the wife turned to me and asked, "How long has it been since you have had a cold beer and a turkey sandwich?" I looked at her quizzically. "Probably been a year since a turkey sandwich, maybe four months since a cold beer," remembering that I had a few on R&R in Australia. She said she had turkey and beer in the refrigerator, and it would be their honor if I would go to their home. I couldn't refuse. The husband said he would make sure I got on the right road that would go straight up to Grand Rapids. To their apartment we went. I sat with the little one on my lap and drank a cold beer coupled with a wonderful turkey sandwich. I was in heaven. I kept thinking that less than a week ago, I was on the first bird in on the combat assault near Dak To, scared shitless I was going to get killed or wounded with but a few days to go. And now I was sitting here with this beautiful couple who were so thankful to meet me, and am so happy that I had survived.

After saying goodbye, the husband drove me to the highway that led directly to Grand Rapids. He told me I wouldn't have any problem getting a ride from here. I thanked him and away he went. I stuck my thumb out and moments later a car pulled over. I ran up and got in. The driver started asking me the same questions and was very friendly. He was a traveling salesman who was headed for Muskegon, meaning he would have to drive right through Grand Rapids. I lived about ten miles off the expressway, but I would be in my hometown. Surely I would get another ride.

I wanted to pinch myself. It felt like I was dreaming. I couldn't have written a script like this, no way. We conversed for a bit. I may have told him where I lived, I may not have. I may have told him my parents' name, I may not have. But since being called out of the field three days ago, processing out of base camp, having little sleep, catching flights, etc., I was tired. I found myself leaning my head against the window of his car. I nodded off.

I awoke later to the man touching my shoulder. At first I thought it was my turn for guard duty. Then I realized what was happening. He looked at me and said, "Is that your house, Tim?" and pointed.

I looked out the window and there, to my total amazement, was 2079 Woodcliff St. My home. Tears welled. I couldn't thank him enough. He said he was so happy he could do this for me. To this day I have no idea how he found my residence.

I grabbed my duffle bag and got out of the car. My heart raced as I walked up to my house. I love surprising people, but this would top all. The garage door was open and one of the cars was gone so I cut through instead of knocking at the front door. I walked into the garage and looked around. Goosebumps. Then I proceeded to the back door. As I was about to open the door and enter the kitchen, I saw a guy I didn't know talking on the phone. I stopped when we made eye contact. He put the phone down and opened the door to greet me. He said, in disbelief, "Are you Tim?" I said yes. "I'm Terry, Charlee's boyfriend," he said. He shook my hand and hugged me, smiling from ear to ear. "Your parents and sisters went to the airport, thinking you may be coming home on the next flight from Chicago, but there is someone on the phone that may want to talk to you."

I picked up the phone and said loudly, "Hello!" The voice on the other end was Frank, one of my very best friends, who had called because he hadn't received a letter from me in a while and was worried. He said abruptly, "Who is this?" I said, "It's Keenan." He said, "Don't bullshit me, man. Is this really you?" I said, "Yes, come on over, brother. There is going to be a party at the Keenan home tonight."

Terry and I shot the shit for a few minutes in the living room. I sat in a spot where I could see the arrival of my parents and my sisters. Soon I would be springing the ultimate surprise. Terry told me the family was worried about me because I hadn't written in a couple weeks. I asked how they knew I might be coming home, because I hadn't told them. He didn't know. Finally, the car pulled into the driveway. All looked sad as they pulled into the garage; mom, dad, Cindy, and Charlee. Terry and I had a plan. He leaned against the sink in the kitchen with a sober look on his face as I hid behind the door. Charlee, 24, came in first, followed by my little sister Cindy, 11. My parents followed.

Terry said something like, "What's going on? Wasn't he there?" Charlee said no. They were glum. I waited until all were in the kitchen talking about me before I swung the door open and said, "Here I am! I told you I'd be back in a year. No need for worry." My mom wept, as did my sisters, as did I. My dad hugged me close, not wanting to let go. Terry sat grinning. It was a moment I will never, ever forget. I wished I could bottle it. I had completed my tour. I was home.

Later that month, when I was home on leave, I received a letter from one of the guys in my company letting me know that they had been ambushed--that many had died, including Lieutenant Hadley. Many were wounded. They were digging in after a long day of moving through the jungle when they were hit. They had no cover.

I isolated myself that day, staying in my room for a few hours. I was fortunate to have my friend Bill Lewis around, because he could relate to the war I had experienced, as he was also an infantryman. I could talk to him.

Vietnam changed me. My parents and sisters saw a different person when I came home. I had nightmares, was more intense, impatient, short, and argumentative. I yelled. I was and am a good person, but I could and did "go off." Over the years since then, I learned to control some of those outbursts. I had fewer nightmares. I tried my best to cope with what Vietnam had done to me.

Hiking the AT has taken me to a new level of inner peace. It's a peace I hope to carry with me always. The journey helped me sort through much of the anger and sadness that I brought home from the war. And I was so fortunate to have a special friend hiking with me, someone I could lean on, unbeknownst at times to her.

I will always remember my Vietnam experience as it was. But I know that writing about it, remembering all that happened, has given me a clearer perspective. Along the trail I was able to look deeply within and consider my own post-traumatic life with greater understanding and clarity. Enjoy, relax, be grateful.

If nothing else, I can now hike and camp without fear, although I must admit that my future hikes will be somewhat shorter than 2,178.3 miles.

Epilogue I

Some 25 years after I came home from Vietnam.

I was wandering around my house in Traverse City early December, 1993. The phone rang and I answered. "Tom Ellis, Atlanta, Georgia," was the reply. He was a friend from high school whom I hadn't seen in years, although we did stay in touch by phone after he moved south. Tom is a trivia buff with a mind like a steel trap. We shot the shit for a bit and then he said, "Now, Tim, you were in the 4th Division in Vietnam, were you not?" Amazed, I said, "Yes, Tom, I can't believe you remember that. I barely remember." Then he went on. "Barbara (his woman friend at the time) and I had Thanksgiving dinner on Tybee Island, near Savannah, Georgia, with this guy and his wife. He said he was in the 4th Division." I chuckled, saying something like, "There were thousands over the course of the war who were in the 4th ." Then he said the guy was a colonel. "I knew no colonels, Tom." "Okay. His last name is Hendrix." I paid little attention. We went on with our conversation, talking about this and that. But for some reason, the name Hendrix stuck in my mind. Finally, as we were about to say our goodbyes, I said, "Tom, that name Hendrix, the colonel. That sounds vaguely familiar. I think our battalion commander's name was Hendrix. I think. I remember him by his radio call sign, Grizzly." Tom paused, then excitedly said, "They call this guy Grizzly on the island." My jaw dropped. "No way!"

Tom said I had to call him up. I said, "I would never call that fucker, never. He was the cause of so many deaths while I was in that war. He had no regard for our lives, just his fucking medals." Tom said, "Okay, I understand, but I'm calling him. Do you mind?" I said, "Have at it." Tom said, "Give me some ammo. What event can you tell me that would assure he is the same guy?" I said, "Ask him about Hill 1338, the one he was referring to when he ordered us: 'Don't come down off that hill till you've taken the son of a bitch.' If he distantly remembers that, ask him about Captain Foye, my company commander. And if he is in tune to that, then you may tell him that in June of 1968, he pinned a Silver Star on one of your best friends. See how he responds." Both of us a bit amazed, we agreed to talk again soon.

Right away, all my anger resurfaced. The disdain for Grizzly. In more ways than one, I was hoping it wasn't the same guy. Twenty minutes later the phone rang. It was Tom. He was wound up. He said, "It's him, it's him." My heart jumped. "What did he say?"

Here is how it went according to Tom:

Grizzly answers the phone: "Hello."

Tom: "Hill 1338, sir, do you recall?"

Momentary silence.

Grizzly:" How do you know about Hill 1338?"

Tom: "How about Captain Foye, remember him?"

More silence.

Grizzly: "Where are you getting your information, Tom?"

Tom: "You pinned a Silver Star on my friend in the jungle back in June of 1968."

Silence.

Tom told me at that time Grizzly seemed overcome with emotion and could not speak. Eventually he gathered himself and asked Tom to have me call him. "You have got to call him, Tim." And I said, "No way. Do you know how much I despise that man?" He pleaded with me. Eventually, I said, "Look, my wife Dawn and the kids are going to take a vacation in March. Maybe we will come to Atlanta or Tybee and visit. Right now I need time to think about this."

In March of 1994, my family and I headed to Atlanta, met up with Tom and Barbara, and headed to Tybee Island. I was going to meet Grizzly. I kept shaking my head, wondering why I would want to do such a thing. I actually thought to myself, "What would the brothers in my platoon think?"

A four-hour drive later, we arrived on Tybee, a small island at the end of Highway 80, a beautiful place, near Savannah, Georgia.

After hanging out at the beach all day with the kids, we were to meet Colonel Hendrix, aka Grizzly, at Margo's, a small bar and restaurant in town. Tom had set up the meeting. Others in this town had heard about it, too, as word travels fast, and everyone knows of the Colonel.

We were supposed to meet at 6 p.m. and we were on time. When I walked into the bar I saw lots of people, and I felt the stares. I looked around the room anxiously. Tom told me the Colonel wasn't here.

I breathed.

I grabbed a beer and found myself in a corner. I stood there with Dawn, Barbara, and Tom. Barbara asked me if she could have the honor of introducing the Colonel. I shrugged and said I didn't care.

My palms and underarms were drenched with sweat as I watched the door. No one knew my anxiety. Every time the door opened I held my breath. I thought, "Is that him?" Then again, "Is that him?" And I would ask myself once again, "What am I doing? Why am I doing this to myself?" I recalled he was about 6'2", 180 lbs. or so, handsome as can be, always looking like a Hollywood soldier. Back in the day he always wore tailored, clean fatigues that looked so different from ours. Ours were beaten up from being in the bush. He always had a Bowie knife hanging from his pistol belt. He was a striking figure to be sure.

The door opened once again. In walked a short attractive woman followed by a rather handsome older gentleman who walked like he commanded respect. Grizzly! It was him. It seemed like the entire crowd looked his way, and he was greeted by many.

Barbara hurried over and grabbed his hand. She led him to me. My heart raced.

The crowd gathered around as I was now face-to-face with Colonel Jamie Hendrix, retired.

Barbara said, "Colonel Hendrix, I would like to introduce you to Tim Keenan, a good friend. He served in the infantry under your command in Vietnam in the years 1967 and 1968."

I looked him straight in the eye. He did likewise as we grasped each other's hand in a strong handshake. He held on as the crowd applauded.

We simply stared at each other for what was a few seconds, but seemed like minutes. No words were spoken. And then he took me by the hand and walked me to the other side of the bar. He placed his hands on my shoulders. I looked at him and saw tears coming down his cheeks as he said, "What did my men think of me? Can you please tell me what my men thought of me?"

Oh, my God. All these years I am thinking, "This guy is going to rot in hell." He had no conscience. But as I looked at his forlorn and pitiful face, that's not what I saw. He knew how we felt. He must have. Six hundred-sixty-plus casualties under his command? How could he not know?

I thought quickly. What purpose and what good would it do if I relayed my real thoughts, those thoughts that have been with me for years? I looked at him and said, "Colonel, you were our leader. We looked up to you." He continued to cry.

I wondered if I was copping out. But what good would come of lashing out? What purpose would it serve of telling him exactly how I felt? I already saw the respect he had on this island. People loved him. Showing my disdain would serve no one. I let it go.

After that first encounter, I've visited "The Grizzled One" annually for the next fifteen years, either by myself or with a friend. I came to love the Colonel. We would fish, drink beer, go for walks, feed his raccoons, go out to dinner. I learned he was a soldier. He was a proud soldier. I guess I was a soldier as well, but for him, being a soldier was his identity. He graduated from The Citadel, a military college in South Carolina. I couldn't relate, but I soon recognized that commanding an infantry unit in Vietnam had been an extreme honor for him. Yet he told me more than once that 1967 and 1968 were the worst years of his life.

Over the years we had many interactions. One stands out in particular. We were trolling in a boat in the bayou country near Tybee one sunny day. I had been reacquainted with him for a decade by then. I asked him, out of the blue, "How would you feel about being my battalion commander in Vietnam if you knew me then like you know me now?" He sat silently for a moment, his lips quivering. Finally he said, "I couldn't. That's why it was so hard for me. I couldn't get to know my men. Do you understand?" I nodded and said, "I do understand."

The Colonel died in the summer of 2014. I spoke with him when he was on his deathbed. I told him how grateful I was to have made his acquaintance after the war. I told him his presence in my life meant the world to me. And I told him that I thought all the brothers in my platoon would love him as I do had they had the opportunity to see him in the same light as I have.

A few days later, I spoke at his funeral.

Epilogue II

November 14-23, 2014

Were it not for the encouragement of my trail-hiking partner, Cosmos, the thought of returning to Vietnam would not have entered my mind. But she mentioned several times on our hike of the AT how important it would be for me mentally and emotionally to return. Make peace with myself. Make peace with the people. She said something like, "You have negative feelings for an entire race of people. If you go back those feelings could diminish, perhaps disappear."

I returned to Vietnam in November of 2014. With me were my son, Jake, and two filmmakers, Neal and Robert. I can tell you now, without hesitation, I could never have gone back without the support of my son.

My goal in returning was to clearly address and confront the concerns of the PTSD that has troubled me for more than forty-seven years: Racism. The Vietnam jungle. The North Vietnamese soldier. I wanted to meet my enemy. I wanted to see the people of this country in a different vein. I wanted to go back to the scene of a horrific battle. I wanted to remember my comrades. I know all of those horrific war thoughts will never go away. But for me, the more positive experiences related to that country I can have, the more positive I, myself, can become. The AT showed me I could enjoy hiking and setting up camp again, and not equate it with combat. I hoped the same kind of enjoyment could engulf me in a return to Vietnam.

As soon as I landed in Vietnam, and as nervous as I was, I felt more relaxed. I was fortunate to be seated on the plane next to a Vietnamese man who was heading to Da Nang to visit family. We had a wonderful conversation. He had no idea the touch of relief he was giving me, as one of my fears was that people would be wary of my presence.

Racism? I have often contemplated how the war caused me to dislike, even hate, an entire race. Gooks, Chinks, they were not humans to me. These were emotions inflicted on me by war. Over the years, through hard work, I had erased most of these feelings of negativity. But spending nine days in-country, in both Da Nang and near Dak To, totally erased those toxic emotions. The people were so kind, so gracious, so warm. They would go out of their way to smile, to shake hands, even to touch me, adults and children alike. All the while I am thinking, "We devastated this country. We occupied. We bombed. We killed. We sought them out. We used chemical warfare. We tortured. We left ordnance that have killed over 80,000 since the war's end. And they still treat me with utmost respect and love." I learned through them, to forgive. We are all children. We are brothers and sisters.

The NVA? Our translator and guide, Ahn and Bill, set up a meeting. I had requested speaking to NVA who were the same age as I. Perhaps had fought in the same area that I had. I wanted to know them on a different level.

I had what turned out to be an emotional meeting with five former enemies, four of which showed up in uniform. When I met them as they arrived via taxi for our meeting, I didn't know what to do or how to welcome them, as they were not smiling, so I gave a half-ass salute to them. They smiled guardedly. The last one out of the taxi was an older man. He struggled getting out, and I offered my hand to help, hoping he wouldn't reject my offer. He didn't. And he held onto my arm the entire walk to the table and his seat. He thanked me graciously. Inside I felt deep thanks to him for not rejecting me.

The former enemy and I talked for over two hours. They wanted to know why I wanted to talk with them. What was my motive? I explained I wanted to make peace. I wanted to know them as human beings. They were my enemy that wasn't supposed to be my enemy. They seemed suspicious at first. All spoke. When I mentioned I was president of the Veterans for Peace in Northern Michigan they seemed to smile and relax and were more willing to talk. There was acceptance. When Ahn served us lunch, three of them pulled chairs next to them and asked me to sit. And when our meeting was nearing completion, all spoke beautiful words to me. Words of peace. Words of brotherhood. Words of forgiveness. All hugged me as we said our goodbyes. One stood at attention and saluted.

The following day we left Da Nang and drove cross-country to Dak To, where I had been "humping the bush" for months back in 1967 and 1968. Hill after hill we took. On November 17, 1967, we took hill 1338. Many wounded, many dead, both NVA and American soldiers. I wanted to climb that hill once again, minus the firefight. And so my son and I did, on November 17, 2014. Amazingly, nothing had changed, save for no enemy. The terrain was identical. I remembered the sights as I climbed. We didn't make it to the top, stopping near a spot that seemed eerily similar to the site we carried our wounded and dead as the battle raged. After my son Jake and I lit candles, I was able to remember many of those friends I fought alongside. Some had been killed, some had been wounded, and some had made it home. All were changed forever. I also paid tribute to the NVA, who gave so much of themselves in that war. And to the families and friends of all the soldiers, who worried and endured so much in that time of turbulence.

Mr. Theut, the older soldier I had helped out of the taxi, had called Ahn several times requesting a one-on-one meeting with me. After the meeting with the rest of the NVA and my journey up 1338, I was emotionally fatigued. I didn't know if I had it in me. But my decision to meet him ended up being the highlight of my tour. The most peaceful man in the world was Mr. Theut. A man who was wounded seven times throughout the war. A man who was raised only ten kilometers from My Lai, the site of the worst massacre inflicted on Vietnamese civilians by U.S. troops in the history of the war. A place we slaughtered more than five hundred women, children, and elderly. I apologized to him. On behalf of me, who represented infantry, on behalf of the men I served with, and on behalf of the American people. I asked him about PTSD, and if he has horrible memories of the war. He told me, through tear-drenched eyes, that his most vivid memory is of attempting to bury six of his close friends after a firefight. He had buried five and was in the process of burying the sixth when "the Americans were coming" and he had to abandon his friend before proper burial. He is pained to this day remembering that moment.

Mr. Theut held my hand and told me to pass this on to my fellow soldiers who were haunted by memories and visions of war: "Those that experience war change into someone they are not. Many of us did things in wartime we would never think of doing, because war changes us. It is important to tell your friends that we, the Vietnamese people have forgiven you. You are now our brothers. We all seek peace within ourselves. Please bring this message home with you."

And so I will.

Cosmos and I had a wonderful hike together. Originally, she was to hike only one hundred miles or so, but she changed her mind and hiked almost eighteen hundred with me, all the way to Katahdin, Maine. She then took a plane back to Irwin, Tennessee, where she first met me on the trail, and hiked the three hundred fifty miles south to the beginning, Springer Mountain in Georgia, alone, to complete her thru-hike. A strong and powerful woman and hiker is she. The peace she brought to me was immeasurable. We physically parted ways sometime after our hike of the AT, but remain close friends. The trusting and loving bond we formed on the trail was eerily similar to the bond formed by my fellow soldiers and me in Vietnam. I will never forget her.

In heartfelt memory of

Lloyd Slack
Lucius Winfield
Leroy Kling
John Terrell
Thomas Herring
Adolf (Tex) Albrecht
Bobby Ray Jones
James Buchner
Ronnie Eskew
John Lobsinger
Dennis Magrie
Kenneth Andrade
Hilaire Andry Jr.
Richard Grier
Abelardo Malave-Rios
Ruffin Satterwhite Jr.
Duane Johnson
Robert Brown
Pedro Camacho-Rodriguez
Raymond Daniels
Roy Edelstein
Leo Hadley
Scott Henry
Steve Lee
Gary Maloy
John Mularz
Bobby Riley
Robert Santoro
and Francis Schwarz

all killed in action in 1967 / 68
and members of
A CO, 3rd BN, 12th Infantry

THANK YOU

Cosmos
Mom and Dad
My sisters Charlee, Eve and Cindy; beautiful sibs indeed
My children Jonathon, Morganne, Colin, Jake, and Larinda
The Put-n-Bay Crew: Thom, Mac, Kevin, Mick, Bid, Egg,
        Pauly, Matt, Dave
Mike Lawton
Mary Dangerfield
Col. David Foye
A Company, 3rd Battalion, 12th Infantry, 4th Division
Richard Holm
My loving and supportive friends
Teresa Scollon
Tom Emmott
Mardi Link
Joe Meredith
AT hiking friends
Neal Steeno
All who gave me the gift of trail magic
Rick Vanderweigh
Emily Bert
Ryan Bilinski
Veterans for Peace, Chapter 50

Combat vets of all wars ... we share the pain.

And to my Grand Rapids friend Lloyd Slack, C Company, killed in action near Christmas of 1967.

My cousin Rod, combat Vietnam vet. We all miss you.

And to all who contributed to my charities. $9,000 was donated by my friends and family, and their friends. The John Lewis Veterans for Peace scholarship is given annually to a financially needy veteran or his or her child. Almost $4,000 was donated to the Women's Resource Center in Traverse City, Michigan, to help the victims of domestic violence.

The author is the subject of an award winning documentary, NANEEK, directed by Neal Steeno.

www.naneek.com

Made in the USA
Columbia, SC
11 July 2017